KU-589-612

HOW TO MANAGE PUBLIC RELATIONS
Practical Guidelines for Effective PR Management

How to Manage Public Relations

Practical Guidelines for Effective PR Management

Norman Stone

McGRAW-HILL BOOK COMPANY

London · New York · St Louis · San Francisco · Auckland
Bogotá · Caracas · Hamburg · Lisbon · Madrid · Mexico · Milan
Montreal · New Delhi · Panama · Paris · San Juan · São Paulo
Singapore · Sydney · Tokyo · Toronto

Published by
McGRAW-HILL Book Company (UK) Limited
Shoppenhangers Road, Maidenhead, Berkshire SL6 2QL, England
Tel: 0628 23432; Fax: 0628 770224

British Library Cataloguing in Publication Data
Stone, Norman,
    How to manage public relations.
    1. Public relations
    I. Title
    659.2

    ISBN 0-07-707454-8 ✓

Library of Congress Cataloging-in-Publication Data
Stone, Norman,
    How to manage public relations : practical guidelines for
effective PR management / Norman Stone.
        p.   cm.
    Includes bibliographical references and index.
    ISBN 0-07-707454-8
    1. Public relations—Management.   I. Title.
HD59.S76   1991
659.2—dc20   90-27807
                                                                        CIP

1234 CUP 9321

Typeset by Cambridge Composing (UK) Ltd
and printed and bound in Great Britain
at the University Press, Cambridge.

Contents

Acknowledgements

So much help to acknowledge, and so many influences: the question is where to begin?

Chapters 4 and 8 grew out of articles I wrote for *PR Week* in the *State of the Art* series edited by Norman Hart, Managing Director of Interact International. I can never adequately acknowledge his support and encouragement.

Chapter 10 owes a great debt to Dr Steve Tibble, Senior Planner with Valin Pollen. Chapter 11 leans heavily on Barry Leggetter, Joint Managing Director, Countrywide Communications, and Roger Haywood, Managing Director of Roger Haywood Associates. Research results in Chapters 1, 5, 7, 9 and 10 are courtesy of John Fowler, New Business and Marketing Director at Burson-Marsteller. They cannot be expected to bear any responsibility for what I have done with their ideas.

In singling out another three dozen people for specific mention, I am conscious that many others may be just as deserving, if less readily identifiable. My thanks, then, to Philip Allan (Philip Allan Publishers), Tony Attwood (Hamilton House Mailings), Nick Band (The Quentin Bell Organisation), David Barnes (American Express), Mary Bartholemew (Shandwick), Quentin Bell (The Quentin Bell Organisation), John Bellak (Severn Trent), Mike Brewer (Marketing Solutions), Bruce Bulgin (National Provincial Building Society), David Burnside (British Airways), Valerie Cooksley (Ernest Ireland), Annette Crocker (The Tea Council), Dick Fedorcio (Institute of Public Relations), Julia Hobble (The Fawcett Society), Sheelagh Jefferies (Women's Royal Voluntary Service), Frank Jefkins (Frank Jefkins School of Public Relations), Robert Keen (Charles Barker Traverse-Healy), John Lavelle (Institute of Public Relations), Dermot McKeone (Infopress), Nicola McLaughlin (PR Selection), Clive Keen (Leeds Polytechnic), Charles Mills (V&A), Maurice Milward (Association of Market Survey Organisations), David Morris (Coventry Polytechnic), Nigel Rigler (Philips), Fergus Robertson (British Institute of Management), Joanne Rule (Barnardo's), Janet Salvoni (Paragon), Gail Sheridan (Gail Sheridan Communications), Harvey Smith (Institute of Public Relations), Nigel Snell (Nationwide Anglia), John Spratt (Shoosmiths and Harrison), Colin Thompson (Public Relations Consultants Association), Flora Thompson (Hampstead Health Authority), Julia Thorne (Paragon), Peter Todd (Market Research Society), John Turner (British Telecom) and Reginald Watts (The Watts Group).

Thanks to the team at McGraw-Hill—Roger Horton, Kate Allen, Christina

Langan, Lavinia Porter and Isla Quinn—and admiration for their patience and professionalism.

None of it could have happened without the support and understanding of Angela, my wife, whose word processing, manuscript management and helpful criticism have been invaluable.

Introduction

So, where do I begin?
A bit before the beginning.

Gavin Lyall[1]

There is no shortage of books on management and there is an increasing number on public relations. More often than not they end with a checklist. This book is about the management of public relations. It starts with a checklist.

1. Are you a user of public relations?	YES/NO
2. Do you provide public relations?	YES/NO
3. Are you a student of public relations?	YES/NO
4. Do you teach public relations?	YES/NO
5. Are you in advertising?	YES/NO
marketing?	YES/NO
sales promotion?	YES/NO
market research?	YES/NO
6. Are you a line manager in industry?	YES/NO
7. Do you need to understand what managing communications is about?	YES/NO

If you have answered 'YES' to even one of these questions, this book will be useful to you. If you have answered 'NO' to Questions 1 and 7, this book is urgently essential to you. Everybody in industry and commerce, in national and local government, in education, and in the voluntary sector needs to understand how communications are managed. Knowingly or not, intentionally or not, everybody is part of the two-way communications process that is PR, and is therefore a user.

How to Manage Public Relations aims to bring together the disciplines of management and the creativity of public relations in a business that is not only about change but is also itself constantly changing. The approach is systematic but flexible, quoting actual case histories as well as summarizing theory, and suggesting guidelines rather than imposing rules. Some of the examples appear more than once, each time seen from a different angle or illustrating a different point. Others make solo appearances, sometimes very briefly, sometimes more substantially. Sources and references are acknowledged wherever possible, and I apologize for any inadvertent omissions. The importance of coordinating public relations with other aspects of the business is stressed in Chapter 5 but is a recurring theme.

Of course, you would not expect PR in the real world to be anything like as straightforward to manage as it is in books—not even this book. Life does not happen page by page, each chapter concluding before the next begins. Nor is it made up of block diagrams, flow charts and checklists. Out there, where we earn our livings, effects can be remote from causes, or occur at about the same time or even appear to precede them. Programmes have to be up and running while objectives are still being discussed. Adequate resources are provided, if at all, only when the job for which they are needed is nearing completion. When things are going well, you are told you don't need a PR budget: when they are not, you are told you cannot afford it. How can anyone make sense of it all?

I think there are only three believable explanations of the way PR works in practice.

1. *The conspiracy theory.* You get together with people with whom you have common or compatible interests, to secure an advantage over everybody else.
2. *The foul-up theory.* The conspiracies don't work and you lose the advantage.
3. *The bran tub theory.* What happens may be affected by conspiracy or by foul-up: but only by accident can it be anything like what you actually deserve.

Whatever theory is nearest to your own experience, I hope you find something in the book that will interest you and help you.

Whereas nothing I have written is incontestable, it is all based on experience— by no means only my own—and is heavily in debt to everyone I have ever met and everything I have ever read. As writer, I bear the responsibility for every word. As reader, you have the power. If you decide not to pay attention—to switch off the receiver, as it were—nothing I write will have the slightest effect. You, the reader, are in control.

Sources and references

1. Gavin Lyall. *Blame the Dead*. Hodder & Stoughton. London, 1972.

CHAPTER 1

PR in the management context

> The next generation of chairmen and chief executives who have
> worked alongside PR practitioners will have seen for themselves the
> key role we play not only in presenting the company, its people and
> its products externally but also in providing key advice and counsel
> internally.
>
> *Tony Spalding*[1]

Probably most people in industry and commerce have a pretty good idea of
what management is. They may disagree on exactly how to go about good
management, though they would be very likely to recognize it when they came
across it, especially if they have benefited from it themselves. Likewise with bad
management: there is much difference of opinion about just how to avoid it,
but very little doubt about knowing it when you see it, still less when you suffer
from it.

Because of this general consensus about management, there is no great need to
define it. There are definitions, of course. In the dictionaries, and in the
substantial body of literature, management is equated with conducting an
undertaking and controlling an institution; with taking charge and with
contriving; with direction and administration; and with wielding power.

Igor Ansoff, master of corporate strategy, argues that management is the active
process of determining and guiding the course of a firm towards its objectives,
and is a very large complex of activities, including analysis, decision, communication, leadership, motivation, measurement and control.[2]

Management manuals accept all this and stress that economic performance is
the central function of management.

About public relations there is no such consensus. Dictionary definitions tend
to be circular, on the lines of 'public relations means relations with the public'.
It would be very difficult to argue against that, but where does it get us?

American academics and the French Government have produced their own
definitions. So have interested associations in Britain. None of them, nor the
several international variations, seems to be the same as any other. It is easy to
get the impression that all 60 or so countries which have their own national PR
organizations, from the Arab Republic of Egypt to Zimbabwe (see Appendix C)
also have their own national PR definition.

In attempting to be comprehensive and exhaustive, definitions get longer and
longer, full of qualifying clauses and adjectives. I hesitate to add to their

number, but the issue of what PR is cannot be ducked. At the end of this chapter some ideas are put forward. But first, what kind of human activity are we talking about?

This PR business

To members of the Institute of Public Relations, PR is a *profession*, with its own council and officers, its own criteria, register of members and code of practice, its own definition of public relations—'The planned and sustained effort to establish and maintain goodwill and mutual understanding between an organisation and its publics'.[3]

The Institute aims to

- *represent* public relations practitioners in the United Kingdom;
- *regulate* and represent the practice of public relations in the United Kingdom;
- *raise* and maintain public relations standards in the United Kingdom;
- *encourage* the attainment of professional academic qualifications;
- *provide* advice, information and opportunities for discussion on all aspects of public relations work and to maintain contacts with practitioners throughout the world.[4]

From 1992 full membership of the Institute will be only by examination plus work experience.

However, many distinguished PR practitioners who do not belong to the Institute would consider themselves to be at least as professional as those who do. They could well be right.

One major source of recruitment into the PR business is the press. Ex-journalists and others who like to be thought of as practical and down-to-earth tend to make a point of referring to PR as their *trade*.

The people who are concerned with providing specific PR services, such as exhibitions or direct mail, have particular skills and know-how. Between them they command a wide range of technologies. They might perhaps be content, indeed proud, to talk about their *craft*.

Undoubtedly there are those, for example on the planning or research side, who are habitually numerate and analytical in all they do. They might rather like their own work to be classified as a *science*.

On the other hand, most of us have come across men and women who make a virtue of their ignorance of all things technical and who give the impression that to them PR is an *art*. Somehow that art is exclusive to them and beyond ordinary mortals like you and me—well, me, anyway.

Aspiring graduates, new entrants and young hopefuls know nothing of all this.

In their ignorance and innocence, all they want is to believe in a public relations *career*.

At one time or another, PR can be any of these, or any combination. But in-house PROs and external consultants, from organizations big and small, whether in the private or public sectors, in Westminster, the City or Whitehall, all have one thing in common. Whatever else they may be, they are all in the PR *business*.

What *size* of business are we talking about? In 1988, the PR industry as a whole (in-house and consultancy) was worth £500–£800 million. Between 24 000 and 34 000 people were employed in the business. Not all were PR practitioners, of course; probably between one-third and one-half were support staff.[5]

At the end of 1989, the picture was a little different. PR earnings approached the £1000 million mark. Around 20 000 practitioners were employed in the industry[6] distributed as shown in Figure 1.1.

Table 1.1, based on a survey of the top 1000 firms, shows the ages of in-house PR managers. The same survey gives salaries of PR professionals (Table 1.2).

A survey of in-house and consultancy incomes, undertaken jointly by *PR Week* and The Lloyd Group, aided by Numbers Research, and published in July 1990, included data on average UK salaries by job title, gender and specialization (see Figures 1.2 (a), (b) and (c)).

Each year's *PR Week* salary survey shows an increasing number of women working at all levels within the PR industry. Their pay is slowly catching up, but there is some way to go yet. Men still earn substantially more than women –

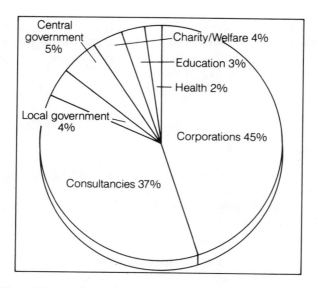

Figure 1.1 Where PR people work[7]

Table 1.1 Ages of in-house public relations professionals[8]

Age	%
Under 25	1
25–29	9
30–34	14
35–39	13
40–49	36
50–59	23
60+	4

Table 1.2 Salaries of in-house public relations professionals[9]

Salary	%
Less than £10 000	1
£10 000–£14 999	3
£14 999–£19 999	13
£20 000–£29 999	32
£30 000–£39 999	18
£40 000–£49 999	14
£50 000–£74 999	10
£75 000–£99 999	4
£100 000+	2
Not stated	3

35 per cent more on average—whereas women are significantly better qualified educationally than men.[10]

Setting the British scene in the world context, there seems little doubt that whatever difficulties the international advertising industry is going through, public relations is expanding in the United Kingdom and abroad. The first international survey of PR consultancies said that the market was worth £2500 million—a huge business. And because public relations is a business, like any other it has to be managed.[11] How?

The public interest

Anthony Sampson suggests, rather unfairly, that 'Whitehall finds PROs very convenient for explaining unpopular actions'.[12] At least he doesn't say 'explaining away'. Whether Whitehall or town hall, the public sector certainly does pay a good deal of attention to public relations. It spends a lot of time and money on it, and contrary to popular belief, it is rather good at it.

Expertise is especially strong in two main areas: media relations and information publications. Read any serious newspaper. Watch any television news or current affairs programme, national or regional. Listen to the radio news bulletins.

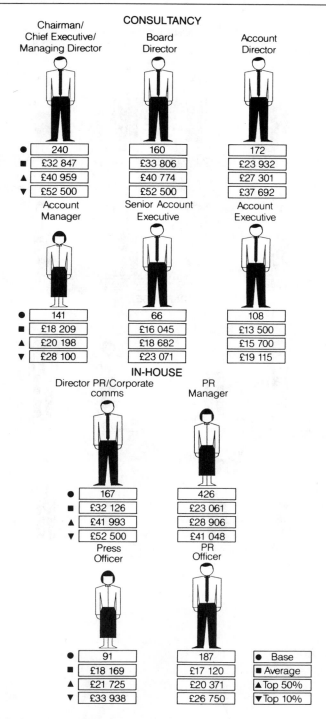

CONSULTANCY

Chairman/ Chief Executive/ Managing Director	Board Director	Account Director
● 240	● 160	● 172
■ £32 847	■ £33 806	■ £23 932
▲ £40 959	▲ £40 774	▲ £27 301
▼ £52 500	▼ £52 500	▼ £37 692

Account Manager	Senior Account Executive	Account Executive
● 141	● 66	● 108
■ £18 209	■ £16 045	■ £13 500
▲ £20 198	▲ £18 682	▲ £15 700
▼ £28 100	▼ £23 071	▼ £19 115

IN-HOUSE

Director PR/Corporate comms	PR Manager
● 167	● 426
■ £32 126	■ £23 061
▲ £41 993	▲ £28 906
▼ £52 500	▼ £41 048

Press Officer	PR Officer
● 91	● 187
■ £18 169	■ £17 120
▲ £21 725	▲ £20 371
▼ £33 938	▼ £26 750

●	Base
■	Average
▲	Top 50%
▼	Top 10%

Figure 1.2(a) Average salaries by job title[13]

Figure 1.2(b) Average salaries of men and women[13]

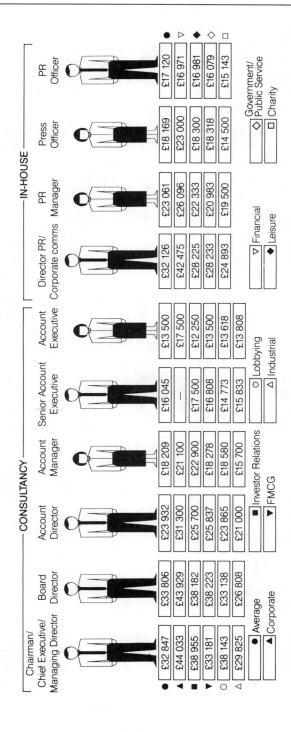

Figure 1.2(c) Average salaries according to specialization[13]

Analyse the news stories and identify their probable origin. The hand of the public relations official may not always be readily detectable, but it is pretty often there. Study the range of material available to the public on health, safety, welfare, education and so on. Trace the origin of serious books and pamphlets on the arts and sciences or popular books on antiques and crafts. The presence of central and local government PROs is strong, if not always overt.

Not that media relations and publications are all that Whitehall and town hall can do. Conferences, exhibitions, presentations, briefings, films, videos, direct mail, receptions, telephone canvassing, cold calling—all these techniques, and more, are used by officials in the pursuit of public relations objectives. Yet there is considerable reluctance to admit that this is public relations at all.

Even on the political side, where departmental accountability constraints do not apply, Ministers may have their 'special advisers' or even 'special communications advisers'. They tend to come from the world of advertising but their job is essentially concerned with the presentation of policies to the publics affected by them, i.e. public relations.

About 130 organizations are listed in the official directory of information officers in government departments or public corporations—the so-called 'White Book'. There is much variety, from ACAS (the Advisory, Conciliation and Arbitration Service) to the Welsh Office; the British Museum to the National Audit Office; the Charity Commission to the Police Complaints Authority. Two out of three do not acknowledge the existence of public relations staff. Press officers, information officers, marketing managers and publicity officers abound, at all levels, from director to assistant. Writers and editors, draughtsmen and illustrators, librarians and executives—all have their recognized job titles.

Sometimes a board, corporation or council has an officer who looks after press and public relations. Others perceive a distinction between public relations and public affairs or corporate affairs. One or two have directors of communications. Interestingly, only a very few, such as the Cooperative Development Agency, admit to employing a public relations consultant or adviser.[14]

Whatever they are called, there can be little doubt that hundreds—if not thousands—of officials are engaged in public relations, though not all are listed in the 'White Book'.

The great departments of state which are headed by Cabinet Ministers—Treasury, Home Office, Foreign Office, Trade, etc.—are among the Whitehall heavyweights with highly professional and proficient PROs, most of whom are very close to their Ministers. The Prime Minister's office is no exception. What are the regular, frequent and officially non-existent lobby briefings by the Prime Minister's Press Secretary intended to be, if not public relations? (The PR expenditure of some departments is discussed in Chapter 8.)

So far the only mainstream Whitehall department in the 'White Book' to own up to having public relations officers on the staff is the Ministry of Defence.[15]

This may be particularly appropriate because it was surely someone with a well-developed sense of PR who first suggested changing the name of the Ministry. It used to be called The War Office.

Systems of management

By its very nature, business management is hazardous and subject to errors, inconsistencies and uncertainties. If it were not so, every manager would be effective and every business would be efficiently managed.

In an attempt to reduce the risks and increase safety margins, many theories, principles and practices of management have emerged. Unfortunately, the most common are usually the least effective, in the PR business, as elsewhere.

Everybody must have come across managements which seem short of hard information. Objectives are very general and quite unquantified. There is a certain vagueness about completion dates and a lack of precision on work in progress. Financial data are on the sketchy side. Markets are not so much researched as taken for granted. This is management by *guesswork*.

At the other extreme, there are managements where everything is codified and regulated, where things are invariably done by the book. What happened yesterday exactly determines what happens today and what will happen tomorrow. In this type of structure there is a set response to every situation and a set procedure for every eventuality—in other words, management by *formula*.

A very popular method turns the perfectly sound notion of making a decision when it is necessary, not before, into the bad one of never making a decision if you can get away with not making it for so long that it goes away—you hope. Management by postponement or by procrastination—what might be called management by-and-by—is management by *default*.

Many managements, whatever their theoretical basis, incorporate some of these elements, though hardly by intention. It is a question of management by *mistake* or *misadventure*.

More successful, for a time, is management by the *big stick*, particularly when unemployment is high or rising and when competition is excessively fierce. But that approach, being based on fear, is doomed to destruction. It literally frightens itself to death.

Fashions in management come and go. Nevertheless, management *à la mode* can be surprisingly effective and long lasting. For example, management by *objectives* (MBO) and management by *exception* (MBE) are widely recognized. MBO might be defined as agreeing with all concerned what is to be done and then doing it. By contrast, MBE is letting people get on with doing it until something goes wrong and then putting it right. These systems are made use of in the public relations business, as they are elsewhere, the world over.

Then there are the personal styles of management—management by *charisma*, as it were. What this really means is management by *example*, usually through the high profile leadership of one individual. In its weakest form, personality substitutes for management; in its strongest, it is management by *Messiah*. There are as many disadvantages as advantages in this type of management, so much depending on one man or woman. It is actually quite rare, and certainly much rarer than many of its apologists believe. It is not the same thing as management by *heroes*, which is different from management through *figureheads*.

Guide to good management practice

Descriptions of what good managers should do are fairly plentiful. It would be hard to better the guidelines in the *BIM Guide to Good Management Practice*. They range from objectivity and self-appraisal to considering the requirements of suppliers and customers and are reproduced here with the permission of BIM.[16]

1. As Regards the Individual Manager
   The Professional Manager should:
   (a) make proper use of the resources available to him.
   (b) appraise his own competence, acknowledge potential weaknesses and seek relevant qualified advice.
   (c) take every reasonable opportunity to improve his professional capability.
   (d) be objective and constructive when giving advice or guidance in his professional capacity.
   (e) accept accountability for the actions of his subordinates as well as for his own.
   (f) in pursuing his personal ambitions, take account of the interests of others.
   (g) never maliciously injure the professional reputation, or career prospects, of others nor the business of others.
   (h) be aware of and sensitive to the cultural environment within which he is working.

2. As Regards the Organisation
   The Professional Manager should:
   (a) by leadership, co-ordination, personal example and commitment direct all available efforts towards the success of the enterprise.
   (b) apply the lawful policies of the organisation and carry out its instructions with integrity.
   (c) define and maintain an organisation structure, allocate responsibilities and encourage the achievement of objectives, by team work where appropriate.
   (d) demonstrate his loyalty to the organisation by promoting its interests and objectives.

    (e) promote effective communications within the organisation and outside it.

    (f) make immediate and full declaration of any personal interests which may conflict with the interests of the organisation.

    (g) refrain from engaging in any activity which impairs his effectiveness as a manager.

    (h) act in accordance with his own judgement in any instance of conflict of interest arising from his membership of trade union, trade association or other body.

    (i) ensure that plant, processes and materials committed to his charge are maintained and operated as efficiently and safely as reasonably practicable.

3. As Regards Others who work in the Organisation

The Professional Manager should:

    (a) strive to minimise misunderstanding and promote good relations between all who work in the organisation.

    (b) consult and communicate clearly.

    (c) take full account of the needs and problems, ideas and suggestions of others.

    (d) ensure that all his subordinates are aware of their duties and responsibilities especially in relation to those of others.

    (e) encourage the improved performance of his subordinates and the development of their potential, by means of training and in other suitable ways.

    (f) be concerned in the working environment for the health, safety and well-being of all, especially those for whom he is responsible.

    (g) promote self-discipline as the best form of discipline both for himself and for his subordinates.

    (h) ensure that disciplinary or other corrective action is constructive and respects the dignity of all concerned.

    (i) using his judgement, advise senior colleagues in advance of situations in which they are likely to become involved.

4. As Regards Customers and Suppliers

The Professional Manager should:

    (a) ensure that the requirements of customers and suppliers are properly considered.

    (b) ensure that all the terms of each transaction are stated clearly.

    (c) ensure that customers and suppliers are informed of any action which may materially affect the terms of transaction and take all reasonable action to minimise risk to the parties involved.

    (d) avoid entering into arrangements which unlawfully inhibit the process of open competition.

    (e) respect the confidentiality of any information if so requested by customers and suppliers.

(f) establish and develop with customers and suppliers a continuing and satisfactory relationship leading to mutual confidence.

(g) neither offer nor accept any gift, favour or hospitality intended
as, or having the effect of, bribery and corruption.

(h) accept or deliver the product or service within the quality,
quantity, time, price and payment procedures agreed.

5. As Regards the Environment, Natural Resources and Society
The Professional Manager should:

(a) recognise his organisation's obligations to its owners, employees, suppliers, customers, users, society and the environment.

(b) make the most effective use of all natural resources and energy
sources for the benefit of the organisation and with minimum
detriment to the public interest.

(c) avoid harmful pollution, and wherever economically possible,
reprocess or recycle waste materials.

(d) ensure that all public communications are true and not
misleading.

(e) be willing to exercise his influence and skill for the benefit of
the society within which he and his organisation operate.

Words importing the masculine gender only shall include the feminine gender.

Five of these guidelines are very obviously relevant to the management of public relations:

2(e) promote effective communications within the organisation and outside it.

3(a) strive to minimise misunderstanding and promote good relations between
all who work in the organisation.

3(b) consult and communicate clearly.

4(f) establish and develop with customers and suppliers a continuing and
satisfactory relationship leading to mutual confidence.

5(d) ensure that all public communications are true and not misleading.

Although some of the other points may at first sight seem a little removed from
the everyday world of PR, all are relevant to a greater or lesser extent.

The only way to manage PR

What is inescapable is that no system of management can be successful for very
long if it does not have the support, cooperation and commitment of all those
involved, whether they are doing the managing or being managed. That is
management by *consent*.

Nor can any management be justified or maintained unless it is contributing
towards the economic performance and success of the undertaking—that is to
say, management by *results*.

The theme running through this book, the very reason for writing it, and the test of relevance to be applied in every chapter, is that the best way to manage public relations is by *consent and by results*. In truth, it is the only way.

It is essential that the two go together. Otherwise, a kind of managerial Butskellism pervades the organization. Consent dilutes into consensus and all too readily into connivance, characterized by a general unwillingness to oppose anything, even when it ought to be opposed.

Management by results should not be confused with guaranteeing results, nor with payment by results.

It is only very rarely that public relations practitioners have total control over the outcome of the work they do or the campaigns to which they contribute. It would therefore be wrong for them to guarantee a particular result. For example, to guarantee the publication of a press notice would not only be misleading, it would imply a possible breach of clause 2 ('corruption of the media') in the IPR Code of Professional Conduct (see Appendix B).

The Code is quite clear. Clause 9 states 'A member shall not negotiate or agree terms with an employer or client which guarantee results beyond the member's direct control to achieve'[17] (see Appendix B).

As in many other professions, the fee agreed between public relations practitioners and their clients (or employers) should properly take into account such factors as the practitioners' experience, skills, knowledge and resources, the complexity of the problem they are to tackle and the importance to the client or employer.

It can be argued that if a public relations campaign is successful in achieving its objectives, there is no reason why the value of the practitioner's contribution should not be recognized by an employer or client by a payment in addition to the agreed fee or salary. However, it would generally be considered bad professional practice to agree, say, a nominal fee relying on the success of the campaign to produce a substantial additional payment to make up the balance or perhaps an amount much larger. In no circumstances should the additional payment exceed the sum of the originally negotiated fee.

Any client or employer has to assess the effectiveness of the public relations service being provided. This assessment is likely to depend upon the attainment of a variety of achievable public relations objectives agreed in advance, ranging perhaps from improved employee relations to a defence against a takeover bid. The results which have been obtained need to be evaluated and management decisions made on future action and expenditure.

What is really needed is a determined attempt to find the common ground and compatibility of objectives shared by all the stakeholders in an enterprise. There will be more to say about stakeholders later.

Some definitions

The public relations business does not exist for its own sake. It needs to be understood in relation to the other communication businesses—marketing, advertising and so on—which make up the total business. Here are some definitions:

BUSINESS	This is about making products and providing services, about distribution and marketing, buying and selling. It is, of course, about making money and about making customers. Business is about satisfying the needs of consumers and reconciling the needs, demands and interests of shareholders and directors, employees and employers—in fact, all those affecting the business and affected by it.
MARKETING	This is about managing a business to provide customers with the products or services they want.
SELLING	This is about managing a business so that customers buy the products or services available.
PUBLIC RELATIONS	This is about managing the strategy and tactics of communication as an integral part of a business's policy making and decision taking[18] and is also about managing the reputation of a business.[19] Ultimately, PR is concerned with the management of behaviour—the behaviour of organizations and of publics important to them.
ADVERTISING	This is about controlling the form, content, placement and timing of a communication by paying for it.
PRESS RELATIONS	This is about influencing and assisting the media to communicate and is therefore not controlled.
FREE PUBLICITY	There is no such thing.

Some misapprehensions

Far from being static, public relations is constantly changing and developing. Although the old images of 'vodka-and-tonic' or 'gin-and-Jag' PR have practically faded from view, other myths and misapprehensions have arisen and are eager to take their place. They should be firmly resisted.

Anyone who reads this book may end up painfully aware that public relations is *not* 'being nice to everybody on company time' (William H. Whyte) or 'organised lying' (Malcolm Muggeridge) or 'free advertising' (a client). Nor is it a way of being paid for extending your social life into working time, despite the impression given by some PROs.

Perhaps the specialist mailing house which announced some newly available lists was trying to tell us something. For £50 per 1000, you could buy labels addressed to 'prisons, remand centres, young offender institutions, police headquarters, named PR consultants . . .'.[20]

None of the definitions and descriptions of PR, in these pages or elsewhere, can possibly be comprehensive. Even so, it is worth while constantly striving to improve them. 'The point of spending time arguing through definitions of the practice [of PR] is not to satisfy an academic need to fill time. The future and quality of the practice—and our capacity to train people to work in a clearly-defined professional practice—depends on it.'[21]

Conclusion

The management of public relations is no different from any other major management responsibility. It calls on the same order of knowledge, ability and skills. It is subject to the same errors and uncertainties.

At the outset, it is important to realize that PR is not a body of knowledge, like accountancy. Nor is PR a technique, in the sense that advertising is a technique. Still less is PR a bolt-on goodie to be applied after the real management job has been done. Above all, it is not a substitute for action.

Chernobyl's nuclear power station disaster hit the headlines in 1986 only after the fallout had reached detectable levels in countries outside Russia. A story journalists told each other at the time, in those pre-glasnost days, went like this.

When the Russians realized they had a crisis on their hands that could not be kept secret any longer, they appealed to the world's leaders for help.

American response was swift. The President announced through the international media, in prime time, that the US government was sending 5000 experts and $5 million by supersonic transport. It also sent five TV crews.

China held meetings in every town and village and reached a collective decision to send $5000 and 5 million people. They are expected to arrive any day now.

France returned the request to the senders, unanswered, because it wasn't in French.

The most economical response came from the UK Prime Minister's Press Secretary, who said 'Change the name'.

None of that is true, of course, and none of it is PR, which involves a coordinated approach to the real world of business and politics and education and consumerism. PR is about managing the interfaces between buyer and seller, manufacturer and wholesaler, retailer and customer, landlord and tenant, head office and regions, government and electorate, and all those groups whose interests may appear sometimes to be contradictory but are also interdependent.

Efficient, effective and systematic public relations will become increasingly essential to the success of any enterprise.

WARNING   Beware, because even the best PR cannot transform a bad business policy into a good one. Unfortunately, bad PR can severely damage even the best business policy, and indeed the business itself.

Sources and references

  1. Tony Spalding. *Public Relations* 40th Anniversary issue. Summer 1988.
  2. H. Igor Ansoff. *Corporate Strategy*. Penguin, London, 1979.
  3. *Professionalism in Practice*. Institute of Public Relations, London, 1990.
  4. *Register of Members*. Institute of Public Relations, London, 1990.
  5. *Facts about the PR industry*. Institute of Public Relations, London, 1988.
  6. Simon Hatherstone and Diane Taylor. 1989: PR rides high on a wave of changes. *PR Week*, 21 December 1989.
  7. *Report and Accounts 1989*. Institute of Public Relations, London, 1990.
  8. *The Survey of United Kingdom Public Relations Professionals*. Burson-Marsteller, London, 1990.
  9. ibid.
 10. Incomes in PR, *PR Week*, 5 July 1990.
 11. as source 6.
 12. Anthony Sampson. *The New Anatomy of Britain*. Hodder & Stoughton, London, 1971.
 13. as note 10.
 14. *Information and Press Officers in Government Departments and Public Corporations*. Central Office of Information, London, 1990.
 15. ibid.
 16. *BIM Guide to Good Management Practice*. British Institute of Management, 1990.
 17. as source 4.
 18. *Executive MBA Programme*. Cranfield School of Management, 1987.
 19. Traditional: also attributed to Warren Newman.
 20. Tony Attwood. *Hamilton House Mailings*.
 21. Jon White. PR Training Conference, 1987.

CHAPTER 2

A systematic approach

There are only two golden rules.
Golden rule No 1: There are no golden rules.
Golden rule No 2: When in doubt, refer to rule No 1.

Anon, twentieth century

Management gurus give out plenty of guidelines and suggestions but very few rules. Their reasoning is that management is not so much about applying the right rules as about getting the right results. What works is what matters.

Management, whether of PR or anything else, is not a matter of all-purpose solutions and foolproof formulae. Cast-iron systems are like the metal they are named after—rigid, inflexible, immensely strong for some applications but surprisingly brittle for others.

Still, a relatively small number of guidelines works so often, in so many situations, for so many people, that they acquire the status of, if not golden rules, at any rate the nearest to them that the PR business is ever likely to have. Call them golden guidelines.

A golden guideline

The first guideline is that because you cannot do everything, you should make sure you do what matters. This is consistent with the well-known Law of Diminishing Returns—that after a certain level of results has been achieved, any further improvements require an unacceptably disproportionate amount of effort.

A respectable academic basis for these popular beliefs is found in the work of Vilfredo Pareto (1848–1923). An Italian sociologist, economist and engineer, Pareto studied the distribution of incomes and noted that even in relatively stable economies the general equilibrium concealed huge inequalities. Society was always made up of an élite minority and a large mass. Most of the power was in a very few hands. A small fraction of the people owned an overwhelming percentage of the wealth. He looked for significant ratios to express these imbalances.[1]

The value of the Pareto Principle to a manager is that it focuses attention on separating the 'vital few' from the 'trivial many'. One company finds that a small number of establishments accounts for a high proportion of total purchases. Another observes that the majority of sales derives from a minority of customers. Identifying these vital few and concentrating effort upon them is seen as the key to success.

These unequal patterns are traditionally described as the 20/80 distribution rule. It is much used in business forecasting, particularly in Europe. In the somewhat harsher economic climate of the United States, it became the 10/90 rule although movie-genius Woody Allen supported the Pareto Principle when he said that 80 per cent of success is showing up.

In its classic form, the 10/90 rule states that 90 per cent of effects follow from 10 per cent of causes. The converse is that 10 per cent of events account for 90 per cent of results.

Science fiction writers are said to acknowledge a more severe rule propounded by one of their own breed. What they know as Sturgeon's law states that 95 per cent of everything is rubbish.

Thomas Alva Edison went much farther even than 20/80, 10/90 or 5/95. Like many an innovator and inventor before him (and since) he could take extreme positions. He asserted that genius is 1 per cent inspiration and 99 per cent perspiration. However, that particularly idiosyncratic insight—we might think of it as Edison's 1/99 rule—was extemporized during a newspaper interview. So the exaggeration is quite understandable.

Is any one of these ratios preferable to all the others? Observation suggests that none is consistent enough. To qualify as a golden guideline in the United Kingdom, a more characteristic relationship might be 1/3 or thereabouts. If we accept that as reasonably likely, we could perhaps express it as a 25/75 ratio. Shall we call it Stone's supposition?

Stone's supposition

Once you start looking for this particular ratio, it can be surprising what you find. Here are some examples.

- A well-known British publisher's production manager found that 25 per cent of the product range generated 75 per cent of the volume.
- The sales manager of a video-hire company noted that 25 per cent of the customers placed 75 per cent of the orders.
- A major screen writer says that 75 per cent of a script is structure and 25 per cent is words.
- For one in-house PR team, Stone's supposition meant that 25 per cent of the staff thought up 75 per cent of the usable ideas.
- The director of a very successful PR agency ruefully admitted that 25 per cent of the clients gave it 75 per cent of the aggro.
- In the consultancy world at large, research confirms that an executive has to generate four times his or her own salary to cover overheads and make a

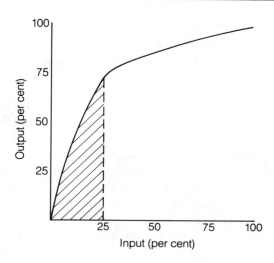

Figure 2.1 Stone's supposition—the 25/75 golden guideline

profit. We could say 25 per cent of clients' fees pays for time and 75 per cent pays for everything else.
- On the bottom line, a very senior accountant reckoned that 25 per cent of what the business did was responsible for 75 per cent of what it earned.
- The other side of that coin is that for many firms 75 per cent of what the business costs accounts for 25 per cent of what it earns.

All these expressions of the 25/75 Stone supposition have a characteristic shape as shown in the graph (see Figure 2.1) which plots input against output but could just as well have plotted customers against orders or sales against costs.

An obvious question

Don't misunderstand me. I'm not saying that once you've identified the vital 25 per cent you can totally forget about the rest. What is true is that the more management's work can be done in the triangular area of the 25/75 golden guideline, the more effective it will be.

Yet it is a fact that most managers spend most of their time and effort, and indeed nearly all their working lives, in the other area, where by definition they are bound to be least effective. Why?

Is it largely because that is where the 'interesting' problems lie? By nature, experience and training, managers do love to solve problems. Think of the intellectual challenge. Think of the demands on creativity and inventiveness, on perseverance and drive. Trying to solve problems can draw on a lifetime's expertise and know-how. It can engage the firm's ablest brains. It can lead to the setting up of task forces, working parties, project groups, think tanks, brain stormings and all manner of special arrangements, exciting to belong to and enviable to those who do not belong.

And oh! that sense of personal achievement and corporate satisfaction when the problem is finally cracked.

Amid all this involvement and commitment to solving the problem, and the elation that follows a successful solution, the obvious question can so easily be overlooked.

According to one of the characters in an Anita Brookner novel that did not win the Booker Prize, 'problems to which there is no solution waste a lot of one's time'.[2] It can be very difficult, if not impossible, to predict in advance whether a problem is actually capable of solution or not. But even more serious is the amount of time wasted on problems that do not need to be solved. Instead of asking 'Can we solve this problem?', the question ought to be 'Do we have to solve this problem?'

The road to successful PR management is littered with discards: the problems that it was not imperative to solve and the questions that never needed to be answered. That is the moral of a salutary case history from the days when decimal coinage had been introduced and metric weights and measures were supposed to follow, and when for a time going metric was thought to depend on knowing metric.

Case History 1
Going metric

Between 1965 and 1975, the Metrication Board expended considerable amounts of time and money on programmes of education and information in the schools and in selected industries, designed to give people a sound working knowledge of the metric system. Going metric was being introduced on a non-statutory basis spread over at least a decade. The principle was that if people could understand metric as well as they understood imperial, they would be able to adapt to whatever changes took place.

Regular research was carried out into people's knowledge of metric weights and measures, and as time went on, detectable improvements were noted after each and every survey.

Yet despite these consistent, if modest, gains in knowledge, there seemed to be no corresponding reduction in errors and complaints—all very baffling. Then someone at the Metrication Board had a bright idea.

The assumption had always been that no matter how easy or difficult it might be to learn the metric system (and logically it must be easy, given its simplicity), the hard thing was to unlearn the imperial system everybody had been brought up on and thoroughly understood.

So how much imperial was there to be unlearned? The Board members decided it was about time they found out. A very large random sample of the adult population was asked seven questions about common imperial weights and measures, from 'How many ounces in a pound?' to 'How many pints in a gallon?' The results of this survey were shattering.

Only 11 per cent of respondents could answer all seven questions correctly. Two out of three did not know how many stones in a hundredweight. Nearly three out of four did not know how many fluid ounces in a pint, even though at the time of the survey the fluid ounce was an everyday measure for liquids.

In fact, the message coming back very strongly from this research was that in many ways the people of Britain were at least as well—or as ill—informed about metric units of weights and measures as they were about imperial units. The conclusion was swiftly reached that effective use of units of weights and measures does not depend upon knowledge of them.

The folklore that everybody in the country thoroughly understood their traditional weights and measures was exposed for the myth that it was. Knowledge of a measurement system is not essential to its use.

Almost immediately the Metrication Board switched the emphasis of its campaign from knowing about the metric units to using them in practical situations. This shift from education to familiarization had quite dramatic results, and the pace of going metric started to gain momentum.

It was no fault of the Board that in 1980 the government of the day backtracked on the national commitment to metrication. With this conspicuous dilution of official backing, the campaign slowed down, leaving the country with a curiously hybrid weights and measures 'system' that was part imperial, part metric and wholly unsystematic.[3]

This case history provides many lessons. The most relevant to this chapter is that unless solving a problem (e.g. improving public knowledge of the metric system) contributes significantly to the achievement of a specified result (e.g. more effective use of metric weights and measures), it is better left unsolved.

Another golden guideline

All this is entirely in line with BIM's insistence, in its guidelines, on making proper use of resources, being objective and constructive, and directing all efforts towards success.[4]

What is needed is to build these first golden guidelines of PR into a structured and formal approach to the whole business of public relations, step by step and

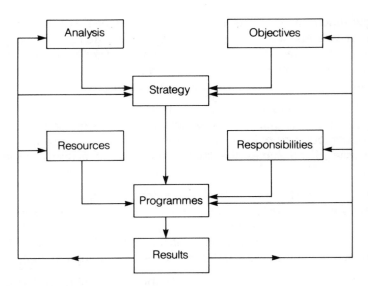

Figure 2.2 Systematic management approach to PR

stage by stage, according to a system which itself becomes a golden guideline. This is shown diagrammatically in Figure 2.2.

The system

Analysis

The first step of the first stage is directed inwards. You need to identify objectively and with precision the present position of your organization. What is done well? What are the reasons for that? What about those things that are done less well? Why is that? Does everyone concerned know what results are expected? What immediate changes can be made to bring about improvements in company performance? And longer term changes—how will they be managed?

Step two is to direct the same objectivity and precision outwards, to all the circumstances surrounding the organization, starting with the problems, that is the gap between what exists and what ought to exist.

Every manager knows that problems are opportunities in disguise. Consequently as much care should be spent in analysing opportunities as problems. According to Francis Bacon, a wise man will make more opportunities than he finds[5]—and what manager does not want to be wise? Nevertheless, if every cloud does have its silver lining, it is also true that every silver lining has its cloud. The down side of newly created opportunities is newly created problems, and these in turn need to be analysed. It is a never ending process.

Objectives

The second stage in your systematic approach to the management of PR involves moving from the relative certainties of analysis, and the reporting of where you are, to the as yet unrealized landscape of intentions and their quantification. What exactly are the changes that have to be achieved? If you need to increase awareness of what your organization is doing, by what percentage and among what audience? Define what other changes you want to bring about, from knowledge to behaviour. What quantity will you measure and in what units? The more specifically you can quantify your objectives, the better chance you have of being able to measure how successful you are in attaining them.

Strategy

Books and courses on management use military analogies to explain what is meant by strategy. Taking the hill by sending up the tanks, in the moonlight— that sort of thing. It may not seem all that relevant to the workaday world of business, but it is. Strategy is about achieving your objectives by out-generalling the competition, so that they are prevented from achieving theirs. Before any PR programme techniques or events can be thought about sensibly, let alone decided on, there is one big, crucial, decision to make. To use another popular metaphor, you need to know what bridge you are going to build to get you from where you are to where you want to be; in other words, to close the gap between analysis and objectives.

Programmes

This is the stage where you plan everything that has to be done and specify the methods you will use. It is a matter of making practical choices about audiences and messages, techniques and timetables, distribution channels and costs. Management preoccupations are with content, form and execution and the contribution they make to the achievement of specific results over a specified timescale. It is through the implementation of programmes that your objectives are realized.

Resources

A great deal of the time of a PR manager is taken up with the management of time. There is never enough. The same is true of money and of human resources. Education, training and retraining are now recognized as resources to invest in. Information is an undervalued resource.

In the public sector, PR management capacity is usually in-house—although the job titles of the people concerned rarely include the actual words 'public relations'—and services are bought on direct contract as required. In the private sector, some of the major companies have their own PR divisions: others engage PR consultants from outside the firm. Increasingly, a combination of in-house and bought-in is the norm and that can produce management challenges of its own.

Responsibility

If something is to happen, someone has to be responsible for making it happen. Otherwise not only will it not happen but the gap is likely to be filled by something else happening.

As a manager, you are responsible for more work than you can do personally—in the final analysis that is what being a manager is about—and you need to assign, allocate and delegate parts of it to other people. As well as being clear about who is doing what, you need to be sure that everyone concerned knows the limits of his or her authority. Traditional linear and pyramidical structures are no longer appropriate.

Evaluation

Measuring the effectiveness or otherwise of your results involves comparisons. Strategically, you compare your overall expectations, quantified, against your overall achievements, quantified. Tactically you compare the intention behind each programme element, and the resources expended on it, with the individual result. Could you have achieved the same with fewer resources? or a better result for the same outlay? Are you sure you know what to measure, how to measure it, and what to do with that information when you've got it?

Accountability

Ultimately, the chief executive or equivalent is accountable for all that is done in the name of the organization. Except in the smallest concerns, that accountability is discharged and channelled through board level directors or people in corresponding positions.

There are very few heads of public relations at that level in the United Kingdom today. PR consultancies excepted, for reasons that are self-evident, most PR directors are accountable to other directors who are at board level—for example, directors of marketing or of corporate services.

The full potential and power of PR will only be unleashed when this state of affairs is corrected. That is a major and urgent task for PR people themselves. Never mind the sometimes niggling concerns about image and status that seem to preoccupy the media. What matters is getting the reality right. Good PR is central to the success of an organization and belongs at the centre. Anything less is a limitation that amounts to self-inflicted damage.

Over the next few chapters, each of these PR management stages will be examined in detail. It is not, of course, as tidy as that in practice. The book implies an orderly sequence—first you analyse, then you set objectives, then you devise a strategy and so on. That is the theory.

But you and I know better. We know that even as you are collecting information for the analytical stage you are roughing out your main objectives, and also getting to grips with the constraints there might be on certain strategic options, including the comparative costs and timescales of some programme techniques. 'Management theory' says Robert Heller 'is full of practical conflicts that neither time nor talent can permanently resolve.'[6]

So although you should find it helpful to keep the systematic approach in mind, be prepared to accept that:

- if something can go wrong, it will.
- if something can't go wrong, it will anyway.

Take the case of the giant South American louse—a real life-and-death matter. The story was going the rounds at the United Nations in Geneva some years ago. It also surfaced in a somewhat different form in a monumental American book on effective public relations.[7] My version draws on both sources.

Case History 2
The giant South American louse

Analysis

In one South American country, health officials were concerned about the unusually and persistently high incidence of typhus. Research pinned it down to the continuous transmission of the disease by a particularly tough and atypically large body-louse.

Objective

Operationally, the objective was virtually self-evident: to eradicate the louse by total destruction. But there was a major difficulty. The population was host to a great variety of different body-parasites, only one of which carried typhus. This was the one that had to be identified and destroyed. To eradicate all the others was out of the question.

Strategy

The crucial decision was that everyone in the country—men, women and children—was to be taught to recognize the giant louse on their own bodies and destroy it. So in a relatively short period the disease should be under control, perhaps even extinct. The cost to the public health departments would be minimal.

Programme and resources

Because the understaffed Health Department had a very tight budget, and because so many different health education programmes were competing for these limited resources, what was needed was a low-cost way of reaching a large number of people quickly and with impact. The answer was a saturation poster campaign.

The posters had to speak for themselves. They were a triumph of graphic design—very few words of simple, hard-hitting text tied in with a superb picture blow-up of the actual body-louse in question. As long as the printed versions were of adequate quality, they were bound to make an impact.

Responsibilities

Things were getting urgent. Because of high-level political pressure, there was no time to do a test run or set up a control experiment. Huge numbers of the poster were produced very quickly. To maintain quality, they were approved and printed centrally and rushed to regional distribution points throughout the country. Local medical staff and volunteers were authorized to get them to any and every place where people lived or gathered so that nobody could avoid seeing them. In places where the level of literacy was low, local readers were recruited as 'town criers', putting across the words on the posters and drawing attention to the pictures. The nationwide health education campaign was rolling.

Evaluation

To the astonishment of the Health Department officials, it made not the slightest difference to the number of typhus cases. Even over a long period of time there was no measurable improvement. Eventually the campaign was recognized as a failure and stopped. Then the inquests began. Did the posters get to their target audience? They did. Were they prominently displayed in suitable places? They were. Could the target audience under-stand the words? Yes, either direct or through the 'town criers'. Yet the education programme had obviously failed to educate. Why? Was it perhaps because not enough money had been spent on design? artwork? production? What had gone wrong?

The answer was in those beautiful, poster-size blow-ups of the typhus-carrying louse. They were perceived by the villagers as being actual size. Because no one had ever seen a louse that big, let alone had one on their body, it was nothing to do with them, was it? They switched off and closed their minds, not only to the posters, but to the entire health campaign.

The alternative version of this case gives film as the chosen method, not posters. The result is the same, for the same reason. Typhus continued to flourish because nobody had checked whether the visual conventions and interpretive skills of the mass population were the same as those of the city sophisticates, which the strategists and planners took for granted. They were not. The inescapable conclusion is that for a PR programme to be cost-effective, it must first actually be effective. If it is not, even a low-cost campaign is unaffordable.

Accountability

Whatever heads may have rolled in the design studio or out in the field, accountability should have rested with those who made the crucial strategic decision, authorized the programme for carrying it out and delegated the responsibility down the line. There is no information on what happened to them.

Summary: The eight-stage approach

A systematic management approach to public relations has these eight key stages.

1. ANALYSIS	What precisely are the problems to be solved? And the opportunities to be seized?
2. OBJECTIVES	What specific results do we aim to achieve? What changes do we want to bring about?
3. STRATEGY	What are the crucial decisions we have to make to attain our objectives?
4. PROGRAMMES	Which methods and media will we use? How? When?
5. RESOURCES	How many people do we need? How much money? What services and materials? What will we actually get?
6. RESPONSIBILITY	Who is going to do what? On whose authority?
7. EVALUATION	How well did we do? How do we know?
8. ACCOUNTABILITY	Who is answerable for what was done?

Sources and references

1. V. F. D. Pareto. *Sociological Writings*.
2. Anita Brookner. *A Start in Life*. Jonathan Cape, 1981.
3. David Morris (ed.). *Economics of Consumer Protection*. Heinemann, London, 1982.
4. *BIM Guide to Good Management Practice*. British Institute of Management, 1990.
5. Francis Bacon (1561–1626). *Essays: Of Ceremonies and Respects*.
6. Robert Heller. Back to basics. *Management Today*. March 1990.
7. Cutlip, Center and Broom. *Effective Public Relations*. Prentice Hall, New York, 1985.

CHAPTER 3
Analysis and audit

Motorist [*after an hour's fruitless search along country lanes*]
   'I say, fellow, can you tell me the way to Steeple Snodgrass?'
Yokel [*after long thought*]
   'If I was you, Mister, I wouldn't start from here.'
Motorist [*scathingly*]
   'Oh yah? Tell me, what are you—the village idiot?'
Yokel [*quietly*]
   'I'll tell you what I baint, Mister. I baint lost.'

                                                                    Trad.

Most of the examples and case history summaries in this book include a brief analysis. For example, Dr Barnardo's, the child care charity, analysed the nature of the support they were getting from voluntary contributors. They were surprised to find that they were being given money for the wrong reasons. Can there ever be a wrong reason for giving money to charity? Yes, if the funds generated as a result of misunderstanding are having an inhibiting effect on a much larger potential total. Dr Barnardo's discovered that too many people thought of them as a charity solely for orphans, whereas their true concern is for all disadvantaged children. Once Dr Barnardo's knew that, they knew where they stood and the direction they had to go to put things right (see Chapter 6).

For the Tea Council, analysis was equally revealing, though in a quite different way. Their analysis showed that the under 35 age group had gone off their favourite non-alcoholic drink—tea—and were much more likely to prefer coffee or a soft drink as their first choice. The Council turned this problem into an opportunity by maximizing an unexpected advantage; it just happened to be the 70th anniversary of the Brownies (see Chapter 4).

In their distinctive ways, both these analyses pointed the way to the need for specific repositioning campaigns. The Tea Council repositioned the product; Dr Barnardo's repositioned itself. Before you can reposition, you have to know the existing position. That is what analysis is about—the drawing of clear and accurate positional maps. It is a relatively common procedure in relation to sales, advertising and marketing, but still fairly new as far as PR is concerned, though that is now changing.

In the absence of any agreed methodology, PR consultants and in-house managers either make up their own rules or they don't have any, in which case they pull out their standard menu of techniques and media—putting à la carte before the horse. There has to be a better way.

Management consultants and accountancy firms are interested because what is needed looks remarkably close to what they are already doing. Could they move into the territory which public relations consultants think of as their own? No wonder PR people are now starting to apply the disciplined methodology that the best practitioners insist is essential. Some of them call it a PR audit.

Essentially an audit is a professional opinion, based on judgement applied to information, or evidential matter as the accountants call it. The judgement is not only on *how* this evidential matter is to be interpreted, but *what* information should be amassed.

In one well-known version of the process, there are three clear stages:

1. *Information gathering:* identifying and collecting relevant data.
2. *Strategic analysis:* weighing all options and choosing the most appropriate.
3. *Communications programme:* putting the chosen option(s) into effect.

This calls for a good deal of work, carefully done and well documented, geared to the organization's goods and services that are being communicated as well as to the communications process itself.

There may be some times when this kind of audit is more useful than others. Certainly you need to do it when a major PR campaign is being contemplated. Other appropriate times include 'when a new managing director takes the helm . . . and needs a snapshot of the company. The same is true during an acquisition or merger.'[1]

On occasions such as those, a major organization might well spend 75 per cent of a sizeable PR budget on information gathering and analysis, leaving 25 per cent to pay for the actual communications programme. To justify this scale of endeavour, the audit has to be comprehensively and professionally carried out. Unfortunately 'most consultancies miss the point—namely that it is reputation management for competitive advantage'[2] which no doubt explains why 'the average audit isn't worth the paper it's written on',[3] let alone the fee that may be charged.

The PR business will get better at communications analysis and auditing, because it has to if it is to survive.

A leading figure in the methodology, Reginald Watts, argues that a company's position map should be unique, flexible enough to change with the climate, and draw together external perception against internal hopes. To do this, he suggests taking an overview through a three-segment process (see Figure 3.1).

The first segment involves collecting information on attitudes and trends, by means of internal and external interviews against a common topic menu.

The second segment is a strategic analysis which draws out the key 'image dimensions', from which several alternative strategies are articulated in a 'preferred strategy matrix'.

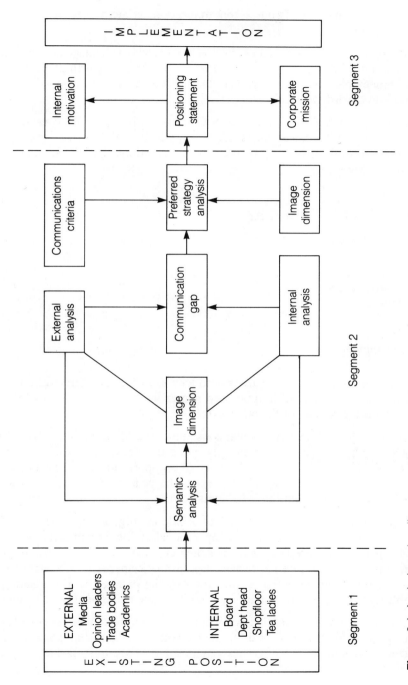

Figure 3.1 Analysis and audit—an overview[4]

The third segment spells out a communications strategy, programme, action plan and timetable.

This structured approach makes effective use of a classic management technique known as the SWOT analysis (Strengths, Weaknesses, Opportunities, Threats). The mnemonic conveys very well the notion of hard, sustained, detailed study—in a word, swotting.

I would like to suggest a variant of SWOT which is developed from the same four elements. The mnemonic is ADOPTS, which might be taken to imply the idea of choice, of picking up or taking over something that already exists, and making it one's own.

The ADOPTS system

The mnemonic stands for

- *A*dvantages
- *D*isadvantages
- *O*pportunities
- *P*roblems
- *T*ime factor
- *S*takeholders.

The first and second of these are inward looking, while the third and fourth are outward looking. The fifth applies no matter which way you are looking and the sixth is the reason for the other five.

In the language of the management consultancy world, you have internal levers (the strengths you can turn to advantage and the weaknesses that will prove to be disadvantages) and external drivers (the opportunities and problems that make up the context in which you exist, the economic, social, political and competitive environment that surrounds you).

If you take a long, hard, objective look inside the organization, whether client or employer, you can expose your operational strengths and weaknesses and relate these to the needs of your stakeholders—customers, agents, suppliers, staff and so on. This internal review of performance needs to be matched by an equally tough and objective examination of the external world, relating the problems and opportunities that you identify to the needs of your stakeholders.

Such external and internal reviews of context and performance lack one further dimension if they are to add up to an entirely convincing portrait of the organization and a map of its present position. That missing factor is time, which does not stand still.

For each and every stakeholder, the advantages and disadvantages, opportunities and problems, all have to be set against a timescale. What is true now

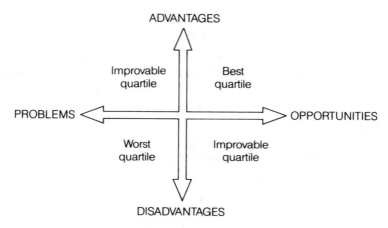

Figure 3.2 The ADOPTS system of analysis

need not be true forever. Today's demoralized staff can become tomorrow's well-informed and well-motivated workforce. A change in legislation can wipe out a complete customer group. New products or services can affect potential market standing.

But when you have collected all this analytical material, this evidential matter, what do you do with it?

Sales managers are accustomed to producing situation reports, or sitreps, on sales, while personnel managers do the same on staffing. Accountants expect to report on the company's financial situation, legal advisers on the legislative position, and so on for all the functions of an organization. When these are put together, you have a situation sitrep. The contribution of PR managers is a sitrep on communications, or a reputation sitrep. That is what the ADOPTS system aims to do.

In the representation shown in Figure 3.2, the best quartile corresponds to the vital 25 per cent of the 25/75 ratio expressed in the Stone supposition. That is where your main effort should go. The two improvable quartiles are next in order of importance and will require a commensurate level of effort. Trying to improve the worst quartile will almost certainly take a disproportionate effort in terms of the likely benefit. If you can forget about it, do.

How does ADOPTS work in practice?

Stakeholders

Whatever other purposes an organization may have, it must also have the purpose of serving the interests of all its stakeholders—that is, all the people affecting the organization and affected by it.

All stakeholders are not necessarily of equal importance, nor does their relative importance or lack of it remain unchanged for all time. Before you start the ADOPTS analysis you first need to identify and rank your stakeholders.

Who and where they are will depend on who and where you are. There can be no standard list, although some stakeholders—for example, customers—are bound to occur on pretty well every list. It is easy to miss out a complete category of stakeholders altogether. Your customers may be your consumers, but they may not. You need to make sure both are included.

To explain this in more detail, let us assume that you have identified the following stakeholders in your own enterprise:

academics	investors
agents	lobbyists
analysts	management
board of directors	media
consumers	neighbouring community
customers	policy community
distributors	pressure groups
finance providers	shareholders
government (central)	shopfloor workers
government (local)	suppliers

That is not a definitive list. For you and your organization, local MPs could be very important stakeholders. So could local industry groups and trade unions, whereas you may have no agents or shareholders at all. Only you can decide who your stakeholders are, but note that your company cannot choose its own competitors; these are actually selected by one of the other groups—your customers. Indeed, to an extent your customers are themselves competitors, because any advantage they secure is going to be at your expense.

There is likely to be considerable variation in the needs and expectations of the different groups and in the effectiveness or otherwise of your dealings with them. Stakeholders are not necessarily the same as programme targets or campaign audiences. They may well be, of course, and certainly the one will contain the other. But you need to be clear in your own mind which is which.

The media will almost certainly be on the list of stakeholders of most organizations. But what media? National press? Trade and technical journals? Regional TV and local radio programmes? These are broad questions requiring broad answers.

Try not to be concerned at this stage with programme targeting, where you will need to look deeper, if more narrowly. When defining stakeholders, you do not need to know precisely which individual titles and editorial staff you need contact to help get your message across. For advice on when and how to answer that kind of question, see Chapter 6. ADOPTS analysis is not about programme targeting or getting coverage. It is about meeting the needs of stakeholders. You are not asking the media to write about you, only to understand you, as you try to understand them.

For your own ADOPTS analysis, you have to give an importance rating to each group of stakeholders. On a scale of, say, 1 to 5, how would you rate them? Give a high number to high importance:

Very important	5
Important	4
Quite important	3
Not very important	2
Unimportant	1

Some of the various ways of helping you to arrive at this kind of grading are discussed elsewhere in this book.

For the purposes of the present chapter, let us assume that you have arrived at the following importance gradings:

academics	1
agents	4
analysts	1
board of directors	5
competitors	3
consumers	4
customers	5
distributors	4
finance providers	2
government (central)	2
government (local)	3
etc.	

For convenience, I have only dealt with part of the list. You would handle the rest in the same way.

Rearrange your selection in order of importance

5	board of directors
	customers
4	agents
	consumers
	distributors
3	competitors
	government (local)
2	finance providers
	government (central)
1	academics
	analysts

Remember this is only an exercise and not an attempt to give a universal importance rating to these or any other stakeholders.

Performance analysis

If your organization happened to be fully equipped and competent to meet all the needs of all your stakeholders, that would be a position of 100 per cent advantage and zero disadvantage. There may be such organizations, but none that I know of.

Every organization I have ever come across has an imbalance, advantages in respect of some stakeholders being more or less offset by disadvantages to others. For instance, a common Japanese view of British industry is that directors are more concerned to keep the shareholders informed than to communicate with the staff. This criticism—which may not be recognized as such by some of the worst offenders—is a kind of performance analysis.

To make your own internal analysis, you need to carry out a review, stakeholder by stakeholder, of the extent to which your organization meets their actual and perceived needs.

Just as you graded the stakeholders on a scale of 1 to 5, so you should grade performance, from 'outstandingly good' to 'gravely deficient'; or, since neither of these two extremes is likely to apply in your case (is it?), from 'very effective' (5) to 'ineffective' (1).

Very effective	5
Effective	4
Quite effective	3
Not very effective	2
Ineffective	1

Gradings of 5 and 4 are advantageous, gradings of 1 and 2 disadvantageous. A grading of 3 corresponds to the minimum acceptable performance.

There are no hard and fast rules for arriving at these gradings, but remember, you are looking at outputs not inputs, performance not intentions.

How well do you know the concerns, preconceptions and expectations of your stakeholders? To what extent are their perceptions and values the same as yours? Are your standards and procedures visible to and understood by them? Are they getting a true and fair view of you?

Your organization—international conglomerate, small local firm, government department, local authority, charity, educational establishment or whatever it may be—is not an abstraction, it is a personality. Whether that personality is working for you or against you is determined not by what you believe about

Table 3.1   Performance analysis

Stakeholder	Importance rating	Performance rating	Context rating
Board of directors	5	2	
Customers	5	4	
Agents	4	3	
Consumers	4	4	
Distributors	4	3	
Competitors	3	3	
Local government	3	5	
Finance providers	2	2	
Central government	2	5	
Academics	1	5	
Analysts	1	1	

yourself but by what your stakeholders believe about you. Some of the ways of finding out about that are discussed in Chapter 10.

When you have some answers that give you a reasonable assessment, make a simple matrix as shown in Table 3.1.

Clearly the very best position is when the needs of a stakeholder of top importance are met with top effectiveness. That would be a grading of 5:5, a winner to be backed.

At the opposite extreme, the worst position is a grading of 5:1, which means that your most important stakeholders are getting your worst performance. This is a signal of extreme danger calling for instant corrective action. A grading of 1:5, though equally out of balance, is not so catastrophic. It suggests that too much high quality resource is going into meeting needs that are not important enough to justify the effort. Remedial action is certainly called for, but it is nothing like as urgent as the demands of a 5:1 grading.

Other gradings indicate relative positions on the scale of advantages and disadvantages, and may give useful pointers to switching resources.

In our notional example, there is overperformance against the needs of local government (3:5) and underperformance as far as the board of directors is concerned (5:2). An obvious adjustment to the balance of advantage and disadvantage is indicated. I know which would cause me most concern.

The golden guideline is to concentrate on the more important stakeholders; maximize existing advantages, improve underperformance and, where it matters, reduce overperformance. In this particular case it would mean putting most resources into meeting the needs of customers (5:4) and consumers (4:4): increasing performance in respect of the board of directors (5:2), agents (4:3) and distributors (4:3); and reducing effort in relation to academics (1:5). The ratios give a good idea of the scale of change needed: 5:2 justifies more effort to improve than 4:3; 1:5 demands a bigger cut in effort than 3:5.

Stakeholder: The media	Importance					Capability					GAP
PR Activity	5	4	3	2	1	5	4	3	2	1	
A Personal contact	✔							✔			6 points
B Press notices		✔					✔				4 points
C Radio notices			✔						✔		5 points
D Press conferences	✔								✔		7 points
E Press cuttings		✔								✔	7 points
F Embargoes	✔									✔	8 points
G Distribution system	✔							✔			5 points

Figure 3.3 Importance/capability analysis

For all practical purposes, the other stakeholder groups in our imaginary example are probably best left to get on mostly by themselves. Competitors' needs are evenly matched by company performance (3:3). Likewise the less important groups—finance providers (2:2) and analysts (1:1).

You can refine your analysis by taking each major group of stakeholders in turn and assessing to what extent you have the capability to meet specific needs. To do this, you set down all the PR activities you carry out with and for that particular stakeholder group. Rate each activity for its *importance* to your organization, and your *capability* to deliver what is needed.

Suppose the stakeholder is the media. Your main PR activities will include personal contact, press notices, press conferences, etc. List them, and for each assign an *importance* rating and a corresponding *capability* rating, on a scale of 1 to 5. The maximum gap between the two is when importance is at its highest (5) and capability at its lowest (1)—a difference of 8 points. The minimum gap is when importance and capability are rated the same (5:5, 4:4, etc.)—a difference of 4 points. Differences of 6, 7, 8 points demand action, 8 being the danger signal calling for immediate response (see Figure 3.3).

In the example of Figure 3.3, clearly you must take immediate action to improve F—are your embargoes absolutely necessary? Do you embargo too often? Are they geared to suit your convenience, whereas they should be to help the media? Activities D and E require urgent attention, and activity A as soon as you can. B and G can be left alone for the moment, though if you leave them too long, the points gap will widen, and then they too will need urgent attention.

The thumbnail sketch of the imaginary organization begins to take shape. Basically market led, you are very good on customers and consumers, and quite good with your intermediaries (agents and distributors). You are needlessly keen on your relationships with central and local government and with the academic world. Could this reflect the background and interests of one of your key directors? Perhaps you yourself? Though you are presumably not a publicly quoted nor heavily-borrowing company, you keep in with the financial sector when it matters. Your media contacts are quite effective, but nobody takes any notice of your embargoes, your press briefings are better than your press conferences, and you ought to look at the way you monitor your performance through press cuttings. You must make sure pretty quickly that your board of directors sees things your way.

Context analysis

In this part of the communications analysis you are looking outside the organization to the opportunities and problems that make up the external context. Because it is usually harder to spot opportunities than to be aware of problems, let's consider opportunities first.

Crown Eyeglass, of Blackburn, supplies spectacles direct to the public through 90 franchised and company-managed outlets. The firm was set up specifically to exploit the de-regulation of the optical industry in 1984, when the opticians' monopoly in supplying spectacles was removed.

Four years later, Crown researched the market and found that 50 per cent of the 27 million people in Britain who wear glasses still did not know about the 1984 change in the law. They were unaware that while opticians were required to issue prescriptions for lenses, customers could buy the actual glasses wherever they liked.

Crown concluded that the Government had failed to publicize the legislative changes anything like enough. The firm used the survey results as powerful ammunition in a lobbying strategy with the Government as target.[5]

What sort of opportunity are you looking for? Is it unique, that is, capable of being seized in only one way? Are there several options? Is it a once-only chance which has to be taken at a specific time or not at all? Will comparable opportunities occur again? If so, when?

For your situation report you need to describe the nature of the opportunity. Is it to do with strategy rather than tactics? Is it an opportunity to improve or modify something that already exists, for example systems, procedures, structures? Will it lead to something entirely new—an opportunity to innovate?

What is the size of the opportunity? Or rather what is the scale of the expected benefit? Will it affect a few stakeholders or many? Remember, you want to take a broad view at this early stage in the management process. Too much detail will only bog you down with matters that should belong in the programme planning phases. What you really want is a grading figure on the 1 to 5 scale, just as you had for stakeholders and for performance analysis.

Although it is important to be aware of the overall context in which all

Table 3.2   Context analysis

Stakeholder	Importance rating	Performance rating	Context rating
Board of directors	5	2	3
Customers	5	4	4
Agents	4	3	3
Consumers	4	4	4
Distributors	4	3	3
Competitors	3	3	1
Local government	3	5	3
Finance providers	2	2	5
Central government	2	5	4
Academics	1	5	3
Analysts	1	1	1

organizations operate, the assessment and ranking of opportunities and problems needs to be carried out according to the potential impact on the success of your particular enterprise (see Table 3.2).

In an ideal world, your very important stakeholders would be matched by equally high performance and context analyses. The perfect matrix line would be 5:5:5, the worst would be 5:1:1. A safe, if unexciting average line would be 3:3:3. Rankings 5:5:5, 5:4:4, 4:5:4, 5:5:4, 4:5:5, 4:4:4 and 5:4:5 would all qualify for the best quartile (see Figure 3.2) and would therefore merit the fullest possible support. You will have to make your own judgement on other gradings, following the clues and cues as before.

It ought to be obvious that no matrix can make a decision for you. What it can do is help focus your attention on the areas that matter most. There is then the matter of interpretation—fleshing out the numerical simplifications with the real advantages and real opportunities they represent. Your professional know-how will be called upon and you will be very conscious of how much you depend on the accuracy and reliability of your information.

The time factor

In analysis, you are trying to deal—no, you *have* to deal—with the past, present and future all at the same time.

There is usually no shortage of information about the past. What you do is select what you need, test it for reliability and decide how you interpret it. Data about the present are harder to come by, and again you need to assess them for reliability and relevance. You are also more reliant on your own judgement, because there are fewer opinions expressed by others against which to match your own.

Reliable information about the future is clearly impossible to obtain, so you have to think in terms of probabilities. Remember that what you expect to happen can be influenced by what you intend to happen. There is no way of altering the past, but there are many possibilities for altering the future.

It is not much use just snapshotting the current position, because each time the shutter falls the situation can have changed, sometimes fractionally, but occasionally quite dramatically. Perhaps the image we should keep in mind is of computerized weather maps, which constantly shift and modify in line with updated forecasts that keep coming in.

The relative importance of some stakeholders compared with others can be very sensitive to time. For instance, when the government decided that something had to be done to help tackle long-term unemployment, they knew they would need the support and involvement of a wide range of people and institutions, each with their own prejudices and preconceptions.

These stakeholders included sponsoring organizations who would provide the necessary temporary work, taxpayers who would finance it, journalists and broadcasters who would report on it, employer and trade union organizations who would have mixed feelings about it, and the long-term unemployed who would actually do the work.

This is how government analysts ranked the main stakeholders in order of importance during the pre-launch and launch phases of the exercise.

Ranking	Stakeholders
5 Very high	Sponsors and potential sponsors
4 High	TUC members and trade union leaders
	Members of Parliament
	Local government officials and their professional organizations
	Local business/charity organizations such as Rotary clubs
	The media
	Voluntary organizations
3 Quite high	Trade union rank and file
	Advisers of the long-term unemployed
2 Quite low	CBI and other senior businessmen
	National business organizations such as chambers of commerce
	The long-term unemployed
	The local community

It is not surprising that there was no 'Very low' category. What government would want to be perceived as allocating the status of 'Very low importance' to any section of the electorate?

After the launch, some of the stakeholders began to shift up and down the scale.

Initially it made sense to rank the obvious beneficiaries of the scheme—long-term unemployed people—lower in importance than the providers of the work—the sponsors. Once the latter had committed themselves, it became necessary to ensure that the specially identified vacancies were filled, so that worthwhile work got done that would not otherwise have been undertaken. That put a higher importance ranking than before on the long-term unemployed, and their advisers.[6]

If rankings of stakeholders can change over time, so too can performance. What may be a disadvantage in year one of a longish PR campaign could be an advantage in a few years' time, and vice versa. That is particularly true of PR specialisms. For example, your company may not need much expertise in financial PR now, so not having anyone on tap with that know-how is no disadvantage. But if the business plan for the next five years culminates in a flotation on the Unlisted Securities Market, you will need to have the advantage of a financial PR capability in place not later than year four, whether in-house or bought in.

Time factor effects can be very important, though less foreseeable, in the contextual analysis relating to your hypothetical USM flotation. According to Shoosmiths & Harrison, solicitors: 'It is expected that the Stock Exchange will shortly announce that the USM and the Third Market are to be merged. An EEC Directive will require the main market to accept companies with a three year trading record as opposed to a five year record. Since this is one of the chief features distinguishing the main market from the USM, it is thought likely that the USM and the Third Market will be combined to form a new second tier market requiring a two year trading record.'[7]

Those changes could have had a profound effect on your company's business plan and communications programme. And wasn't it good PR for Shoosmiths & Harrison to provide their clients with this information?

The timescale element of the ADOPTS analytical process helps to direct minds towards the future, which may not be predictable with any certainty, but should not be a total mystery, either. You can be absolutely sure of one thing—the pace of change in your own business and in your client's will be faster next year than it was last. Managing the timescale includes spotting the time bombs.

FUN auditing

It is not always practicable to apply the intellectual discipline of a Reginald Watts, nor the methodology of SWOT or ADOPTS. But applying the golden guideline that there is always something useful you can do, a more modest approach is better than none. It is perfectly feasible to assess how the company informs without striving to pin down every possible piece of information or consider every conceivable option. In his analysis of the economics of consumer protection, David Morris had this to say about information and reputation: 'In the absence of perfect information on the reputation of a seller, the consumer may resort to signals which proxy for reputation, such as the amount of advertising done by the seller or the guarantee given with the product.'[8]

These are enlightening references to the reputation value, the image factor, the public relations implications, for good or ill, that flow from the sheer volume of advertising, irrespective of its content or style, and from the existence of a guarantee, whether or not it is ever called in and honoured.

PR by advertising as proxy for reputation is well understood by the Westminster/Whitehall axis. According to Rowland Morgan's 'Index' column in *The Independent on Sunday* the Department of Employment's TV advertising budget in the run-up to election 1986/87 was £16 400 000. In 1989/90 it was £2 800 000. The Department of Energy's TV advertising budget in the same election year, 1986/87, was £16 300 000 and in 1989/90 was nil.

The idea of signals which proxy for reputation is expressed by Norman Hart of Interact International in this way: 'The impression gained by an individual of an organisation comes from a multitude of signals he receives from all manner of sources. Some of these are quite deliberate by the organisation, e.g. advertising. Others are unintentional but can nevertheless be very important, e.g. the telephone manner of the sales department or the appearance of a delivery van.'[9]

It is good practice to make a list of all the message sources relevant to your own organization, from the annual report to attendance at conferences, customers to competitors, logotype to labels, social activities to service engineers.

When British Telecom changed the prefix for London telephone numbers from 01 to 071 or 081, the company issued a useful little checklist of types of material that would need to include the new numbers and an explanatory message about the change:

Stationery
Letterheads
Business cards
Compliment slips
Invoices
Computer stationery
Memoranda

Literature
Internal directories
Advertisements
Company brochures
Direct mail
Product brochures
Specification sheets

Other material
Signage
Public notices
Display fronts
Packaging
Vehicle livery
Emergency instructions
Hazard control signs[10]

That is not a bad starter list of message sources. For your own organization you should have no difficulty in jotting down another 30 or so without having to think very hard. Put your mind to it and you could come up with 100. For each of these message sources, or reputation proxies, you make an objective and realistic assessment of the value to your organization. Rate them Favourable, Unfavourable or Neutral (FUN). Try not to rely solely on your own judgement.

You might, for example, ring up some journalists you trust and ask them for their honest opinion on every aspect of your press relations—receptions, releases, news conferences, etc. You may find that their evaluation agrees with your own. If not, believe theirs rather than yours.

Ask your complaints department to show you what customers are concerned about—more data for your FUN audit.

As for the switchboard operators—well, you can telephone when you are away from base and make your own assessment.

Do the best you can to grade each and every message source as F, U or N. Do not overlook the routine paperwork like delivery notes and price lists, nor external sources like trade associations. Remember that ex-customers are very definitely a message source.

As far as you can, verify your own judgement in some independent way. You shouldn't want to believe only what you want to believe.

At the end of the exercise, you may not have a strict and intellectual evaluation. What you will have is a very good idea indeed of what proxy reputation signals are being sent out and how they are being interpreted. That will give you a 'starting point for a comprehensive and planned campaign to create a more favourable reputation'.[11]

When you have your FUN audit results (Figure 3.4), concentrate your best resources on exploiting the advantages of the F evaluations. They belong in the best quartile (see Figure 3.2). It is also worth putting considerable effort into turning the Ns of the improvable quartiles into Fs. The distance between Neutral and Favourable is much easier to bridge than the gap between Favourable and Unfavourable.

You will want to find out the reasons for any U gradings before you decide what, if anything, to do about them.

Assess each message source for its 'proxy reputation' value to the organization.

F = Favourable
U = Unfavourable
N = Neutral

	Message source	F	U	N
51	Notice boards			✔
52	Open days	✔		
53	Packaging		✔	
54	Quality marks			✔
55	Reception area		✔	
56	Staff newspaper	✔		
57	Visitors' toilets		✔	
58	etc.		✔	
59	etc.	✔		

Figure 3.4 FUN audits

Keep in mind the time factor. FUN audits are not once-for-all exercises. They need regular reviewing to plot the changes over time and to feed these back into the analytical process.

Conclusion

This chapter has been an attempt to present concepts and methodologies which should be of help in the management of public relations. It falls very far short of being a complete explanation of the process of analysis, neither does it lay any claim to scientific or academic respectability. What it does do is to provide a starting point for practising managers in the struggle to forge links between public relations and competitive advantage.

It is not necessary to collect all the relevant data and have them at your fingertips. Not every opportunity has to be seized nor every problem solved. You can be rather more realistic than that.

You will want to identify the one subgroup in four in every stakeholder group which influences the other three quarters. You will want to look out for the problems from outside that pose the biggest risks to your company, and to open whatever windows of opportunity give the best view.

In short, you will do best if you concentrate on the vital 25 per cent of stakeholders, advantages, disadvantages, opportunities, problems and time factors.

For the rest, you will of course do as well as you can within the constraints of the real world that is subject to all the usual pressures. Be sensible—settle for the day's best bet.

Some BIM guidelines are particularly relevant to the analysis and audit stages of management.

- Appraise your own competence, acknowledge potential weaknesses and seek relevant qualified advice.
- Take every reasonable opportunity to improve your professional capability.
- Be aware of and sensitive to the cultural environment in which you are working.
- Using your judgement, advise senior colleagues in advance of situations in which they are likely to become involved.
- Ensure that the requirements of customers and suppliers are properly considered.
- Establish and develop with customers and suppliers a continuing and satisfactory relationship leading to mutual confidence.
- Recognize your organization's responsibility to its owners, employees, suppliers, customers, users, society and the environment.[12]

Sources and references

1. Donough O'Brien, quoted in 'When is an audit not an audit?' *PR Week*, 11 June 1990.
2. John Smythe. ibid.
3. Reginald Watts. ibid.
4. Reproduced by permission of Reginald Watts.
5. Seeing the benefits of market research. *The Independent*. 7 July 1988.
6. *Guide to the Community Programme*. Manpower Services Commission, 1983.
7. Public companies. *Bulletin No. 17*. Shoosmiths & Harrison. January 1990.
8. David Morris (ed.). *Economics of Consumer Protection*. Heinemann, London, 1982.
9. Norman Hart. *Conducting an image audit by assessing*. Course paper, College of Marketing, 1986.
10. *Guidelines for print, stationery and signage*. British Telecom, 1989.
11. as source 9.
12. *BIM Guide to Good Management Practice*. British Institute of Management, 1990.

CHAPTER 4
Setting objectives

Authorities differ as to the exact nature of objectives for business enterprises.

Robert P. Appleby[1]

Analysing and auditing the advantages and disadvantages, the opportunities and problems, of an organization enables you to draw a serviceable map of the position that organization is in. The better your information input, the better the map and the more realistic, with alternative routes signposted, hazards identified and, with any luck, dead ends indicated, all against a general timescale.

All this tells you where you are. But the best map in the world cannot tell you where you want to be. For this, you need to specify your objectives.

You would be well advised not to concern yourself overmuch with the distinction between objectives and aims. Whole books could be written about that, and doubtless have been. They are so much word spinning. Nor should you get too excited about precise definitions purporting to prove that objectives are not the same as goals. That there are differences between objectives, aims and goals is undeniable. The question is, do they matter? It can be argued that a goal is an actual destination, whereas an aim is somewhat less definite than that—perhaps more of a hope that you are going in the right direction. After all, the word 'aim' has the same origins as the word 'estimate', with its implications of guesswork, however well informed. On the other hand, the word 'goal' comes from a root meaning a post, or a point, and therefore has a more physical sense. Indeed, strictly speaking, a 'goal post' is a 'goal goal' or a 'post post'.

What are you to make, then, of the word 'objective'? It is a slightly more elaborate form of the word 'object', which expresses the idea of 'point to be aimed at'. Therefore an objective embraces the ideas of both 'aim' and 'goal', which should put paid to any further argument.

The objective is change

In practical terms, PR objectives are to do with specifying what changes need to be made in your relationships with your publics, to further the solution of business problems and the exploitation of business opportunities.

A main requirement will almost certainly be to cause changes in *awareness*, because without that there can be no other change, except by accident. In some cases, increasing awareness may be a sufficient and self-contained objective, with no other changes required.

In other cases, however, it is not lack of awareness that is the problem—quite the opposite. When British Nuclear Fuels defined its PR objective, it can hardly have been concerned with raising the level of awareness. BNFL was faced with a suspicious, sceptical, even downright hostile public: a public that was quite aware enough.

What BNFL needed to do was improve public *knowledge*. That was their vital first stage (the second stage in most organizations) in the interconnected chain of objectives concerned with change.

Increased knowledge can lead to better *understanding* and this is important because PR is about explaining each side to the other.

The British Institute of Management knows the importance of this objective to every professional manager. One of its guidelines is 'establish and develop with customers and suppliers a continuing and satisfactory relationship leading to mutual confidence'.[2] That confidence flows from understanding.

Better understanding will usually lead to a shift in *perception*—what is sometimes called the 'aha!' effect. The British Gas campaign which invited complaints and suggestions from consumers was called Banishing Gripes. A customer survey exercise by direct mail had only four questions. The first asked customers how they felt about 12 British Gas activities, such as attending to leaks, installing appliances, telephone enquiries and gas bills. The second asked what most pleased the customer about the service, while the third asked what was most irritating. All these were not really about the services being provided but about how the customer perceived them. The fourth question gave the game away. 'If you had to pick one thing which we could do which would most improve your view of our service, what would it be?' Not to improve the actual service, note, but to improve the customer's view of it. No doubt British Gas learned enough from the survey to enable it to change the customers' perception, a perfectly reasonable objective, as far as it goes.

From that clearer perception *belief* should flow, as was the case over 900 years ago when William, Duke of Normandy and his half brother, Bishop Odo, were, surely, out to change beliefs in eleventh-century England. From the Anglo-Saxon point of view 'in many respects the Norman Conquest was a non-event . . . It was not in the interests of the contemporaries of the Normans to paint them as they were, uncultured Norsemen descended from the Vikings.'[3] The Normans themselves knew what they were doing. The objective of the Bayeux Tapestry was undoubtedly 'to provide, admittedly with great artistry and often in stunning detail, a picture of what the Normans would have everybody believe happened . . . Its clear purpose was to justify William's assault upon England and to magnify his triumphs in carrying it off . . . The longer one studies the tapestry the more do its deep purposes become clear.'[4]

The marketing plan of an organization may call for public relations support in developing customer preference and brand loyalty. To do this is to bring about a change in *attitude*. Many tracking studies are about changes in attitude—political polls, for example—which may or may not lead to action.

British Airways spelled it out in these words: 'to achieve worldwide recognition and approval for BA, furthering the company's commercial success'. The advertising slogan 'The world's favourite airline' is really an expression of BA's determination to change attitudes.

Probably the most important, and almost certainly the most difficult to achieve, is the objective of changing *behaviour*.

The Flour Advisory Bureau's 'Flour Power' campaign had the explicit aim of promoting greater use and consumption of flour and flour-based products.

Whatever the changes to be accomplished, campaigns could be seen as either mainly preventive or mainly remedial: if preventive PR, the timescale is likely to be long; if remedial, things may have to be made to happen more quickly.

Here is an example of how it might work in practice. A small plating company which has been in business for years, and which is well regarded, suddenly finds itself criticized by a local community group for discharging its effluent into a stream. No matter that it has been doing so for a decade or more without complaints. Times change: today ecology and the environment matter. Now the attack is on and the local media are quick to show an interest. The firm's immediate PR objective must be to refute the criticism if that can be done, and, if not, to contain it. Being a genuinely responsible company, its middle range objective is to respond, and be seen to respond, to the underlying problem—by changing the process, perhaps, or by demonstrating beyond argument that it is not toxic and could even be beneficial in some way. Longer term, the company will want to rehabilitate itself and reposition as a major local asset, well regarded and in even better standing than before.

Of course, it could be argued that if the firm had really cared about relations with its public, it would have anticipated the criticism and pre-empted it. Even 30 years ago, environmental matters attracted very little attention by the media or by pressure groups. Today, environmental matters matter, because more basic needs are largely satisfied. 'An environmental movement is the product of a prosperous society.'[5]

Strategic objectives

The long-range way of looking at objectives is for their strategic value. Any business organization, wrote Peter Drucker, needs to address itself to a limited number of 'general areas of objectives'.[6]

Four such areas, in no particular order of importance, are:

1. Market standing.
2. Innovation.
3. Worker performance and attitude.
4. Public responsibility.

For each of these areas of business objectives there are corresponding areas of PR objectives.

Market standing

Market standing is not the same as market share, but there ought to be a close relationship between them. Take the case of ICL, a wholly owned subsidiary of STC, which manufactured a range of computer systems for use in the retail trade at the point of sale. The trouble was that the company did not seem to have the status that its market share deserved. It was true that its chief competitors, IBM and NCR, between them held over one-third of the market, but in fact ICL's market share was second only to the brand leader, IBM.

A major image research survey carried out by Research Solutions for ICL showed that the company was not perceived as first-choice supplier by any of the following key target markets of decision makers and opinion formers: board level within the retail trade; senior retail management; retail data processing staff; management consultancies; the media.

The business objectives ICL set itself were to

- *produce* high quality reliable products,
- *provide* quick and efficient customer support,
- *offer* value for money systems,
- *become* a safe and secure supplier,
- *charge* competitive prices,
- *develop* a clear and long-term strategy.

Over a two-year period, 1985–87, the firm's PR objectives were as follows:

Phase 1
- To improve image and awareness among retail trade decision makers.
- To improve regularity and effectiveness of communication with consultants and media.

Phase 2
- To demonstrate the product's practicability for networking, data communications and support services.
- To expound a clear strategy for all retail sectors.
- To create a major impact with keynote statement.
- To achieve measurable changes in retailers' attitudes.[7]

The strategies and programmes for attaining these objectives, and the success or otherwise of the campaign, devised and carried out by Paragon, are described in the chapters that follow and are summarized in Case History 16.

Innovation

Many companies, especially those run by entrepreneurs, have a reputation for generating a constant stream of innovations. Not so the Civil Service. Yet the truth is that Whitehall—or in this particular case Sheffield—has its share of original thinkers who are fully competent to cope with the management of change, not least in the difficult area of employment and unemployment.

One of the more disturbing characteristics of the labour market in the 1980s was the large and increasing number of people who had been out of work for at least six months and in some cases for a year or more. These long-term unemployed were caught in a vicious circle—the longer they remained out of work, the less likely it was that employers would want to take them on.

One of the solutions was to identify work that needed to be done to improve the environment and amenities of local communities, and to provide government finance for long-term unemployed people to do the necessary work, which otherwise would not get done.

There were difficult questions of pay levels, the effect on employment benefit and other state provision, preservation of existing jobs, unfair commercial advantage to employers sponsoring the scheme, and so on. Eventually a proposition was hammered out that was broadly acceptable to all concerned and would produce temporary—but genuine—work for hundreds of thousands of people who until then had no prospect of ever working again.

To launch the scheme, there were four clear objectives:

1. To create awareness of the scheme and establish a broad level of understanding of its aims among key sectors of the population.
2. To encourage support from sponsors and potential sponsors (who were, of course, one of the key sectors).
3. To give the long-term unemployed the opportunity to be aware of the existence of the scheme.
4. To find a suitable name for the scheme.

The Community Programme, as it came to be known, went through several developmental stages after the prototype, though it was never fully absorbed into the day-to-day life of the labour market.[8]

Worker performance and attitude

In addition to those PR objectives that come and go, changing as business objectives change, there are more or less continuous PR needs that all organizations have. Once set, the strategic objectives in these cases hardly change at all over time. What is called for is a steady consistent ongoing programme which allows plenty of scope for tactical variation but stays with the underlying strategy.

A classic example of this type of sustained, permanent PR is the maintenance of good communications between the organization and its workforce. Unfortunately, there are far too many instances of management communicating with the staff only when things are going wrong—anything from tightening up security to reducing bonuses, from banning private telephone calls in the firm's time to closing a factory.

The result of this reactive, remedial approach is that the workforce associates internal communications with bad news. 'They only talk to us when they're in trouble or they've got trouble for us.' Small wonder that in circumstances like that the staff are suspicious and apprehensive of any communication from management. Had the organization deliberately set out to alienate its own people it could hardly have been more successful.

'Organisations do not have objectives. Only people have objectives' and unless the corporate objectives of a business are compatible with the personal objectives of the individuals working in it, they cannot be sustained.

Case History 3
The Partnership Programme

After analysing its markets, the Nationwide Anglia Building Society came to two important conclusions:

1. People prefer to buy products from people they like.
2. The costs of obtaining new customers are very substantial indeed compared with the costs of keeping existing ones.

Well, we probably all know that. The question is—what to do about it?

What Nationwide Anglia did was to set the objective of maintaining and developing a quality 'marriage' with its existing customers. It is called the Partnership Programme. It is ongoing, and a comprehensive customer-service campaign involving management, staff and customers.

The campaign is not a simple customer care programme, but encourages staff to develop better working relationships with internal 'customers', that is with colleagues from different departments within the organization, as well as with external customers.

In pursuit of its objectives the company identified four principles:

- First, the campaign is unlikely to succeed if it is not believed in by all staff—hence the concept of management by example.

- Second, it is more likely to succeed if all concerned understand and agree the objectives.
- Third, it is more likely to work if it can be adapted to particular circumstances.
- Fourth, it will only succeed if it is continually monitored and if rewards are given for excellence.

This is what Nationwide Anglia's Chief Executive, Tim Melville-Ross, had to say. 'The Partnership Programme included everybody in the company from the chief executive to the newest recruit . . . The belief is that the adult open relationships which we have with our customers and with our staff is the way by which we will win. We are building a culture in which service excellence is rewarded and where the whole focus of the organization is tuned towards getting it right.'[9]

Public responsibility

The community policy of many organizations includes government departments and the public domain generally. It is accepted business practice—indeed, a right—for commercial interests to communicate with and attempt to influence the public interest. Very often the method chosen is lobbying and that can be very effective, as the case history on changing behaviour demonstrates.

The main limitation is that this approach is often responsive and comes into operation quite late in the decision-making process. Green Papers may be consultative documents but even so a lot of decisions will already have been taken, such as what the issues are and who the main players are going to be.

It is better to put public responsibility on your own agenda, rather than wait for events to set a perhaps quite different agenda. Make public affairs a permanent part of your business plan and a continuous objectives area.

> The benefits of conducting an ongoing public affairs campaign are twofold. On the one hand, establishing a general presence in the eyes of policymakers makes it easier to communicate in times of crisis. Officials will already be aware of who you are, what your areas of interest are, and generally how policy initiatives may affect you. More importantly, it means that the firm's view can be taken into account at an earlier stage in the policy process so that they may influence the decision to place issues on the policy agenda. The net effect is the same—ongoing communication programmes allow business to contribute to, rather than react to, policy debates.[10]

There is opposite traffic as well. Whatever administration is in power in Westminster, all government departments have legitimate, non-political, PR objectives. Some of the better known are:

1. To ensure that the public are aware of their rights, obligations and responsibilities.
2. To keep taxpayers informed about how their money is being spent.
3. To promote safety, health and welfare.

It is perfectly proper—indeed, necessary—to spend public money on objectives such as these.

What is not proper is for government departments and the Civil Service to advocate and justify political policies and decisions. In the 1980s, the distinction between the two functions became blurred, and departmental information programmes were criticized for being political in effect and maybe even in intent.

Sometimes it was the timing that caused concern, for example when a corporate image promotion of a public undertaking, funded by public money, appeared just before a privatization campaign. It is true that the publicly funded campaign did not overtly try to sell shares in the forthcoming privatization. The question is, did it influence public attitudes in favour of buying shares? On another occasion, marked similarities of style between departmental and political campaigns—logo lookalikes, for example—were said to merge the publicly funded effort with the political message in a way not previously thought acceptable.

Leaked documents, allegedly revealing the political objectives of departmental campaigns, were cited in Parliament and the media. Readers drew their own conclusions.

Case History 4
Changing behaviour

You don't have to start from the same point as others to arrive at the same destination. Here is the history of what happened when two governments and two international corporations decided for different reasons that they were in need of public relations.

Towards the end of the 1980s, the Canadian Government became very concerned about the harmful effect of acid rain, especially on farms and forests. The main source of the pollution was identified: it lay outside Canada's national borders.

At about the same time, TransWorld Airlines found themselves threatened by a takeover bid. They perceived this as hostile and were determined to fight off the predator.

Over in Puerto Rico there was great agitation, fuelled by ominous hints that the preferential tax advantages on which the country's economy largely depended were about to be withdrawn.

The Boeing Aircraft Corporation had a new state of the art aircraft that would cost the only possible customer $2000 million—and he already had one.

Four major organizations, each with specific business problems and opportunities, all different. What were the key issues? Canada's acid rain was being generated in the United States. TransWorld wanted US Government intervention to neutralize the takeover bid. Puerto Rico depended on US tax laws. Boeing's customer for AirForce One Mark II was the President of the United States.

From these four very different analytical bases, Canada, TransWorld, Puerto Rico and Boeing all travelled by different routes to arrive at the same PR objective. They all decided that what they had to do was influence the behaviour of the US Government in their favour.

Strategy

It was not only their objectives that were identical. So were their strategies. Out of all the options available, each made the crucial decision to go for lobbying. Nor did the coincidences end there. Out of all the people working in this highly developed area of PR activity, they all commissioned the same man. He was Michael K. Deaver, former Deputy Chief of Staff at the White House. Most famous for his uncompromising and virtually uncontested views on the power of the media—'TV elects presidents' is attributed to him—he was described by the media at the time as a man of 'extraordinary experience and connections'.

Programmes

The essence of lobbying is that it is discreet and low profile. That is not to say that all lobbying is underhand: but it is usually undercover. Consequently there is no readily available information about exactly how this particular lobbying was to have been done. It is fair to assume that specific politicians, civil servants and power groups would have been identified as targets for presentations, briefings, entertainments, and indoctrinations, being persuaded or pressurized as appropriate. Great care would have been taken to get the timing right in relation to the legislative and decision-making processes, and all this in minute and painstaking detail.

Resources and budget

The chief resource was Michael K. Deaver himself. According to media reports, he was paid a six figure fee by each of his clients. If that were indeed the case it would be yet another thing all four had in common. Programme costs would presumably have been extra.

Disaster

Through no fault of the clients, things came unstuck. Deaver was charged with using undue influence, which he denied to a Senate Committee and a Grand Jury, and in 1987 found himself in court. The case is over and done with now. At the time, the trial and subsequent conviction excited great interest, especially in government circles and the PR profession, all over the world. Several factors explained this.

There was the stature of the clients, which was matched by the size of their problems. The fundamental simplicity of the proposed solution—lobbying—contrasted sharply with the technical, legal and moral complexities that developed. As for the reputed scale of the fees—well, that does suggest recognition of the difficulties and imply some confidence in the ability of the lobbyist to deliver. All in all, there has been plenty for the PR world to discuss and argue about.

Learning the lessons

However, there was perhaps one aspect of the Deaver case on which one might have expected general agreement. That was to do with the common objectives of Canada, Puerto Rico, TransWorld and Boeing, and also with some characteristics that are maybe shared by all objectives.

First, there was the aim of influencing the US Government to say and do specific things at specific times, or to refrain from saying and doing other specific things. How that was to be achieved legally and ethically is a matter of conjecture: but that does not affect the legitimacy and validity of the objectives themselves.

Second, the PR objectives were geared to particular business objectives, such as securing a specific contract or preserving a specific piece of legislation. These were to be the ultimate measure of success. Any number of other achievements could have been very welcome, but they were not what was being paid for. It was the expectation that business objectives would be attained through government action that no doubt explains the dramatic fees quoted in the media.

Third, what was to be achieved was capable of clear and simple statement. Classical management theory maintains that objectives can be fully described in two or three words, like 'increase productivity'; 'reduce costs'; 'maintain market share', etc. To spell out a specific PR objective may take a few more words, but not a great many.

Fourth, all concerned understood what was to be achieved. That is not quite the same thing as stating it, however clearly and simply. Clarity of expression should certainly help towards understanding. It does not guarantee it. The Theory of Relativity can be expressed in a single equation: $e = mc^2$. There, that is simple enough. But how many understand it?

Fifth, all that was desired to be attained could be attained. Whatever the difficulties, there was nothing intrinsically impossible, or even improbable, about influencing the machinery of government in the United States. Nor were the required changes so fundamental that the odds were stacked overwhelmingly against them. Whether or not they were actually achieved is another matter altogether.

The Deaver trial was not about that. What he was found guilty of, on three out of five counts, was lying.

Sixth, because the objectives were specific, geared to business aims, clearly stated, fully understood by all concerned, and actually achievable, their success or otherwise was capable of independent verification. In the case of Puerto Rico, for instance, the success was spectacular. The US Congress overrode its own Treasury and kept in place the section of the Revenue Code allowing American companies to keep 25 per cent of their profits on the island free of tax. These funds now exceed $14 000 million and have largely financed the development of the economy in Puerto Rico in recent years.[11]

If lobbying is a well-established fact of life in the United States, so is anti-lobbying. Jay Hedland, lobbyist for Common Cause, the public interest lobbying group, pointed out that members of Congress devote 'more time to fund raising than policy, and more attention to lobby groups than to their constituents . . . Raising campaign funds has become the dominant feature of a US politician's life.'[12]

Not all objectives are headline material, nor do they have to be weighty to be serious. Consider The Tea Council's objectives in 1984, and how they were achieved. It is a cheering story.

Case History 5
The Tea Council scores Brownie points

Analysis

Surveys showed that the under-35 age group were more likely to choose coffee or a soft drink in preference to tea.

Objectives

- To promote tea as the first choice non-alcoholic drink in the younger age groups.
- To position tea drinking as a young, sociable activity.

Strategy

- To run 'National Brownie Tea-making Fortnight' to coincide with the 70th anniversary of the Brownies.
- To gain a high level of media exposure, locally and nationally.

Programme

- Insert in *Guiding* magazine.
- Issue of 'celebration activity kit' which included everything needed to take part, for example a chart on how to make a good cup of tea.
- 'Good turn' challenge to individual Brownies to make at least 30 cups of tea for family, friends and neighbours.
- Tea making certificate.
- 'Celebration tea party' challenge to Brownie packs to devise unusual tea parties in unusual locations, with special guests.
- Press notice proformas for packs to draw on when compiling own local press notices.
- Invitation to submit press cuttings to Tea Council.
- 'Winning' Brownie packs to compete for prizes, for example VIP trip to Paris: holiday: cash for group funds.
- 'Winning' individual teamaker (658 cups).

Evaluation

- 10 000 Brownie packs took part.
- 50 per cent response from *Guiding* insert.
- Quarter of a million mothers involved, mostly in the target under-35 age group.
- 2000 major stories in local and national press, mostly with pictures.
- 51 minutes of TV airtime in news and news magazine programmes.
- 300 minutes of airtime on local radio, including 106 interviews.
- 7 million extra cups of tea made during the fortnight.[13]

Numerical values

The main measure of the success of any PR campaign or programme must be the extent to which the objectives are attained. The difficulty of measuring and evaluating PR results is a major preoccupation, especially in consultancies, whose traditional reluctance (or inability) to quantify what clients get for their money contrasts unfavourably with the performance of advertising agencies.

All that is changing. In Chapter 10 we examine some of the ways in which the results of PR are now being measured and evaluated. One thing is clear. If results are to be measured, they must as far as possible be quantified. This in turn means that objectives also need to be quantified. To what extent is this practicable?

The answer to that question is to ask more questions. For example, let us suppose that an objective of a publicly quoted company is to improve employee motivation and loyalty by encouraging them to buy shares in their own organization. What the company needs to know is how many of the workforce are shareholders now and how many could realistically be expected to become shareholders.

The difference between those two figures, or percentages, becomes the quantification of the PR objective, which might then be expressed as, say, 'to double within two years the percentage of employees who own shares in the company'. Notice that this is not the same thing as doubling the value of the shares held by employees, because in this case the objective is to encourage an increase in the number of people holding shares, rather than just an increase in the number of shares held. As well as putting a numerical value on the shareholders, the timescale is also quantified at two years.

That is an example of a quantified 'behaviour-change' objective. Exactly the same principle applies to all the other objectives and objective areas we have already discussed.

Change in awareness? Quantify it. If 18 per cent of your market now consider your company as their first-choice supplier, what percentage increase can you reasonably expect from your next PR campaign and how long should that take? If your closest competitors are mentioned on average once a month in a group of four trade and technical journals, how often should you be mentioned, in which journals, and how long will you give your press office to achieve a measurable improvement?

Imagine you are the director of a national museum which does not charge for admissions and has made a policy decision to stay that way. To offset government cuts in funding, you need to generate more revenue. Analysis throws up the following business opportunities:

- Increase revenue from voluntary donations.
- Attract more sponsorship.
- Stage special events for fee-paying clients.
- Increase revenue from shop and restaurant.
- Market new products and services (e.g. replicas, library photos).

In each case you would quantify the financial results you intend to achieve. Your PR programme in support of these monetary objectives should also be quantified. For instance, how many additional potential sponsors will you need to reach? What percentage of these should deliver? What is the target figure? When should you reach it?

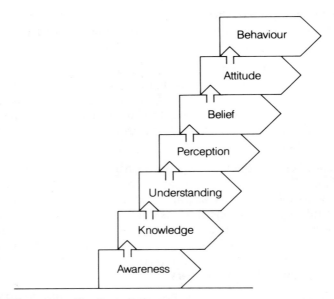

Figure 4.1 The seven objectives of change

The more specific the objective, and the more accurate the quantifying, the more likely it is that successful results can be demonstrated by measurement.

Summary

In this chapter we have looked at a wide range of organizations, each with its own specific problems and opportunities. They have had a variety of PR objectives—short term and long term, local and national, individual and corporate.

Each objective was concerned with bringing about one or more changes (see Figure 4.1). From the diversity, a pattern has emerged of questions that need to be answered before any thought can be given to strategies and programmes, activities and techniques.

These are the questions:

1. Are your PR objectives specific?
2. Are they about doing something?
3. Can they be quantified, for example a specific number or sum of money within a specific timespan?
4. Will they contribute to the achievement of specific business objectives?
5. Can your PR objectives be stated clearly and simply?
6. Does everyone concerned know and understand what is to be done?

7. Are your objectives actually attainable?

8. Will success or failure be measured and verified?

If the answer to even one of these questions is NO, an immediate re-think is called for. Two negatives would suggest that the re-think needs to be radical as well as rapid. Should only three or four questions get a YES, there must be serious doubt that there are any real PR objectives at all.

Sources and references

1. Robert P. Appleby. *Modern Business Administration*. Pitman, London, 1987.
2. *BIM Guide to Good Management Practice*. British Institute of Management, 1990.
3. Lloyd and Jennifer Laing. *Anglo-Saxon England*. Paladin, London, 1987.
4. Edwin Tetlow. *The Enigma of Hastings*. Peter Owen, London, 1974.
5. Wyn Grant. Pressure groups—New trends in their influence. *Contemporary Record*, November 1989.
6. Peter Drucker. *The Practice of Management*. Pan, London, 1968.
7. Julia Thorne. *Case histories*. Presentation at Interact Seminar, 1990.
8. Manpower Services Commission handouts on the Community Programme.
9. Case history authenticated by Nationwide Anglia.
10. Sarah-Kathryn McDonald. Corporate strategy and the public domain. *MBA Review*, March 1990.
11. Robert Graham. Puerto Rico. *Financial Times*, 24 February 1989.
12. John Lichfield. Congressmen buy their way to a cleaner image. *The Independent*, 17 November 1989.
13. Case history authenticated by The Tea Council.

CHAPTER 5
Strategic decisions

> Strategy is too important to be left in the hands of junior analysts and planners. It has to be handled as a priority by the management team of the company.
>
> *Milan Kubr*[1]

Analysis tells you as exactly as possible where you are starting from. You set objectives when you know where you want to get to.

Bridging the gap between analysis and objectives, between where you are and where you want to be, involves making strategic decisions. In what way are these decisions different from any other business decisions?

In the cut and thrust of day-to-day life, decisions often have to be made very quickly. Indecision can be costly, and if all the information you need is not to hand—too bad. You do the best you can, relying on instinct, or experience, or know-how, or luck. The overriding need is to make a decision and then get on with it. This kind of day-to-day decision making is operational, not strategic, and even a 'wrong' decision can be better than no decision at all.

Press officers and exhibition assistants often find themselves having to make operational decisions on their own, pretty well instantly. The fact that they are quick, solo, decisions does not mean that they are trivial. They have to be factually correct and in line with policy.

On a somewhat longer perspective, there are decisions to be taken about annual plans, about deploying resources and selecting techniques, about tracking budgets month by month over the year. More than one person is involved in making the decisions, and more than one in carrying them through. Generally speaking you know what your programme objectives are and how you intend to attain them. This kind of executional decision making is tactical not strategic.

If the operational PR timescale is from hour to hour over days, and the tactical from month to month over the year, strategy looks further ahead. It is not so much taking a view as sharing a vision, which should be 'as rational as possible and not a result of wishful thinking'.[2]

How rational can strategic vision be? It is not a skill, although you may need very advanced skills indeed if your strategy is to be successful. Nor is it about budgets, although considerations of cost must be part of your strategic thinking. All these things have their place because they all matter. Nevertheless, they are not strategy. Nor is planning in itself strategy, although every organization ought to have a strategic plan for public relations.

Even in the top companies and financial institutions, only about one in three people (37 per cent) who are responsible for PR say they are actively involved in strategic planning.[3] Could this be at least partly because they are not sure what strategy actually is?

Can the management gurus help towards a definition? This is what Coopers and Lybrand had to say 'In the absence of any universally accepted definition . . . we have made up our own . . . Strategy is concerned with solving problems which involve a long-term commitment of significant resources and which affect competitive position.'[4] Nice try, C and L. But will it do?

The word 'strategy' is of Greek origin and was to do with generalship and making war. Forcing the enemy's armies to fight when you wanted them to, where you wanted them to, and under conditions of your choosing—that was strategy. Air raids that disrupted the enemy's economy and shattered their morale—that was strategic bombing in the major wars of the twentieth century. We have since become accustomed to hearing and reading about Strategic Arms Limitation Talks, Strategic Arms Reduction Talks and Force de Frappe—meaning the Strategic Nuclear Force. The glamorous and remote-sounding Star Wars come very much closer to home under their official name of the Strategic Defence Initiative. Indeed, the very phrase 'strategic capability' is commonly understood to mean the capability to make nuclear war and to take nuclear reprisals, while the Institute of Strategic Studies carries out 'scholarly analyses of the role of military and para-military force in international relations'. This is 'considerably wider and more political in character than military or war studies'.[5]

What all these applications of military strategy have in common is that they are all about war with the enemy. The same is true of business strategy, which is about war with the competition. Coopers and Lybrand got very near it with that phrase 'which affect competitive position'. But it is more than that. However gentlemanly you may be, your strategic purpose is to beat the competition and win the competitive war.

You pursue maximum advantage to yourself, your organization, your client, at minimum cost. You throw in all the resources, skills and know-how that you can muster. You think about all the strategic options, evaluate the pros and cons, and make rational choices between them. 'However, total rationality is not achievable for one simple reason—the future is unknown and is being shaped by a myriad independent actions all over the globe.'[6]

Perhaps a better way to get to grips with strategy is not so much thinking about what it is as observing how it works.

Strategy in action

When Puerto Rico, Canada, TransWorld and Boeing had each analysed their economic and political problems and opportunities, they all decided that they needed to secure favourable consideration by the US Government. They then made the strategic decision to go for lobbying (see Chapter 4).

British Airways has a multi-stranded strategy geared to gaining worldwide recognition and approval by presenting the 'true view' (as it sees it) to key audiences. For example, to the external financial world and its own shareholders BA promotes the airline's commercial performance and reputation over other airlines (see Chapter 6).

The strategy behind the Flour Advisory Bureau's PR programme (described in Chapter 6) had six key elements to bridge the analysis/objectives gap.

Analysis

Consumers and to some extent retailers of bread, flour and other flour-based products have deep-rooted misunderstandings and mistaken beliefs about health, low nutritional value and unwanted weight gains. Bread consumption per person in the United Kingdom is lower than in many other European countries and very much lower than in some.

Too little is known about many of the types of bread available in this country. Purchasing patterns are seasonal and unadventurous. Retailers are missing out on a significant percentage of the market—for example purchasers of the bakery convenience foods known as morning goods. In the catering sector there is greater potential for cost cutting and profit raising through increased use of flour and flour products.

Objectives

To promote greater awareness and knowledge of flour and flour products among consumers, retailers and caterers, and so encourage higher purchasing, consumption and use.

Strategy

1. Reach all target audiences through a cohesive, sustained umbrella theme campaign.
2. Focus primarily on bread.
3. Exploit consumer ignorance to create publicity.
4. Develop attention-grabbing events and activities.
5. Promote via the media and direct to target audiences.
6. Coordinate with sales promotion.[7]

Many organizations make the strategic decision to mark a change of corporate policy by a corresponding change in corporate identity. When Dr Barnardo's children's charity relaunched as plain Barnardo's, they made the strategic decision to engage an outside PR consultancy to handle the corporate identity programme, while in-house they maximized the public relations value of their President, the Princess of Wales (see Chapter 6).

A main strategic decision made by ICL, in a three-year plan to reposition the company as the leading authority on information technology (IT) in the retail sector, was to position itself alongside top UK retailers by working with them on joint development programmes which were then promoted as demonstration projects (see Chapter 6).

One of Nationwide Anglia Building Society's central strategic ideas is to engage all its staff in a 'Partnership Programme' with customers, and also with colleagues from different departments in the organization. Everybody in the company is involved, from Chief Executive to rawest recruit. Management leads by example. Excellence is rewarded (see Chapter 4).

In the 1980s, vocational training in England and Wales was 'higgledy-piggledy and uncoordinated'. A review headed by Oscar DeVille made recommendations that would lead to fundamental changes in the English approach to education. More than 40 per cent of the workforce had no formal qualifications whatsoever, academic or vocational. DeVille's strategy to overcome the barriers was 'a matter of bridging the gap between the vocational and the academic . . . you had to go for the hearts and minds of the people involved'. By 1986 the specialists had been won over, and most of the head teachers and personnel directors. 'Now,' said DeVille, 'it was a question of going for managing directors and finance directors.'[8] The strategy shows every sign of succeeding.

A crisis precipitates operational and tactical decisions. It can also generate strategic thinking. It was as a result of the Lockerbie air disaster, just before Christmas 1988, that the Chief Executive Officer of the town decided to move PR people out of the economic development department into his own office. Of course it helped in the handling of the crisis at the time, but it was not an administrative re-shuffle, nor a response to operational pressures and heightened media interest. It was not even a tactical decision but a genuine strategic innovation. Public relations should always be part of the top management function. It took Lockerbie to bring that home to the county council of Dumfries and Galloway.[9] Other local authorities please copy.

Another example in the field of crisis management is what happened when pieces of glass were found in jars of baby food, presumably having been put there deliberately. One of the things Heinz did was to speed up the introduction of tamper-evident shrinkwrapped jars into the stores. The strategic question was what to do about communicating this to the public. 'On advice from the Home Office and the police' said Young and Rubican, Heinz's agency, 'Heinz decided that a public campaign could be provocative, challenging the culprits to find a way round the packaging. They took a wise decision in trying a more private approach.' This 'wise decision' was to do a huge, personalized mailout to nearly 1 million mothers of young children. The mailshot explained the benefits of the new packaging and rebutted some of the more damaging criticism in the press and on the air.[10] This was not, however, a media decision but a strategic one.

Case History 6
Floating water

Privatization of the water industry involved the setting up of 10 public limited companies. According to chairman John Bellak, the plus points of Severn Trent PLC were that it was landlocked, had no sea discharges, possessed a good management team and was the second largest of the 10.

'There was a need,' said Bellak, 'to uplift Severn Trent's PR operation, from a low profile reactive response to enquiries, to a proactive coping with the impending dramatic interest. Bear in mind that our publics include over 8 million domestic customers, some of the country's major industrial concerns, local authorities, local MPs, Government ministers, civil servants and over 7000 staff.'

Because of the need to communicate with such a diverse audience, and because of the expected opposition to privatization from some quarters, Severn Trent developed a strategy to 'enhance our own business objectives, meet the new demands and in the longer term convince the City that it was a worthwhile investment'.

An external consultancy and parliamentary consultant were appointed, which, with Severn Trent's own in-house PR resource, made a strong team for the two-tier campaign. First, a communications programme by the industry as a whole, aimed at increasing national awareness that water is an industry, and a very large one. Second, regional programmes via the individual authorities.

There were four key messages to get across:

1. We're responsive, well managed and environmentally responsible.
2. We will be profitable.
3. We're the best of the 10 water companies.
4. We will continue to provide first class service.

Tactics were conventional, embracing news stories, briefings of and meetings with key publics, customer literature and limited advertising ... 'we spent a lot of time and effort on City analysts—some 40 individual visits over 12 months—hard work but time well spent.'

Although Severn Trent was surprised by the vehemence of the 'green' campaign and the lack of understanding among journalists, the low level of understanding shown by politicians was not unexpected. 'There were difficult moments', recalled Bellak, 'but it worked in the end. Altogether over 2 million people invested in shares, of which we attracted 300 000.'

'There is still much to do, but with two years' experience, the right structure, and the freedoms of the private sector, we will see success. Public relations will continue to play a vital part. There are extra audiences to be informed. To help management meet our business objectives, the intention is to expand our core businesses. The emphasis now is on product quality.'[11]

All these cases of strategic thinking are underlined by Quentin Bell, Chairman of the Quentin Bell Organisation, who consistently champions the strategic function of PR. 'PR professionals will sit on the main boards of companies, advising managing directors and chairmen on strategy before commissioning marketing subcontractors (advertising, design, direct marketing, sales promotion) to come up with the creative tactical solution.'[12]

In the continuing promotion of equal opportunities, education can have a key role. The head of one school for boys, age range 11–18, devised a three-point strategy for changing perception.

> The first strategy was to get rid of the Brylcreen-sodden chairs in the staff room and to change it from an entirely male enclave to a friendly mixed environment.
>
> The next strategy was to appoint more women staff, including a number in senior positions . . .
>
> The third strategy was to make sure that the ancillary staff, who tend to be female, are seen to be, as they are, equally valued members of the school community so that the pupils could see that it was the job to be done that was important, not the sex of the doer. Thus, the school secretary, the librarian, the lab technician, all women, were equal to the teacher in the contribution they made.[13]

And if all that sounds a bit remote from the warlike origins of strategy, let me reaffirm that the best strategic PR can be a lethal competitive weapon.

Strategic options: The generation game

Strategic decisions affect the long-term future. You should be very suspicious of any strategic question that absolutely has to be answered here and now. If it is that urgent, either it is not a strategic matter at all, or you have neglected strategy to such an extent and for so long that you are managerially incompetent—and who will admit to that?

There is nearly always time to think about strategic decisions before you have to make them. In fact, the real risk is that because by its very nature strategy cannot normally be urgent, it tends to be forever at the bottom of the in-tray. As a result, PR resources are devoured by what is operationally and tactically urgent, rather than by what is strategically important.

In a properly managed organization—which must include yours, mustn't it?— the run-up period before strategic decision taking is used creatively. All the possible strategic options are identified, and a choice made between them. There are many different techniques for doing this.

What they all have in common, or should have, is that they involve a group of people at top management level. A survey of 80 companies in membership of the Strategic Planning Society showed that 95 per cent made their strategic decisions in a group, and that roughly 10 per cent used computers on-line during decision-making sessions.[14] Their work is both enabling and decisional: enabling, because it is through them that all the options are put up for consideration; and decisional, because it is by them that the final judgements are made. Strategic thinking does not exist on its own, somehow remote from line management decisions. According to the *Financial Times*, 'In a well-run organisation it is impossible to distinguish clearly between line and staff roles. As many companies have found in recent years, the most effective strategist has one foot in line management.' The report warns of the danger of conflict of interest, personality, etc., that can arise, if an outside consultancy is charged with responsibility for the client's strategy.[15]

The consultancy issue is discussed in Chapter 11. Here let us look at some ways of involving managers in the two-stage process of speculating on the options and of choosing from them.

A great deal depends on the company culture, which will determine to a large extent how the strategy group is constituted and the way in which it operates.

One very effective procedure is to get together a group of people of roughly comparable rank and background, covering all the experience necessary to the decisions. Under the chairmanship of someone of recognized authority, put them to work on dissecting past performance, identifying current best practice, and systematically applying some analytical system with which they are familiar, like SWOT or ADOPTS (see Chapter 3).

They may take some time to work through the options but they are likely to come up with the maximum number of sound, uncontroversial and workable choices. Because of self-censoring, the more creative options are literally non-starters in sessions of this kind. Consequently, the next, decisional stage, may be relatively brief.

Another popular way of generating strategic options is to get a highly disparate bunch together, without too much reference to rank, background or specialism. Set them brainstorming in a freewheeling manner, with no options barred, even the most outrageous. There are no self-censored non-starters. Steered by an experienced enabler, the process can be intensive and powerful, throwing up the maximum number of options fairly quickly, many of them quite useless, but some quite brilliant. Because of the richness of material that can be generated, the decisional stage needs time.

Strategic options: Decision time

Paradoxically, once you have generated the maximum number of possible options, your next stage is to reduce them by selecting only the most probable. Only you and your organization will know what they are. Remember that the word *decision* comes from a Latin word meaning 'cut out' or 'cut down'. Here is a process for helping you to cut down and cut out. The first stage is to review your objectives and single out the essential stakeholders and their essential needs. Options that do not meet both these criteria are ruled out.

That could be enough to leave you with a short list of, say, four or five which you will then want to rank in order of preference. However, it is more likely that your freewheeling sessions will have produced quite a large number of options that get past the first stage of selection. What do you do next?

You go beyond the strictly essential by looking at the most desirable needs of the most important stakeholders. Options that score well on both counts stay in, those that do not are omitted.

If you need a further filter, assess the options you have retained by comparing the benefits the stakeholders stand to gain if all goes well against what they would lose if things do not go well. Favour the options with high gain/risk factors, or low risk/gain factors, depending on the culture of your organization. Entrepreneurial? High gain/risk. Blue chip? Low risk/gain. Of course, if you are lucky enough to identify any low risk/high gain options, you will know what to do.

In the extremely unlikely event of this elimination process leaving you with only one option, then in fact you have two, because doing nothing is always an option. You would then assess the pros and cons, using a simple plus and minus technique, to arrive at the best bet, and that would be your strategy decision.

More probably, you would end up with a handful of options. The standard way to deal with this is by using a decision tree. They became popular in the 1960s and were based on the application of logic to present actions within the control of management and to future events outside that control. Algorithms are a simpler form of the same approach. Most people are familiar with the idea—humorous versions of it appear in popular magazines and the tabloid press—and, if not, there are plenty of management manuals that explain the technique very fully.

Figure 5.1 shows how it might look applied to the process of reducing the number of strategic options to manageability and ranking them.

Here is a different way of organizing a number of options, into a series of pairs

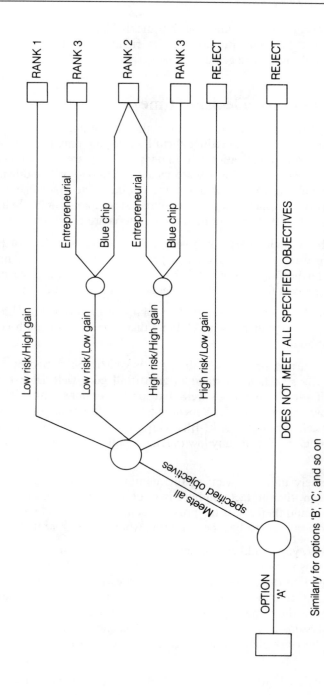

Figure 5.1 Strategy by algorithm

so that there are only two at a time to be considered. The method can perhaps best be explained by illustration and example. Assume that for your particular objectives you have identified six different types of campaign strategy, each with its own specific pros and cons. For the purpose of illustration only, we'll say that these options are:

A Drip feed   Low level doses at frequent intervals with a cumulative effect over a period of time.
B Pulsing   Bunching the low level doses so that intermittent levels are somewhat higher, but the average remains the same.
C Salvoes   Grouping the pulses into longer bursts, with longer gaps in between.
D Knockout   All effort concentrated into one make-or-break operation.
E Response only   Activity stimulated by the competition.
F Nil activity   Heads below the parapet.

Your first decision is whether nil activity is a genuine option. Let's say that for political/presentational/expediency reasons it is not. That leaves five options, which permute into ten pairs. For each pair, using the plus and minus balance sheet approach, you decide whether one choice is clearly preferable to the other (score 3), or an obvious loser (score 1). If the pair actually balances, or if you don't know, score 2.

First compare the drip feed strategy (option A) against pulsing (option B). We'll say that after you have compared all the pros and cons, pulsing is your preferred option, so A = 1, B = 3.

Next, compare option A against the salvo approach (option C). Again, let's say you find salvoes better than drip feed, A = 1, C = 3.

Continue in this way, comparing every option with every other, making the decision each time on the basis of a pros and cons assessment.

The outcome might look like this:

A:B = 1:3   B:C = 2:2   C:D = 3:1   D:E = 2:2
A:C = 1:3   B:D = 3:1   C:E = 1:3
A:D = 3:1   B:E = 3:1
A:E = 3:1

Adding up the scores, you have

A = 1 + 1 + 3 + 3 = 8
B = 3 + 2 + 3 + 3 = 11
C = 3 + 2 + 3 + 1 = 9
D = 1 + 1 + 1 + 2 = 5
E = 1 + 1 + 3 + 2 = 7

On this totally notional basis—it is only an illustration of the method—you have a clear indication on strategy.

Best option—pulsing (scored 11)
2nd option—salvoes (scored 9)
3rd option—drip feed (scored 8)
4th option—response only (scored 7)
5th option—knockout (scored 5)

For a matrix version of this technique, see Chapter 7.

These rankings are not, of course, absolute. Nobody is expected to believe that a pulsing strategy is always the best option, or a knockout strategy always the worst. It is the decision-making method that has been explored. The results of this particular example are irrelevant.

What is relevant is the realization that even the most reasonable decisions are not entirely rational. Other factors come into play, such as habits of thought that always point us in a certain direction, fear of the unknown, group pressures and so on. As long as you are aware of them, you can to a large extent discount them, or, better still, use them.

A useful cross-check is to ask the following questions of every strategic option.

1. What effect will doing it have on our stakeholders?
2. What effect will it have on our organization?
3. What will it cost, in money?
4. And in other resources?
5. What will happen if we don't do it?

Coordination

In a company where the culture encourages and esteems cooperation, people keep each other informed about what they are doing. Diary clashes are avoided. If someone is absent, his or her work gets done by others without any fuss. At the tactical level, there is a good deal of informal coordination. All that is excellent. But it is not enough. A major strategic decision has to be taken. PR needs to be coordinated strategically as well as tactically with the other communication disciplines.

Three out of four PR managers who took part in a survey claimed that they were actively involved in just such coordination, bringing in senior executives from other departments. The particular mix varied from organization to organization. The departments most often involved are shown in Figure 5.2.

There is no standard way of achieving coordination. Some do it under the marketing umbrella, others as a central communications function, or as the ultimate service to customers.

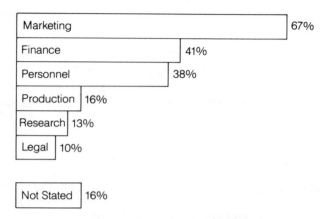

Figure 5.2 Non-PR departments involved in PR coordination[16]

American Express has a Marketing Review Board with sign-off power over all company communications.

Texaco set up a public and government affairs department with a coordinating remit that included political analysis, issue management, exhancing public awareness of the company, the management of corporate advertising and meeting the communication needs of the company as a whole. In addition to its strong in-house PR team, Texaco uses several outside PR consultancies and advertising agencies.[17]

The National & Provincial Building Society coordinates external communications centrally.

British Telecom has a full-time properly staffed Customer Communications Unit that coordinates advertising, public relations, direct marketing, exhibitions and sales literature, controlling budgets and hiring agencies.

Companies which take coordination seriously expect their agencies and consultancies to do likewise. Increasingly, client expectations are being met by consultancies appointing one director to coordinate all services used or on offer to them. Research, marketing, advertising, PR, etc., are welded into one strategic whole.

A strategic decision that should always be made, so invariably that it counts as a golden guideline, is to match your media relations to your markets, both horizontally and vertically. You will want to research your markets and tailor your message specifically to each part or sector, but always from one, consistent point of view. How you do it is a matter of tactics and targeting, review and renewal, all in meticulous detail. But do it you must as a strategic necessity.

Case History 7
Flour power coordinated

Earlier in this chapter we looked at the Flour Advisory Bureau's six-point PR strategy. Programmes for carrying them out are described in Chapter 6. Here we focus on the element of coordination, involving caterers and retailers.

Caterers

Research showed that almost one-third of all the flour produced in the United Kingdom was used in the catering sector. This included pubs, restaurants, hotels, industrial canteens, institutions, fast-food outlets, takeaways, cafés and snackbars. In addition to bread, the other main products of the sector are biscuits, cakes, quiches, pies, pizzas and sauces.

The Bureau presented to the catering sector four powerful arguments for using more flour and flour products.

1. Using wholemeal flour with its recognized health benefits can add greater variety to the caterer's menu and can help to ring up additional profits through the higher premium it commands. For the institutional caterer—who is concerned more with cost control than profit—it represents a simple way of introducing innovative and nutritious dishes to the menu.
2. As cost is still the primary factor affecting consumer choice about what and where to eat out, more value for money in the form of flour-based foods on the menu could be the deciding factor.
3. For low-cost, large-scale catering, flour is the obvious starting point. Crumbles, pastries, pies, quiches and dough-based pizzas are economical to produce and yet can make a valuable contribution to a well-balanced diet.
4. The popularity of pastas and pizzas continues to grow: both represent value for money meals for the consumer and significant profit margins for caterers.

Third party endorsements from caterers and catering consultants reinforced and supported these arguments.

The conclusion was that promotions on all flour-based goods, including bread, would be a simple and effective way to attract new customers and keep existing customers. To assist the catering trade to carry out such promotions, the Bureau produced, free of charge, a catering kit, with guidelines and specific advice, by sector, for:

- the volume sector—cafés, takeaways, fast food and roadside outlets,
- hotels, restaurants and pubs,

- the industrial sector, and
- the institutional sector.

The kit was backed up by a series of recipe leaflets on such topics as large-scale catering, bread in pub catering, sandwiches and toasted snacks.

Retailers

To help high street and in-store bakers increase profits, the Bureau produced a six-point action plan which drew on the experience of the major multiples.

1. Include detailed shelf labelling for unwrapped bread on display. Give serving suggestions as well as price and nutritional information.
2. Educate staff on the varieties sold, their uses and nutritional benefits, so that staff can provide customers with helpful information on request.
3. Encourage staff to be professional salespeople, by equipping them with positive sales techniques and perhaps offering them incentives or prizes for high achievement.
4. Make more of displays by using posters and leaflets, focusing interest on unusual or high margin lines. Run tastings for new or unusual lines.
5. Take advantage of specialist firms which provide good quality volume lines such as gateaux, doughnuts and sponges, which can then be finished off by hand.
6. Investigate the bake-off system (buying in partially cooked or uncooked frozen dough to fresh-bake on site as needed) and see how this could improve efficiency and profitability.

In the morning goods sector—buns, baps, croissants, crumpets, muffins, pykelets, rolls and teacakes, etc.—only three out of four working people buy, and purchasing patterns tend to be seasonal. To help the trade reach the missing 25 per cent, the Bureau developed a six-point action plan.

1. Exploit customers' willingness to buy morning goods throughout the day for different purposes. Serve warm croissants in the morning. At lunch time prepare hot items such as bacon in a bap, or salt beef on rye. In the afternoon, offer warm crumpets or toasted teacake.
2. Promote seasonal goods, not just hot-cross buns at Easter, but specials for Mothers' Day or Fathers' Day, treats for bank holidays, heart-shaped items for St Valentine's Day, etc.
3. Innovate—introduce new products to exploit consumers' willingness to experiment.
4. Offer multi-packs of popular goods for home freezing.
5. Exploit the impulse purchase factor with high impact displays in the window and at the till.
6. Promote with special offers and tastings of new lines.[18]

Sources and references

1. Milan Kubr (ed.). *Management Consulting*. International Labour Office, Geneva, 1986.
2. ibid.
3. *The Survey of United Kingdom Public Relations Professionals*, Burson-Marsteller, London, 1990.
4. Steve Wall and Chris Outram. The Coopers and Lybrand approach to manufacturing strategy, *MBA Review*, September 1989.
5. Bullock, Stallybrand and Trombley (eds). *The Fontana Dictionary of Modern Thought*, Fontana, London, 1988.
6. as source 1.
7. Janet Salvoni. *Case histories*. Presentation at Interact Seminar, 1989.
8. DeVille sees it through. *The Financial Times*, 31 January 1990.
9. Helen Slingsby, When disaster strikes in your own back yard, *PR Week*, 30 November 1989.
10. Consumer terrorism nearly killed the Heinz brand. *Campaign*, 1 December 1989.
11. Case history authenticated by Severn Trent.
12. Quentin Bell. Speech at Marketing Superstars Conference, London, November 1989.
13. David Middleton quoted in: Changing attitudes in a boys' school. *Opening Doors*. The Fawcett Society, 1986.
14. Ray Acosta and Paul Finlay. Senior Managers and their use of information technology. *MBA Review*, September 1989.
15. Christopher Lorenz. Using consultants as managers. *The Financial Times*, 13 January 1987.
16. as source 3.
17. Henry Sutton. Texaco's corporate communications gets major revamp. *PR Week*, 18 January 1990.
18. Case history authenticated by Paragon.

CHAPTER 6

Plans and programmes

The PR function should be recognized as central to good management and able to act as a unifying force within the organization in the way it presents itself. That way a schedule of activity can become a campaign. A campaign can become a programme.

Roger Haywood[1]

It is not analysis that gets results, nor setting objectives, nor making strategic decisions. It is not even knowledge, for the uncomfortable truth is that those who know most about public relations are not necessarily the best at actually doing it.

What really matters is taking effective PR action by implementing effective PR programmes. That is what this chapter is about. But first, the programmes have to be planned.

Planning

Planning is tactical thinking. Just as strategic thinking forms a bridge between analysis and objectives, so tactical thinking—planning—forms a bridge between strategy and programmes.

A lot depends on how you approach it. As Michael Madison pointed out in his column 'At the Sharp End', 'Two entirely different methods of planning can be observed. The more popular one is called "writing the plan", i.e. getting right down to the chore of producing a document, and not wasting any time on thinking about it first. This consists of taking the blank planning format . . . and simply filling it up like an income tax return . . . The alternative and less popular method of planning is to think long and deeply about the various opportunities for suggestion and action. Then you formulate a plan. Even if it doesn't contain any giant leaps, or stunning new insights, such a plan can be replete with cunning wrinkles and ingenious wheezes . . . Plans of this character are almost impossible to write down in the straitjacket of a standard planning format.'[2]

While the clear implication of that is that the second method is better than the first, nevertheless a structured and systematic approach to planning improves the chance of success, as you might expect.

Perhaps the most important thing to say about planning is that it provides a framework against which activities take place. Planning should never be mistaken for the activities themselves. The best plan in the world couldn't sell an umbrella to a man in a thunderstorm, nor add even one pound to your credit balance at the bank.

The headmaster of the boys' school described in Chapter 5 certainly had a plan to help change sexist attitudes. The plan was made up of a number of specific activities. Here are some of them.

1. Personal and social development elements were introduced into the compulsory content of all courses throughout the school age range.
2. Sex stereotyping was discussed in the classrooms.
3. Ancillary staff—traditionally female—talked openly about their role, pay and conditions of service.
4. Mothers came into the school and talked to the boys about fair distribution of family incomes.
5. Life skills took on a new meaning—for instance, the boys had to scrounge two cookers for their cookery lessons, because boys' schools were not issued with them.
6. Personal hygiene was made suddenly attractive after an 18-year-old girl lectured at the school on 'why I don't like smelly boys'.
7. A female advisory dance teacher was appointed to the staff and the Contemporary Dance Company spent a week in the school.

The school won a commendation for positive action in the Fawcett Society awards for 1986.[3]

The second important thing about planning is that it can be immensely complex. The French call it 'planification', which nicely catches the detailed and questioning nature of the process.

Case History 8
Farming goes metric

When the Metrication Board planned the metrication of the farming sector, they worked with government departments, agricultural organizations, the farming supply industries, estate agents, schools and colleges, libraries, the media, consumer organizations and other stakeholders in going metric to work out a detailed and coordinated communications, legislative and technical plan. This is a summary:

Politics
1. Individual briefings for Members of Parliament in agricultural constituencies.
2. Presentations to parliamentary committees concerned with agriculture.
3. Presentations to Government Ministers and senior civil servants in agricultural departments.

4. 'Planted' parliamentary questions.
5. Special attention to parliamentary press.

Regulations and documentation
1. Coordination of timetable for change, including agricultural census and annual farm review.
2. Briefing of responsible organizations.
3. Technical help in conversion of units from imperial to metric.
4. 'Instant' validation services.

Farming organizations
1. Open and visible consultation.
2. Staff briefings.
3. Timetables agreed with Metrication Board and Government.
4. Distribution of metrication timetable for farming.
5. Distribution of Metrication Board publications.
6. Assistance with production and promotion of organizations' own material.
7. Film shows.
8. Exhibitions.
9. Speakers' panel.
10. Validation service.

Supplying industries
1. Open and visible consultation.
2. Brief organizations and firms concerned with agrochemicals, fertilizers, soil conditions, seeds, feedstuffs, machinery, fuel oils, etc.
3. Agree and publish metrication timetables.
4. Publish and distribute Metrication Board information.
5. Assist trade to publish and promote own material.
6. Take part in trade exhibitions.
7. Speakers' panel.
8. Conversion and validation service.

Farming media
1. Individual briefing of key journalists and broadcasters in specialist and general media.
2. Group briefings of other relevant media people, for example provincial papers in agriculture areas.
3. Contributed articles to farming press.
4. Interviews on TV and radio programmes on or including farming.
5. Storyline references in *The Archers*—a long-running soap opera about rural life.
6. Journalists sitting in on Metrication Board Agricultural Committee meetings.

Agricultural shows and conferences
1. Major presence at major shows: large exhibition stand; films; competitions; audience-participation, booklets, leaflets, etc.

2. Tailor-made information packages to all exhibitors and delegates.
3. Minor presence at minor shows.
4. Mini-tourer on loan to village halls, etc., in more remote areas.
5. Speakers' panel for conferences.
6. Metrication of exhibition catalogues and other literature.
7. Launch platforms for promotions and informational publications.

Land and estate management
1. Open and visible consultation.
2. Prior agreement with Ordnance Survey on metrication of maps: preparation of specimens.
3. Brief local government; land professions; water/drainage boards; road/construction agencies; and contractors.
4. RICS examination in metric.
5. Conversion and validation service.

Marketing of produce
1. Brief organizations and firms concerned with contracts (e.g. growing, canning, freezing); farm sales; wholesaling; quotas, grading and other standards; statistics; prices, etc.
2. Agree and publish metrication timetables.
3. Assist trade to produce and promote own material.
4. Offer validation service.
5. Provide speakers.
6. Develop interface with retail sector.

Other sectors (e.g. building and building materials, forestry, pharmaceuticals, weighing machines)
1. Develop Metrication Board PR programmes for these sectors.
2. Encourage development of PR programmes by these sectors.
3. Interchange of information between sectors.

Adult education and training
1. Open and visible consultation.
2. Brief government and commercial advisory services.
3. Curriculum development with agricultural colleges, industry training boards, agricultural departments of universities, etc.
4. Joint ventures with the education and training sector, such as setting up practical tests and demonstrations at recognized centres and on specially selected farms.
5. Provision of conversion data, tables and devices.
6. Validation of such devices produced by others.
7. Teacher training.
8. Metrication of examinations and professional qualifications.

Schools
1. Special attention to schools in rural and agricultural areas.
2. Teacher training; teach-ins; workshops; displays; video and teachers' guide.

3. Encouragement of commercial production of metric games.
4. Information on availability and suitability of metric textbooks.
5. Speakers' panel, for example for parent/teacher meetings.

Libraries
1. Seminars and teach-ins for librarians.
2. Free copies of major Metrication Board books.
3. Lists of other books on metrication.
4. Very large issues of free metric bookmarks.
5. Articles in the book/library press.
6. Mini-display sets on loan to main libraries.
7. Speakers' panel.

The rural community
1. General information about the progress of metrication nationally.
2. Specific information about changes affecting rural and farming areas.
3. Speakers' panel for local interest groups.
4. Pilot projects with provincial media.
5. Advance testing of consumer aids.

Logos and emblems
1. The Metrication Board's logo was reserved for use by the Board alone.
2. The Board's colour coding and typographical style were freely available to all. The Board offered guidance on how to use them.
3. A separate 'key to metrication' logo was designed for use by any approved organization. The Board provided artwork free of charge.

Evaluation
1. Baseline research.
2. Awareness and knowledge polls.
3. Attitude surveys.
4. Media studies.
5. Strategic and tactical feedback.
6. Selective publication of results for PR purposes.

For all the blueprint detail and jigsaw precision of such coordination, the principles of planning are straightforward. Think of it as a block diagram showing how a message, supported by reasoning, is projected to an audience whose location is known. The resources employed to reach that audience are timetabled and channelled using the most cost-effective techniques. Finally, the results are measured and fed back to influence the message (strategic evaluation) and the means (tactical evaluation) (see Figure 6.1).

The 'specification sheet' that goes with this block diagram has 10 key sections.

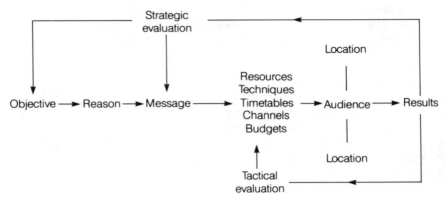

Figure 6.1 Planning—simplified view

These key sections are:
1. Audience
2. Response
3. Reason
4. Message
5. Location

6. Timetable
7. Techniques
8. Cost
9. Contingency
10. Evaluation

Dealing with each section in turn is the easiest way, in a book. Things may not be so tidy in real life.

The audience: To *whom* are you talking?

For reasons that are not entirely clear, the recipients, the targets, the people and organizations towards whom PR programmes are directed, are generally called 'the audience', even if hearing plays a minor or non-existent part in the communications process.

Why are people who read pamphlets called 'the audience'? How can posters be understood by listening to them? Are deaf people not able to receive PR messages?

The point is not trivial. The fundamental notion is that messages are sent out for audiences to hear. Researchers speak of the 'tone of voice' of a press advertisement or editorial. It is as if you are engaging in a dialogue with an individual stakeholder, rather than with a group. In any dialogue, it is the listener who is in control, not the speaker.

So the first question to be decided is 'to whom are you talking?' The more precise the answer, the better.

Suppose you need to influence the traditional attitudes of retired people towards investment opportunities. One strand of your PR programme would be geared to reaching your audience through the media. To whom are you talking? As far as contributed articles are concerned, you are talking direct to the retired people themselves, in the pages of the newspapers and magazines you know they read. You may also want to put out press notices aimed at this audience, but in that case you would actually be talking to the editorial staff, not to the readers. Another audience could be those who advise retired people on what to do with their money. You might approach that audience direct, or through the media, or both.

More than 3000 trade and technical journals are on sale in this country, each with its own special subject area and readership. In Europe, a further 7000 cover 14 countries and a couple of dozen subject areas. The United States has another 5000 'T & Ts', as they are commonly known. Accurate targeting of journals is clearly very necessary—and not too easy—quite apart from the additional task of accurate targeting of staff within each journal.

This kind of pinpointing is one way by which an audience is distinguished from a stakeholder group. The group might be trade and technical journals: the audience is made up of individual people on individual journals.

When tailoring your messages to specific business audiences, as opposed to business media, you might well conclude that it is the size of the firm that matters, rather than its Standard Industrial Classification (S I C). You would position them in one or more of the recognized payroll bands, or turnover brackets.

For a particular PR purpose your decision might be to group recruitment consultants with management consultants; whereas for a different PR purpose, they could belong with personnel officers.

There is even a system whereby you classify people according to their first names. It is said to be highly likely that Kylie, Kelly and Kirsty, for example, are all much of an age, living in much the same sort of place, sharing many of the same interests, and purchasing mostly the same branded goods.

Kylies or consultants, small firms or small investors, you need to put a number on each audience, so that you know how many you aim to reach. Even when fairly large numbers are concerned, it can be a precision exercise. Post-privatization electricity supply companies in the United Kingdom are represented by the Electricity Association, which looks after the industry's common interests, such as industrial relations, wage negotiations and health and safety matters. The Association's PR programmes include a glossy quarterly magazine which is precisely targeted to the 6500 members of the Association, 2400 business managers and—the delicate touch—170 named MPs from Lords and Commons.

The response: *What* do you want them to do?

You know to whom you are talking. They need to know what you want them to do. In the investment opportunities example, used above, the response you want from the retired people themselves might be that they send for your brochures on appropriate investment schemes, whereas the media response you are seeking is that they publish stories or comment on investment opportunities, preferably the ones you offer.

As discussed in Chapter 4, the objective of all PR is to secure a change of some kind, from the most basic change in general awareness to the ultimate change in behaviour of specific audiences.

'Flour Power' for the Flour Advisory Bureau meant identifying three key audiences.

1. All consumers, mostly women.
2. Retailers of flour and flour products, including bakers, the grocery multiples and their independent counterparts.
3. Commercial, industrial and institutional caterers.

The campaign had a different message for each audience. Consumers were encouraged to perceive bread as a healthy, non-fattening food of great variety and good value for money. Retailers were shown the profit-making potential of bread and the possibilities of market expansion. Caterers learned of the cost-cutting benefits, particularly in the volume sector, and the scope for menu innovation.

Those were the messages. What responses were required? First, there were the changes in awareness and perception, including the abandonment of some cherished myths—about bread not being good for you, for instance. Then, the Bureau wanted consumers to try more and buy more, retailers to promote more and sell more, caterers to use more and experiment more.[4]

Once again, the more specific these programmes and campaign objectives were, the more readily their results could be measured. If 25 per cent of working people don't buy buns, baps and crumpets, and you aim to make them more aware of these 'morning goods' and more attracted to them, you have a target figure against which to test the success of your efforts.

Sometimes the required response can be as simple as sending for a leaflet, the first step on a road that could eventually lead to a much more serious response, like switching brand loyalty in the consumer goods area, or investing some money. Certainly the retail and financial sectors put a lot of effort into getting audiences to send for leaflets and brochures. Quite often they use advertising as the hook, but increasingly they rely on editorial coverage in the relevant media, coordinated with mailshots, special offers, database marketing and so on. The literature is promotional, but nearly always contains a further response mechanism—an order form, an application, a redemption, a special offer, money-off, etc.

Everybody in advertising knows the story of the man who drank Guinness not because of the advertising, but because it was good for him. Clearly value signals were working in his case and not only because of the advertising. The whole of the marketing and communications programme was geared to producing that response. Even though the rigour of modern advertising standards means that it is no longer permissible to use the slogan 'Guinness is good for you', plenty of people still believe that it is. What is more, their purchasing reflects that belief.

The reason: *Why* should they do it?

It is not an attack on advertising to say that while it has to be 'honest, decent, legal and truthful', it can and does use confusion and ambiguity—in a creative way, of course. You are not expected to believe that Heineken literally reaches the parts other beers cannot reach, whatever they are. Indeed you might justly ask what the literal meaning is.

Advertising copywriters are notoriously fond of puns, especially in headlines and slogans. Visual puns are much rarer, although they do occur. By its very nature, a pun is unclear, attaching at least two different meanings to one statement.

Another popular style of advertising—popular with the advertising agencies, anyway, and presumably with their clients—centres on vague general all-purpose notions which could apply to so many organizations that it is difficult to see why any of them should want it. The 'Tomorrow Today' approach is particularly pervasive—'Tomorrow's Technology Today', 'The Taste of Tomorrow Today', 'Today Europe, Tomorrow The World', 'Tomorrow Is Already Here' and so on.

Public relations need not be like that. It should be about openness, about clarity, about understanding, about truth. The issues have to make sense intellectually, but also at the emotional level. People are not moved by logic alone, nor are causes won entirely by argument. On the other hand, emotion may be a very powerful agent for change, but unless it is complemented and reinforced by realistic thinking, the changes will not last.

Different audiences will respond to different ratios of intellectual and emotional reasoning. It is not always easy to get the blend right but much more effective when you do.

Voluntary organizations would have a view on the most appropriate head : heart ratio, quite different from that held by, say, multinational conglomerates.

At their annual meeting in London's Albert Hall, and indeed throughout the year, the Women's Institute take a high profile line on contemporary issues which engage the intelligence and the emotions. For all that, there are deep seated concerns that the persistent 'Jam and Jerusalem' image inhibits recruitment. One of the solutions is to project a more lively and modern personality, which is why the WI teamed up with Vauxhall Motors to find the Women's Institute Woman Driver of the Year.[5]

Driving is something members of the Women's Royal Voluntary Service know a lot about. They cover about a million and a half miles a year and deliver 16 million meals on wheels. But there is more to the WRVS than that—tea bars in courts and crèches in prisons, clubs for the elderly and for mothers and toddlers, hospital shops and residential homes, plus the splendid work they do at civil disasters as one of the statutory emergency services. They, too, have concerns about their image—middle aged, middle class, white—and carry out a well-integrated public relations programme aimed at those who have 'Time to spare—Time to care'.[6]

Fund-raising charities, from Barnardo's to Band Aid, know very well that altruism can be a powerful motivator—perhaps more powerful than many give it credit for—but that there has to be room for the acceptable face of self-interest, too.

What it comes down to is the need to reconcile the audience's perception with the reality. The history of painting, music, literature and all the arts shows that there are only two ways of making sense of the world. One—the 'romantic'—is to treat every experience, even the most familiar and workaday, as if it were totally new and unique and you were experiencing it for the very first time. The other way—the 'classical'—is to treat even the most bizarre or distressing experience as if it were an integral part of the pattern of existence, and you had known it all your life, without realizing it.

Either way works, but the most reasonable and convincing arguments are those which use the right combination of both.

The message: *What* are you going to say to them?

If there is one element in this structured approach to PR programmes that is more important than any of the others, it is the content of the message. No matter how you say it, or to whom, or where, it is what you actually say that has to be right. You are not going to be the judge of that; your audience is.

Messages can be expressed in words, pictures or actions or in any combination.

When a health scare blows up, it is usually of the utmost importance to get factual information out as quickly and accurately as possible. Bovine spongiform encephalopathy is not easy to say or remember. If the messages about it are to be understandable and reassuring, is it a help or a hindrance to call it 'mad cow disease'?

Was Edwina Curry's famous remark about salmonella clear or not? 'Sadly, most of Britain's egg production is affected' seemed a clear enough message at the time. But was it? It certainly altered perception. Nature's very own, health-giving, pre-packed convenience food, the one to 'go to work on', was transformed into a potential health hazard. Behaviour changed too. There was a 13 per cent drop in sales of eggs and alarm in the industry. The messenger was attacked. So was the message. Was it wrong? Or was it misunderstood? If so, who did not understand it?

Hampstead Health Authority was not unique in needing to attract and retain more learner nurses. A management consultancy report recommended improvements to accommodation, study and counselling facilities and better targeting to specific audience groups in specific locations. Two of the report's main conclusions were to do with the message:

1. Describe the job better, overcoming 'misconceptions about the role, skills and characteristics needed to perform the job well'.
2. Rewrite recruitment literature, to 'better articulate and sell the many positive features of the School of Nursing'.[7]

The results of Hampstead's programme to increase the supply of staff accommodation is described in Chapter 10.

Possibly one of the best known messages in the English language was delivered to the American people, and the world, at Gettysburg on 19 November 1863. More than one person spoke that day, but the one who is remembered is Abraham Lincoln. His message affected, and still affects, the beliefs, attitude and behaviour of millions. It was a short speech, and 16 words express the core of it:

> . . . government of the people, by the people, for the people, shall not perish from the earth . . .

Phrases like that do not usually spring complete and unrevised out of the heads of even such as Lincoln. Wouldn't it be helpful to us, as PR practitioners, if we could see his first drafts?

Well, in a sense, we can. Five years earlier, Theodore Parker said this at the Boston Music Hall, on 2 July 1858:

> . . . direct self-government over all the people, by all the people, for all the people . . .

Parker's own first draft was tried out at the New England Anti-Slavery Convention on 29 May 1850:

> . . . a government of all the people, by all the people, for all the people . . .

Twenty years before that, and 33 before Gettysburg, Daniel Webster's second speech on Foote's Resolution included these 16 words:

. . . the people's government, made for the people, made by the people and answerable to the people . . .

With such a provenance, small wonder that Lincoln's message achieved immortality.

Can a picture be worth 1000 such words? Vandyke's royal portraits convey very seductive messages about the unquestioned and unquestionable authority of kingship—the Divine Right—as perceived by the monarch and endured by his subjects in the first half of the seventeenth century. The image was not matched by reality and Civil War was not far away. In Mexico 250 years later Diego Rivera's vast murals conveyed messages diametrically opposed to Vandyke's, but no less powerful—the corruption of the rulers and the heroism of the ruled, who became revolutionaries, not by Divine Right but through economic necessity.

The third great embodiment of a message is action. You not only have to be what you say you are and what you appear to be, you also have to do what you claim you do. You do not become environmentally credible just because you use recycled paper and colour it green.

Whatever the physical form your message takes, there are some key questions to be answered.

1. Do you understand the message that your PR programme is going to put across? If you don't, how can you possibly expect anyone else to?
2. Will your audience understand it? Remember the case of the giant South American louse in Chapter 2.
3. Will they believe it? Does it square with their perception of reality? The credibility of the source has a lot to do with the credibility of the message. That is why third party endorsement can be so effective, and why for most copywriters who attempt to update teenage slang, nearly right is ludicrously wrong to those in the know.
4. Can they take it? Some messages can hit so hard that they are self-defeating. Road safety campaigns based on fear can make many road users over-anxious. Consequently they become more at risk, not less. Others simply switch off their minds.
5. Is the message compatible with their own self-interest? Altruism can be a powerful motivator, but don't bank on it.
6. Are they able to take action on it? If they can't do what you want them to, what is the point of asking them?
7. Will they act on it? If you don't make it easy for them to do, don't expect them to supply the motivation themselves. Inertia is an easier option, unfortunately.

Case History 9
Building a quality reputation

Ernest Ireland Construction, building and civil engineering contractors, set themselves the objective of gaining a reputation for quality work. As a visible mark of real achievement, they went all out to win Quality Assurance 5750 of the British Standards Institute. Their method was an extensive campaign of training to meet the required standard. This is what they did.

Stage 1 (1987)
Preparation of a quality and training manual.

Stage 2 (1987/8)
Far reaching programme of seminars covering all the company's operational areas and involving 350 staff.

Stage 3 (1988)
BSI 5750 registration, the first in the building contracting industry.

Stage 4 (1988 onwards)
Coordinated promotion of this achievement, including:
- Award ceremony.
- Policy statements in company literature.
- Support documentation in pre-tender submissions.
- Syndicated articles/pictures for trade and business media.
- Award logo on company stationery.
- Award logo on company advertisements.
- Chief Engineer's speeches at national/international seminars.
- Conference workshop at Human Resource Development Week.

Results
1. Significant new business.
2. Greater efficiency.
3. Turnover increased by 30 per cent from 1987 to 1989.
4. Considerable cost savings.
5. National Training Award 1989.
6. The *Channel 4 Business Daily* Award.

Moral
If you aim to build a reputation for quality, first build the quality.[8]

The location: *Where* are you going to reach them?

When you are identifying your audience, knowing where they are can be as important as knowing who they are. Otherwise, how can you reach them? It is part of media planning. Advertising agencies do it well and systematically. Why not you?

Where people are located shapes to a very large extent how they behave and how receptive or otherwise they are to particular PR messages. What works with bank clerks or shop assistants or managers may have quite a different effect on the same people when they are on the football terraces or the cross channel ferry or at a rock concert. The role they are playing—perhaps even the very people they are—can change as the location changes. PR programmes need to take account of that.

Geography can shape messages, whether they are specific and tailored to the region, or general with a regionalized angle.

Maybe your company has a message for mothers of newborn babies—perhaps to alert them to a health hazard. One location you will certainly want to consider is maternity hospitals and clinics. For most people in hospital, the main common factor is that they are sick. In maternity wards the common factor is that they are mothers—or very soon will be. Any hospital environment affects what you can say and how you say it: maternity hospitals more so.

Location need not be static. If you want to reach an audience of small businessmen, one place to find them is in their cars, on their way to or from work. For that location, radio and tape cassette can be very effective, as long as the message is appropriate.

Much of the planning and execution of PR programmes is to do with identifying all the relevant locations and fitting them into a coherent whole. Better transport systems and improved information technology mean that the message can be taken out to the audience in ways, and on a scale, that would have been unimaginable in former times. For all that, the methods of the day were far from primitive, and more than 500 years ago there were national information networks. The following case history, drawn from history, has something to tell today's managers.

Case History 10
Government PR in the late Middle Ages

The tentacles of royal administration—enabling decisions, grants of taxation and legal pronouncements to be implemented—stretched to the extremities of the British Isles . . .

The king's administration was a cooperative affair. In each county the sheriffs and the new justices of the peace functioned best with the aid of the nobility and local gentry, whose interests in turn were securely tied to the monarch, the greatest single source of wealth and patronage in the realm. Parliament . . . came to play an essential part in the late medieval government. By Edward I's reign, war and domestic upheaval had fortified the king's need to consult his subjects ('the community of the realm', as contemporaries termed them) and to seek their advice in reaching and implementing decisions affecting the realm at large . . .

This institution, unique among the parliaments of medieval Europe, discussed both important matters of business and minor matters raised by individuals. It won a monopoly of taxing Englishmen; it was the highest court in the land; and it made new law and modified existing law through legislation . . .

The commons' representatives had to be informed, courted and persuaded before they returned home to their constituents, considerable numbers of whom desired information about affairs. It was, after all, they who paid taxes, served in war and defence, and who were asked for their cooperation and obedience. The government was, therefore, well advised to weigh carefully the news it transmitted to the realm and the opinions it hoped the king's subjects would adopt. Well-developed methods of communication and propaganda were used to this end. The preambles of official proclamations could popularize a policy and justify a practice: Edward IV's proclamation against Margaret, Queen of the deposed Henry VI, made much of the memory of Archbishop Scrope of York, who had been executed by Henry's grandfather and had since taken on the aura of a martyr. This was skilful propaganda to sustain opposition to the Lancastrian dynasty, for proclamations were sent to every shire for public reading and display. Songs and ballads reached wide audiences too, and some that were officially inspired stressed the glories of Agincourt out of all proportion. Sermons were no less effective in moulding opinion and mobilizing support. In 1443 Henry VI requested that good stirring preachers be sent through every diocese to reinforce from the pulpit royal appeals for money for yet another French campaign. Coronations, royal progresses and the formal entries of kings and queens into York, Bristol and Gloucester (as well as London) were occasions for lavish displays of official propaganda, harnessing mythology, Christianity and patriotism. In 1417, Henry V was portrayed for all to see at his reception by London as a soldier of Christ returning from the crusade against the French. If any citizen harboured lingering doubts about the justice of his invasion of France, this was calculated to remove them.

The circulation of letters to inform, persuade and justify was as near as the pre-printing age came to publication; such letters soon found their way into popular chronicles. In this way, Henry V reported to his subjects the progress of his French campaigns. Even fashionable writers of the day became official propagandists. In the fifteenth century, authors rarely produced their words unsolicitedly. Thomas Hoccleve was a humble government bureaucrat who was paid by Henry V to produce laudatory verses about Agincourt and the English seige of Rouen (1419). John Ludgate was patronized by Henry VI and his court over a long period, implanting in the popular mind all the jingoism that could be wrung out of the successful defence of Calais against Burgundian attack in 1436.[9]

The timetable: *When* are you going to reach them?

The planning and scheduling you put into a public relations programme can be very demanding and complex—much more so than for an advertising programme. What is more, some of the timings may be entirely beyond your own control. If you book an advertisement to appear in a specific format, on a specific day, in a specific place, it will appear, because that is what you pay for. Your press briefing or press notice is not guaranteed to get any particular coverage at any particular time or in any particular place, or at all, though your chance of success will be greatly improved if you get the timing right.

The deadline for a local weekly newspaper is normally 10.30 am—or possibly noon—two days before publication. Give them an extra day or two if you can. National dailies like to gather their hard news by about 4 pm in the afternoon of the previous day. Sunday papers have their own conventions. Freelance journalist Arthur Smith, conceding that it is very difficult to place stories in the business section of *The Sunday Times*, points out that their business desk closes midday Thursday 'and it's pushing it to get in Friday, while the main paper has considerable pressure on space'.[10]

An evening paper prefers to have its news by about 10.30 am on the day of issue, but midday is still acceptable. Similarly with local radio news, though a radio phone-in is for all practical purposes instantaneous. A technical journal, published monthly, could need anything from six to twelve weeks lead time. They start putting their pages together in the middle of a month.

Try to avoid embargoes. If you time your approach right, you do not normally need them. An exception is when you put out on a Friday a story embargoed for Monday, a slack day for news. On a slightly longer timescale, you might start planning a press reception three months before it happens. To make sure that all the associated jobs get done, you could use the reverse countdown method, from D-day minus 90 through to the event itself on D-day. The method is simple and easy to follow, as in this example, from the Frank Jefkins School of Public Relations (see Figure 6.2).

When a PR programme is planned to run for a year or so, the D-day timetable method can still be used. However, consider the advantages of time bands or time bars, which show where the different tasks start and finish in relation to each other, and where the overlaps and gaps are. The method also gives some idea of tempo (see Figure 6.3).

Corporate identity programmes, positioning through sponsorships, reputation building—these can take even longer to bring about, and the risk is that all sense of pace can be lost. A five-year rolling programme is made up of a whole

D − 90   Decide date.
D − 85   Plan programme for press reception.
D − 85   Shortlist venues.
D − 85   Invite quotations, menus, from prospective venues.
D − 80   Complete compilation of invitation list, including checking of names.
D − 75   Compare received hotel quotations and menus.
D − 70   Visit prospective venues.
D − 65   Select and appoint venue.
D − 52   Design invitation card. Agree wording.
D − 50   Seek printer's quotation for card.
D − 42   Receive printer's quotation. Order cards and envelopes.
D − 35   Photograph subject.
D − 32   Receive, check and return proof of invitation card.
D − 30   Write managing director's speech.
D − 30   Order self-adhesive lapel badges, press kit wallets, and visitors' book.
D − 30   Book projector, projectionist, microphones.
D − 25   See contact prints. Order photographs.
D − 24   Obtain approval of managing director's speech.
D − 22   Send special invitations to radio/TV producers of news programmes.
D − 20   Write news release.
D − 14   Delivery of invitation cards and envelopes.
D − 13   Address envelopes for invitations.
D − 12   Despatch invitations.
D − 12   Order studio artwork—tent cards with names of speakers, displays, directional signs.
D − 10   Record acceptances/refusals.
D − 9   Follow up non-replies, important refusals.
D − 8   Photographs supplied. Items at D − 30 delivered.
D − 4   Collect 16 mm film.
D − 3   Give hotel total numbers for catering, seating, together with plan of the room.
D − 3   Caption photographs.
D − 2   Run off news releases, managing director's speech.
D − 2   Prepare name badges.
D − 2   Assemble press kits.
D − 1   Deliver materials and equipment to venue.
D − 1   Prepare room.
D − 1   Rehearsal. Run through film.
D-Day Press reception.

Figure 6.2 D-Day planning timetable for a press reception[11]

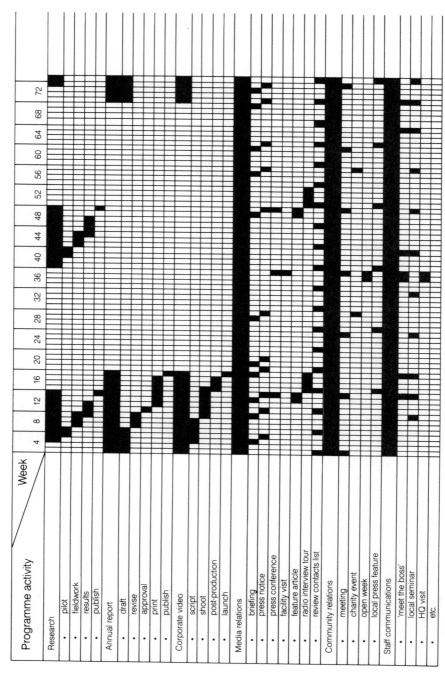

Figure 6.3 Time bars

series of interlocking shorter programmes and to keep the overall shape clear and understandable, network analysis or critical path analysis can be helpful.

The techniques

Most of the examples and case histories in this book have something to say about the techniques used in PR programmes designed to achieve specific objectives. Those techniques were chosen as the most appropriate for their purpose, and the selection was usually made by, or at least on the advice of, PR professionals. How did they know what techniques would be best?

They relied on their experience and training, knowledge and know-how, judgement and instinct, in fact all the facets of professionalism, to steer them in the right direction. The mental process involves matching particular programme requirements with the characteristics of particular techniques or media.

Look first at the size of each specific audience—small, medium or large. For example, if it is essential to get information across quickly to a large audience, advertising, editorial and telephone campaigns would have clear advantages over face-to-face presentations and one-to-one meetings. On the other hand, for a very small audience—say the 170 MPs known to be interested in the power supply industry—advertising would be expensive and wasteful, when you could reach them all quickly and cheaply through presentations and group briefings. You would also have interaction and the likelihood of immediate feedback through on-the-spot response. Of course, you might use advertising to marshal public opinion on your side, and so pressurize the MPs; or you might be able to target your advertising in such a way that the small audience groups are subsumed within the large.

Is your message long and complex? You are not going to get it across via posters or TV advertisements. Editorial would be much more effective, or publications or exhibitions, as long as you had planned far enough ahead to use them. But these are essentially non-intrusive techniques, and if you needed to grab attention, you might consider using TV or posters for teasers and reminders. Maybe you need a programme of deep penetration but low visibility.

There are no 'best' techniques or mixes of techniques. Each needs thinking about in relation to programme needs. A balancing act is required.

Once again, you could use a decision tree to help you arrive at sensible conclusions. A matrix aproach might be easier, one axis for the programme requirements you have identified as important, the other for the techniques at your disposal. Leave out any obvious non-starters.

For a particular audience size, is a requirement—say speed—a good match with a technique—say advertising? If so, put 3 in the appropriate square (see Figure 6.4). If the match is only average, or you don't know, put 2. A poor match rates a score of 1. Fill in all the squares in the same way, trying not have

Figure 6.4 The mix matrix

AUDIENCE / composition / size / location / REQUIREMENT — TECHNIQUE	Complexity of message	Cost factor	Impact	Interaction	Intrusiveness	Penetration	Repeatability	Speed	Visibility	Total	Notional average
ADVERTISING Press	3										
Radio	2										
TV	2										
CONFERENCES	1										
DIRECT MAIL	3										
EDITORIAL Briefings											
Conferences											
Facilities											
Receptions											
Releases											
EXHIBITIONS National	1										
Regional	2										
Mobile	1										
FACE-TO-FACE	1										
LOBBYING	1										
PUBLICATIONS: A/Report	1										
Books	1										
Brochures	3										
Leaflets	3										
Staff mags	2										
SPONSORSHIPS:											
Videos											
etc.											

too many 'average' or 'don't know' scores. Be decisive. Then add up the total for each line and compare it with the notional average for that line, that is as if every score rated 2. The results should give you a good idea of the mix you might find most effective for a specific message to a specific audience.

Above average scores are more convincing than those below average. In thinking about costs, you will want to take account of the absolute figure, the critical mass (the minimum expenditure below which a particular technique cannot do the job assigned to it), unit costs, or cost per OTS (opportunities to see; see Chapter 10).

Case History 11
Spreading the word

British Airways uses 'the whole range of public relations methods' in a well-integrated, worldwide programme. This is its award-winning approach.

Objective

To achieve worldwide recognition and approval for British Airways, furthering the company's commercial success.

> It is crucial that our key audiences—the media, our customers, our shareholders, our regulators and our staff—receive the true view of British Airways.
>
> *Sir Colin Marshall*
> *Chief Executive, British Airways*

Strategy

- To identify the audiences with which BA must communicate, and create and lead a programme of activity that will achieve their support for the company's corporate and marketing objectives.
- Actively to promote British Airways and its people through the world's media, using the whole range of public relations methods.
- To achieve the informed and sympathetic support of politicians and other public opinion formers.
- To foster the support of the company's employees for its aims, missions and goals, through a range of internal communications media.
- To minimize damaging publicity.

Programme resources

Press and media relations:
- Own press office at Heathrow (12 press officers).
- Agencies at Manchester, Birmingham, Belfast and Glasgow.

Worldwide marketing (covering 170 cities in 80 countries):
- Gatwick Press Office.

- Full-time managers in the United States, Canada, Australia, Germany, Italy.
- Agencies in 50 other locations.

City and financial (300 000 shareholders) run by Public Affairs and Finance and Investor Relations departments:
- Reports, accounts, briefings, shareholders' newspaper, presentations, roadshows, AGM, corporate video, brochures, company history, etc.

Parliamentary affairs (650 MPs + 81 MEPs):
- One person plus specialist (lobbying) agency.
- 150 regular contacts.

Internal communications (50 000 BA staff):
- *BA News*: weekly tabloid (43 editorial staff).
- *News updates*: for immediate cascading.
- *Outlook*: quarterly management video.
- *Newsbriefs*: electronic data, daily.

Speechwriting is covered by each of the above sections, depending on audience.

Budget

> Our Budget represents just one-tenth of 1 per cent (i.e. 0.1 per cent) of the company's total expenditure.
>
> *David Burnside*
> *Director of Public Affairs, BA*

Awards

Best in-house PR department 1988 and 1989:
- British Airways in-house PR department successfully took on the airline taboo on selling safety, marrying it successfully with its other activities. By early summer 1988 it was clear that safety in the air was going to be one of the main media issues of the year, even before the tragedies at Lockerbie and Kegworth. BA has already taken preventive PR action to position itself positively in advance of such issues.
- The objective of the PR programme was to strengthen BA's reputation for technical excellence, establishing it as number one in the eyes of the media in all safety matters. The BA team also launched two major products which between them represented investments of £25 million.
- It also ran a major campaign in support of lower fares in Europe which included the publication of its own *Manifesto for Europe* at the time of the European elections.

- BA's in-house team broke new ground in communication with the private shareholder with the creation of the *British Airways Investor*. It continued to publish internally and externally its *Spreading the Word* guide on its activities.

Best use of video:
- British Airways commended for its quarterly video news magazines for managers, *Outlook*. The presentation is styled after the BBC's *Newsnight* or the *Money Programme* and its analytical approach helps make managers feel part of the policy-making process.[12]

The cost

Money as a resource is dealt with in Chapter 7, budgeting in Chapter 8.

It is only necessary here to underline that as a good manager you are always looking for cost-effective solutions to problems. That is fine when what you are planning to do has been tried and tested before. It is more difficult when you are trying to be entirely innovative. By its very nature, a new idea has no track record. The way round that is to check that every step of the way towards the solution has been cost-justified.

Costings ought to be accurate, therefore specifications need to be tight. That booklet you are about to commission—what is your target costing? What format will be most effective? How many pages? What weight of paper? How many colours? What is the economic number of copies? A difference of one gram in the enveloped weight can add 50 per cent to the mailout costs. That might or might not be justified; it ought to be thought about.

Do you always participate in a certain exhibition because your competitors do? Is that reason enough and have you calculated the true costs? The Stone supposition could apply here—25 per cent of the cost of an exhibition is site cost. The other 75 per cent comprises stand design, construction and dressing; videos, demonstrations, working models; brochures and mailouts; press reception; hospitality; advertising support; staff time and expenses; and so on. All of these may be justified: each should be cost-justified.

Can you get what you want for less money? More of what you want for the same money? Could spending a little more bring you a lot of added value, for example by reaching an important secondary audience?

Most people in the PR business would agree that targeted press information is more effective than the scatter-gun approach of firing off the same press notice to everyone. But how many different versions should you afford? What would be the additional cost of producing and delivering purpose-made material for radio stations?

What effect does size of audience have on cost-effectiveness? The relative cost of press advertising falls as the number of readers increases. For which other techniques is that true? Face-to-face demonstration is just the opposite—costs rise with numbers.

The overriding guideline is that costs should be commensurate with objectives.

Case History 12
The Flour Advisory Bureau's programme

This is how the Flour Advisory Bureau spent a £145 000 budget over 12 months with Paragon. Objectives, strategy, required response and coordination have already been discussed earlier in this book. Here is the programme.

Activities

Cohesive campaign theme:
• 'Flour Power—everybody needs it'.

Consumer and trade research:
• Attitudes/misconceptions/varieties
• Product knowledge/staff training/merchandising/range/promotion.

Bread and flour report:
• Retailing study
• Four catering studies
• Consumer education leaflet.

Exploitation via
• Advance consumer/trade press briefings
• Two press conferences
• Targeted mailings (media/industry/educational bodies).

The loafers roadshow:
• Eight key media towns
• Advance publicity via competitions, posters, radio announcements
• Literature/merchandise distribution
• Photocalls
• Media interviews
• Sales promotion.

Beyond the roadshow:
• Regional press competitions
• Media tour
• Syndicated cartoon strips
• Sales promotion.

Sponsored features.
Trade case studies.

Results

	Target audience reach (million)
National consumer press	6.0
National TV and radio	13.8
Regional consumer press	7.1
Regional TV and radio	40.5
Trade press	0.5
Direct consumer contact/literature distribution (est)	12.5
Total	80.4

Cost per OTS: 0.0002p
   (for explanation of OTS see Chapter 10)
Cost per 1000: £1.80[13]

The unexpected

You have worked out your programme most carefully, with cost-justification built into every stage. Your measurement systems are in place and your expectations are realistic. But what about the unexpected?

Michael Regester, an acknowledged expert in crisis management, points out that 'most crises happen bewilderingly quickly. News of what has gone wrong spreads with equal speed.'[14]

Yet the strange thing about the unforeseen is that it is always happening. A good manager expects the unexpected and plans for it. If you do not take charge of a crisis, assuredly it will take charge of you, with the media dictating the agenda and setting the pace.

Every organization needs to know in advance what its potential crises are and be ready to deal with them—if possible before they occur, if not as soon as the signs are unmistakable.

The best way is by mobilizing a well-rehearsed crisis management team, armed with an operational plan that has been prepared in advance and is constantly updated. The team calls in any expertise it needs, from legal to financial, personnel to sales, production to marketing. The team knows what to do and has the authority to do it.

If outside help is needed, there are consultancies which specialize in the management of crises, and even in particular aspects such as product recall. Most large PR consultancies have a crisis management capability.

When is a crisis actually a crisis? When it is a board matter, and that, says Shandwick, is when

- the trading operation is interrupted
- the financial performance is threatened
- the reputation of the organization is damaged.[15]

Perhaps a fourth determinant should be added—when major stakeholders are at risk.

Whether your company handles crises from its own resources, or calls in professional help, there is one crucial decision that has to be made, and that is to put maximum effort into resolving the crisis itself, by accepting responsibility, admitting errors, and taking remedial action.

Alongside this executive commitment to putting things right, you need to run a centralized programme for all information, incoming and outgoing. Present a united, authoritative, well-trained, single *human* voice to the media.

Measure what the people who really matter—your stakeholders—know and think, as well as what the media say: there could well be significant differences. Treat the media fairly. Be open. Take the initiative. Keep your head. Remember that most crises are not fatal to an organization. Stay in control.

These and other golden guidelines should stand you in good stead when the balloon goes up, the bubble bursts and unidentified flying objects hit the fan. But the best guideline of all is Michael Regester's—'the key to crisis management is crisis prevention'.[16]

Of course, not all surprises are crises. Sometimes the unexpected can be an unforeseen opportunity to add to your PR programme. Opportunism is certainly part of the PR mix and some practitioners are brilliant extemporizers. For all that, ideas for unscheduled activities should be put through three hoops or filters. Are they on strategy? Can they be cost-justified? Will they be demonstrably more effective in attaining your objectives than the activities they would replace? Not many stunts and wheezes pass these stringent tests.

The evaluation

A number of ways of evaluating PR programmes, examined in Chapter 10, include monitoring the effectiveness of media coverage and measuring direct what happens to the bottom line.

Media coverage of the target messages of the Quentin Bell Organisation (QBO) PR programme for Firstdirect was measured quarterly, taking account of changing communication priorities. During the launch period they wanted to get across that Firstdirect was a totally autonomous division within the Midland group: a very different alternative to traditional high street banking (words like radical/exciting/different); customer driven (speed/price/convenience); able to provide a complete range of banking services. In the second quarter, as the public and the media began to understand the Firstdirect proposition, new message playback was looked for—backed by but separate from Midland; good/competitive rates of interest; information on products and services; 0800 contact telephone number.

Evaluation of each press cutting or transcript was by pre-agreed criteria: total number of items; advertising value; opportunities to see; quality of message. 'The first three points are quantitative and easy to measure using a variety of media information sources such as DNA and BRAD', said QBO. 'Measuring the quality of the coverage is a slightly more subjective exercise and takes a great deal more time to conduct.'[17] The section in Chapter 10 on measuring media coverage explains how the Quentin Bell Organisation does it.

Case History 13
Dropping the doctor

Media evaluation and direct measurement of results were very much in evidence when Britain's largest childcare charity relaunched. This is what happened.

Analysis

Research showed that most people who supported Dr Barnardo's did so for the wrong reasons. They thought the 120-year-old charity cared exclusively for orphans.

Objectives

1. To inform donors and potential donors of the full extent of the work of the charity.
2. To dispel any stigma there might be about being helped.

Strategy

Relaunch Dr Barnardo's with a new corporate identity, maximizing the involvement of a royal patron.

Programme

1. Brief and train staff in advance.
2. Relaunch at AGM attended by Princess of Wales.
3. Eight simultaneous regional launches.

4. Change name from Dr Barnardo's to Barnardo's.
5. New graphic identity.
6. Fashion show by Bruce Oldfield, a Barnardo's old boy. Princess of Wales present.
7. Lunch honouring 'Champion Children', also attended by Princess of Wales.
8. Major BBC documentary followed the process on camera.

Resources

In-house PR department of 26 people.
Consultancy by Valin Pollen.

Budget

£147 000

Responsibilities

Strategy and tactics by in-house team.
Corporate identity by consultants.

Results

1. Front page news in every UK national newspaper.
2. Morning, noon and night TV news for two days.
3. One-hour TV documentary in prime time.
4. All costs met by sponsorship (e.g. £47 000 for AGM) or extra donations.
5. Substantial increase in postbag.
6. Additional offers of help reported from all regions, often prefaced by remarks like 'I didn't know you do all that'.

Accountability

Chief Executive of Barnardo's.
Council of Barnardo's (voluntary governing body).[18]

Checklist

You will frequently come across a particular set of proposals that masquerades as a PR programme. It is not. Nor is it a campaign, but a standard all-purpose package of four activities.

1. Carry out a survey.
2. Publish a report.
3. Hold a press conference.
4. Set up an information centre or service.

If you want to go beyond that, and develop a real PR programme, here are the 10 key questions. Simple to ask, they are not always simple to answer.

1. To *whom* are you talking?
2. *What* do you want them to do?
3. *Why* do you want them to do it?
4. *What* are you going to say to them?
5. *Where* are you to reach them?
6. *When* are you going to reach them?
7. *Which* techniques will you use?
8. *How much* are you going to spend?
9. *What if* there is an unforeseen problem?
10. *How* did you do?

All those concerned should be involved in arriving at the answers. Quantify wherever practicable. If you have an audience of shareholders (Question 1) how many? If you want them to vote in favour of a particular issue (Question 2), what percentage? The more accurately you can do this, the better your answers will be to Questions 7 and 8, and above all to Question 10.

This is an entirely conventional approach, tried and tested countless times. It still works.

Sources and references

1. Roger Haywood. *All about PR*. McGraw-Hill, London, 1991.
2. Michael Madison. Round and round the planning cycle. *Marketing*, 17 September 1987.
3. Commendations for positive action—Rushden Boys Schools, Northants. *Opening Doors*. The Fawcett Society, 1986.
4. Janet Salvoni. *Case histories*. Presentation at Interact Seminar, 1989.
5. A drive to win new laurels. *PR Week*, 15 February 1990.
6. *WRVS News*. Women's Royal Voluntary Service, published quarterly.
7. A most accommodating service. *Network*. Hampstead Health Authority, May 1989.
8. Case history authenticated by Ernest Ireland Construction.
9. Kenneth O. Morgan (ed.). *The Oxford Illustrated History of Britain*. Oxford University Press, 1984.
10. Midlands IPR meets the National Media. *Communiqué*. Midlands Group of the Institute of Public Relations, May 1990.
11. Frank Jefkins. *Public Relations Techniques*, Heinemann, London, 1988.
12. Case history authenticated by British Airways.
13. Case history authenticated by Paragon.

14. Michael Regester. *Crisis Management—how to turn a crisis into an opportunity.* Hutchinson, London, 1987.
15. Mary Bartholomew. *Crisis Management—a team approach.* Course paper, College of Marketing, 1986.
16. as source 14.
17. *Memorandum.* The Quentin Bell Organisation, April 1990.
18. Case history authenticated by Barnardo's.

CHAPTER 7

Resources

> Management having guaranteed the necessary resources, would these be of the right quality as well as being available at the right time . . .?
>
> *William F. Coventry*[1]

The very first of all the guidelines to management practice spelt out by the BIM states clearly and uncompromisingly that professional managers should make proper use of the resources available to them.

As far as PR managers are concerned, what are these resources? Essentially they are no different from those available to any manager in any business.

In the manufacturing industries, for example, they talk about the 'four Ms'— materials, machinery, money and manpower. The fact that these resources are set out in that particular order may reflect the overriding importance the industry used to attach to the production process.

Playing the M-game can be quite useful if it helps to focus attention on resources. As well as manpower, what about management skill, mental ability and motivation? Is machinery much use without modernization? Do you think of the media as a resource?

Perhaps the most popular 'extra M' is marketing. However, that is not so much a resource as a philosophy. Marketing has been described as the whole business, seen from the customer's point of view. But remember that customers are by no means the only stakeholders.

You could go for Joan Plachta's brilliant simplification, 'Top managers may recognise that they have only two tools at their disposal—finance and communication—but while they are taught accounting, very few are taught PR'.[2] What managers, top or otherwise, can do is to adapt what they know already to the management of PR resources.

The ever-helpful BIM guidelines come to the rescue again. We are told flatly that professional managers need to use processes and materials efficiently. This applies to everything from print to video.

In many ways the most comprehensive of the guidelines reminds managers that by leadership, coordination, personal example and commitment they must direct all available efforts towards the success of the enterprise. Efforts include resources, not least their own inner resources.

In the environment-conscious 1990s, the BIM guideline about making the most effective use of natural resources for the benefit of the organization and with minimum detriment to the public interest is of increasing importance.[3]

The resources which are of most concern to the PR manager are as follows:

- People
- Experience, knowledge and know-how
- Time
- Services, whether in-house or bought in from outside
- Money
- Information
- Consultancies.

Using these resources to the best effect calls for decisions about relative importance and priorities.

People

At some stage in its development, pretty well every business can be called a people business, and usually is. Careers counsellors find that more and more youngsters put 'working with people' high on their list of desirable jobs. Every beauty queen seems to want to 'work with people'.

Predictable and boring, maybe; but good sense for all that. Businesses are run by people who employ people who buy from people and sell to people. It is not the business or organization that sets objectives, devises strategies or delivers results—it is people. 'Business-to-business' really means 'business-people-to-business-people'.

But if every business is to that extent a people business, what is distinctive about the PR business? It is becoming increasingly capital intensive, particularly through investment in information technology. Nevertheless, the main resource is the professional staff who work in the business, whether in-company or in consultancies. Truly, PR is labour intensive, or rather, people intensive.

What kind of people are they? Where do you find and recruit them? What motivates them? What skills do they need? How do you train them, develop them, reward them, retain them?

Few graduates have been going into PR as their first venture into the labour market. Those who have were qualified in disciplines other than PR because until the late 1980s it was impossible to acquire a first degree in public relations anywhere in the United Kingdom. No courses were available.

Stirling University, the Dorset Institute of Higher Education, the College of St Mark and St John, Plymouth, and Leeds Polytechnic are among those starting to change all that (see Appendix D). There are sure to be others. These endeavours are supported by the industry in a variety of useful ways.

The Public Relations Education Trust (PRET) is a cooperative venture between the Institute of Public Relations and the Public Relations Consultants Association. The Trust is pledged to promote the development of public relations education and research, advise the industry on development in public relations education and research, and liaise and cooperate with similar bodies worldwide.

A wide range of educational initiatives, including BA and Masters' degrees, is being encouraged at universities, business schools, polytechnics and colleges around the country and a scheme for all stages of public relations education has been devised with these important criteria in mind:

- The need to ensure the highest levels of skills in public relations practice by all practitioners, whether they are working in business organizations or in consultancies.

- The need to ensure that, at all levels of experience, public relations practitioners are able to fulfil the expectations of them, thus contributing to the professionalism of those they serve.

- The need to take into account the essential difference between working in business organizations and working in consultancies, at the same time recognizing that many of the required skills are interchangeable.[4]

Consultancies and in-house PR departments provide visiting lecturers, give textbooks and prizes, sponsor students, offer work-experience placements, and help to shape college curricula. Some may eventually endow a chair or two.

In the early 1990s, the first PR graduates entering the labour market will be calling into question the seriousness of the employing organizations and putting the employment prospects of newly qualified people to the test.

When—and it must be 'when' not 'if'—PR graduates get jobs in their chosen field, they will still need training that is specific to their employment. What they should not need is training in the basics of PR, as so many do now and so few actually get. For every employing organization that takes training seriously, there are many more who do not. Beyond question that has to change.

People who have been in PR for some time have a range of qualifications to aim at as well as membership of a number of appropriate institutions. In 1989 a survey showed that nearly one in two in-house PR professionals in the top companies had a degree, whereas 26 per cent had no qualifications at all (see Table 7.1).

One in four belonged to the Institute of Public Relations but 34 per cent did not belong to any professional body (see Table 7.2).

Recruitment was through pretty well all the possible channels. Very senior or very unusual positions tended to be filled through head hunters, while recruitment consultants, with or without press advertising, took care of many vacancies. Direct advertising by employers was the most popular way of getting people. Word of mouth was more important than many realized.

Table 7.1   Professional qualifications[5]

	%
Degree	48
Further degree	7
MBA	1
CAM	1
Marketing diploma	4
Other	15
None	26
Not stated	7

Table 7.2   Professional membership[6]

	%
Institute of Public Relations	25
Institute of Marketing	8
National Union of Journalists	8
Marketing Society	3
Institute of Directors	3
Market Research Society	2
Other (none larger than 1 per cent)	24
None	34

After 1992, entrants into the IPR will be required to have approved educational qualifications, although candidates will also have to produce evidence of substantial work experience.

Experience, knowledge and know-how

These resources fall into two main groups. One consists of the experience and know-how which is necessary and specific to the employing organization's industrial sector, or to the organization itself, and is therefore of limited application elsewhere. The other comprises the professional experience, knowledge, skills and competence which apply in a wide range of circumstances and are therefore transferable.

The IPR and PRCA identify four categories of knowledge and skills necessary to any public relations professional, at each of five levels or stages.

The categories are:

A Knowledge
B Writing skills
C Public relations skills
D Business skills

The levels are:

Stage 1   Pre-entry requirements. The basic skills and knowledge necessary for any candidate wishing to pursue a career in public relations. These may be obtained while working in an administrative role.

Stage 2   Professional starter. The specific initial knowledge and skills essential for those developing their public relations career, from assistants and junior executives.

Stages 3 and 4   Developing and operating professional. The development, knowledge and skills, necessarily gained over a period of time, to become a fully rounded and experienced public relations practitioner and public relations operator.

Stage 5   Experienced professional specialist and management. The continuing development phase from functional to team or group supervision responsibility, counselling and management roles in public relations.

An Education and Training Matrix was developed with and endorsed by the IPR and PRCA.[7] Figure 7.1 shows how it works for the nine elements of knowledge at the five stages of professionalism.

It is clear from this matrix that people at all levels in the PR business, from pre-entrant to experienced professional, need constant training and updating in the legal, legislative and regulatory framework of Britain and the EC, whereas management psychology or organizational strategy apply to the higher levels.

The matrix works in the same way for the 14 writing skills, again at the five stages of professionalism (Figure 7.2). Business writing is a skill to be developed at all stages, whereas pre-entrants will hardly be concerned with editorial or presentational writing.

Public relations skills—35 of them are listed in Figure 7.3—do not apply at the pre-entrant stage, with the interesting exception of the skill of compiling contact lists. Students on vacation work and first year YTS trainees probably spend a lot of their time on this skill. The results can be instantly usable by their employers. Counselling and crisis management are among the skills most likely to be needed at the higher stages—3, 4 and 5.

The matrix (Figure 7.4) identifies a group of 18 skills—communication, organizational, analytical—that make up the business skills section. Teamwork, telephoning and meeting techniques are important at all stages, design of financial and quality controls only at the 'experienced professional' stage.
The matrix can be used as a basis for

- self-assessment of training needs and career development,
- appraisal of employees' skills and their development needs,
- evaluation of training and education course suitability.[8]

		KNOWLEDGE Stage:	1	2	3	4	5
A	1	The role of public relations, both in-house and consultancy, in commercial and public sector organizations.	X	X	X	X	X
	2	An appreciation of the range of techniques and media available to public relations practitioners in the United Kingdom.	X	X	X	X	X
	3	The role, responsibilities, value systems and reporting structures of the public relations function both inside the organization and with outside bodies such as the press, clients, local and national government and the trades unions.		X	X	X	X
	4	The role, responsibilities, vocabulary, techniques, ethics, law and regulations of:					
		public relations;		X	X	X	X
		marketing;		X	X		
		advertising;		X	X		
		research and behavioural studies; and production of printed media.		X	X	X	X
	5	The role, responsibilities, vocabulary, techniques, ethics, law and regulations of:					
		sponsorship;		X	X		
		sales promotion;		X	X		
		direct marketing; and		X	X		
		broadcasting.		X	X	X	X
	6	The structure, priorities, distribution, basic economics, organization and operation of:					
		manufacturing industry;		X	X	X	X
		service industry;		X	X	X	X
		financial institutions;		X	X	X	X
		the public sector;		X	X	X	X
		local and national government;		X	X	X	X
		voluntary organizations; and		X	X	X	X
		member organizations.		X	X	X	X
	7	Organizational strategy and policy making, both concept and practice.				X	X
	8	The legal, legislative and regulatory, framework of Britain and the EC.	X	X	X	X	X
	9	Managerial psychology:					
		motivation;				X	X
		leadership.				X	X

Figure 7.1 The matrix applied to the nine elements of knowledge[9]

It is, of course, a practical tool for the analysis and auditing processes described in Chapter 3.

Off-the-job training is increasingly available. The Pims Scholarship, worth £11 000, funds a place on the Cranfield School of Management MBA course. The London Business School has a PR module on its MBA course. Some of the commercial organizations providing suitable training are listed in Appendix D.

		WRITING SKILLS		Stage:	1	2	3	4	5
B	1	Business writing:	agenda		X	X	X	X	X
	2		meeting notes		X	X	X	X	X
	3		memoranda		X	X	X	X	X
	4		letters		X	X	X	X	X
	5		reports: proposals						
			planning						
			progress		X	X	X	X	X
	6	Editorial writing:	photocalls			X	X	X	X
	7		interview calls			X	X	X	X
	8		news releases			X	X	X	X
	9		photo captions			X	X	X	X
	10		briefing material			X	X	X	X
	11		feature material			X	X	X	X
	12		newsletters			X	X	X	X
	13	Presentation writing:	script planning			X	X	X	X
	14		script writing			X	X	X	X

Figure 7.2   The matrix applied to the 14 writing skills[10]

Time

PR consultancies keep very accurate time records. They have to, because they make their money by selling time. Not so all in-house PR departments, though they really have just as much need to know what everybody's time is being spent on. Either way, if they are at all typical of British industry, they could reduce the cost of their controllable overheads by about 20 per cent.

A study by Develin and Partners into corporate overheads—that is, all costs not directly linked with making a product or providing a service—identified three groups of activities responsible for overheads.

- Core activities, which the company expects and requires staff to carry out.
- Support activities, which the staff do in direct support of the core activities.
- Discretionary activities—'work which does not utilise the particular skills of the group, or which has to be done to compensate for previous mistakes made within the company . . . adds cost . . . but no value'.
    'The challenge is to reduce the proportion of discretionary activities and improve the effectiveness of the corework . . . It requires a clear quantified understanding of each activity with its relevance in meeting the needs of the business, followed by a careful consideration of the improvement that can be made.'

There is indeed scope for improvement. Develin and Partners estimate that British companies are spending £18 000 million on inessential activities.[11]

Who pays? Consultancy fees have to cover overheads and show a profit. In-house PR departments either have to carry their own overheads or are themselves an overhead.

Figure 7.3   The matrix applied to the 35 public relations skills[12]

		PUBLIC RELATIONS SKILLS Stage:	1	2	3	4	5
C	1	Understanding public relations objectives and strategies.		X	X	X	X
	2	Identifying publics.		X	X	X	X
	3	Selecting media to reach identified publics.		X	X	X	X
	4	Compiling contact lists.	X	X	X	X	X
	5	Media liaison techniques and operation.		X	X	X	X
	6	Understanding the differing emphasis of different market sectors, such as:					
		consumer;		X	X	X	X
		technical; and		X	X	X	X
		financial.		X	X	X	X
	7	Editorial planning and monitoring.		X	X	X	X
	8	Handling editorial enquiries.		X	X	X	X
	9	The basics of photography.		X	X	X	X
	10	Briefing a photographer.		X	X	X	X
	11	Event planning and organization.		X	X	X	X
	11a	Sponsorship selection, planning and organization.		X	X	X	X
	12	Editorial promotions (competitions, special offer advertising).		X	X	X	X
	13	Negotiating editorial features and interviews.		X	X	X	X
	14	Briefing designers.		X	X	X	X
	15	Print selection, briefing and production management.		X	X	X	X
	16	Audio/visual briefing and production management.		X	X	X	X
	17	Exhibition planning and management.		X	X	X	X
	18	Capabilities of desktop publishing.		X	X	X	X
	19	Reviewing and implementing emergency plans.		X	X	X	X
	20	Understanding the implication of international developments in the media.			X	X	X
	21	Formulating public relations objectives.			X	X	X
	22	Developing public relations strategies—overall			X	X	X
	23	—contingency				X	X
	24	Creating public relations plans for action.			X	X	X
	25	Identifying trends, risks and issues relevant to an organization.			X	X	X
	26	Monitoring and evaluating progress.			X	X	X
	27	Formulating responses to threats and for an organization as they arise.				X	X
	28	Assessing the public relations implications of general management plans and decisions.				X	X
	29	Assessing the public relations implications for an organization of the plans and decisions of other organizations, including:					
		its market place;			X	X	X
		local and national government;			X	X	X
		the European Community;			X	X	X
		national and international regulatory bodies;			X	X	X
		the media;			X	X	X
		special interest groups;			X	X	X
		the local community.			X	X	X
	30	Selecting external resources, such as photographers, designers, printers and researchers.			X	X	X
	31	Public speaking.			X	X	X
	32	Giving interviews.					X
	33	Counselling and advisory techniques.					X
	34	Risk and issue management.				X	X
	35	Crisis management.				X	X

		BUSINESS SKILLS	Stage:	1	2	3	4	5
D	1	Communication:	telephone technique	X	X	X	X	X
	2		meeting technique	X	X	X	X	X
	3		presentation technique		X	X	X	X
	4		working as part of a team	X	X	X	X	X
	5		working as part of an organization	X	X	X	X	X
	6		networking (clients, colleagues, contacts)		X	X	X	X
	7		motivation and leadership			X	X	X
	8		induction and orientation				X	X
	9		interviewing and staff selection				X	X
	10	Organizational:	work flow planning and setting priorities	X	X	X	X	X
	11		time management		X	X	X	X
	12		delegation and supervision		X	X	X	X
	13		budget setting and control			X	X	X
	14		team building and management				X	X
	15		professional development of subordinates				X	X
	16		design of financial controls					X
	17		design of quality controls					X
	18	Analytical:	analysing annual reports and financial data			X	X	X

Figure 7.4 The matrix applied to 18 business skills[13]

In a typical medium-to-large consultancy, fee income might be distributed on the basis of 25 per cent to salaries, 20 per cent gross profit and all the rest on those core, support and discretionary activities that make up the corporate overheads (see Figure 7.5).

There is no shortage of advice on what to do about using time more effectively, and any number of mnemonics. Here are a few.

Appropriately enough, one is called CLOCK.

Cost the time you spend.
Look at every activity.
Order your priorities.
Core work comes first.
Know what to delegate.

Another, MODERNE, brings in information technology.

Measure how you actually spend your time.
Organize it better.
Decide what really matters.
Ensure that it gets done.
Review regularly.
No unnecessary paperwork.
Electronics help.

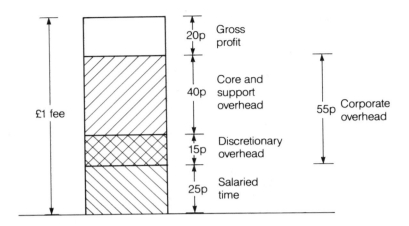

Figure 7.5 Overheads as proportion of fee income

Perhaps the best-known formula for managing your time so that you get everything done in time is known, by some unfathomable logic, as LATER.

List all your activities.
Allocate an 'importance ranking' to each.
Time each one.
Estimate the total time available for doing all the tasks.
Review your activities to be sure that you spend enough time on the important things.

The difficult thing about all that is allocating an importance ranking. Some ways in which you might do this are discussed in Chapter 5; other ways may be found later in this chapter in the section on importance versus priority.

Services

Many in-house PR departments are able to provide a range of services from their own resources. These might include public inquiries, press office and copy writing for leaflets and brochures. Services brought in from outside suppliers might include design studio, print production, direct mail, exhibitions, video production and advertising. To the extent that materials are a resource, they are included in services. If desired, a PR consultancy could provide all these and other services, either direct or on a sub-contract basis.

In Chapter 6, the provision of PR services and the various techniques available for use are explored from the point of view of planning and carrying out programmes. Budget and contract implications are examined in Chapter 8, while the role of consultancies in managing and implementing programmes is discussed in Chapter 11.

All that need be added here is a reminder that great attention should be paid to executional detail. The difference between an outstanding video, exhibition, press reception, etc., and one that is merely competent, may be marginal looked at from within, but can be magical seen from the outside. You are paying others to deliver PR programme services, but the programme itself is in your name. It is you that stakeholders will judge, not your suppliers. Make sure that what you get meets your own executional standards.

Money

It is sometimes said that there are only two sorts of resource in business—one is money, the other is everything else. Consequently there are only two sorts of decision that matter—the ones about money, and all the other ones. Control the money in order to control everything else—that is the assumption behind sound budgeting practice.

The budgeting aspects of money are fully covered in Chapter 8. Here are some more general points.

Timing is very important. No matter how low inflation may be, cash today is always worth more to you than the same amount of cash at some future date. Within the parameters of normal business practice, there is a lot to be said for getting money in as early as you can and paying it out as late as you can. Some organizations, private and public, push this well beyond acceptable limits. That is bad business practice. It is also bad public relations.

Whenever it is legitimate to do so, it makes good sense to use somebody else's money in preference to your own. In-house PR departments can often bill other departments for their services, though sometimes they have to compete with outside suppliers.

For consultancies, the usual procedure is fees in advance, expenses in arrears. When they pass on to their clients the costs of bought-in services, they add a percentage (commonly 17.65 per cent), not so much as a handling charge but more as compensation or cover for the risks they take with their own money on behalf of clients. There is, of course, nothing to stop a client arranging to be invoiced direct from the suppliers.

Discussions and arguments about money are very widespread. They can be disruptive and the cause of many wrong decisions. The trick is to avoid them by turning them into discussions and arguments about objectives and issues. That is what happens—or should happen—in crisis PR.

When some bottles of Perrier water were found to be contaminated with small amounts of benzene, the issue was public apprehension and the objective was informed reassurance. That was what led to the decision to withdraw 10 million cases from the market while tests were carried out and remedial action taken. Undoubtedly the financial cost of doing that was carefully calculated, as well as the financial risk in not doing it. But the driving force was the issue, not the money.[14]

Allocation of the money resource should always be decided on issues and objectives.

Information

Everything in public relations is to do with stakeholders. The information resource is no exception, whether it is information *about* stakeholders—data input—or information *for* stakeholders—data output.

News gathering, company profiles, market research, timesheets, are all examples of data input of concern to PR organizations, whether in-house or consultancy. Some of these, like timesheets, are specific to the organization. Others are more generally available. All need to be managed.

Data output can include programme proposals, analysis of media coverage, presentational graphics, budget control statements and so on. Again, all need managing.

Hardware used in the handling of information is basically of two kinds: computers and telecommunications. Word processors, laptop and desktop PCs, and personal organizers are common examples in the computer stream; portable telephones, faxes, and modems in the telecommunications. Like data, hardware needs to be managed.

So does the software—the programs and processes that enable information to be stored, analysed, retrieved and presented.

There are really only two ways of managing all this. One, the most common, is to allocate particular information tools to particular information functions or services. Personalized letters to customers? Word processing and laser printing. Immediate approval of page proofs? Fax. Fast distribution of documents? Electronic mail. As new data, or software, or hardware, become available, update to the best of your ability and as far as time and budgets allow. Most people in PR are familiar, to a greater or lesser extent, with this approach. They know it works. It is probably the only practical way to manage the information resource in small-scale PR operations.

The other way, which may require a greater investment in hardware and software and a greater time investment in terms of planning and training, affects not only how information is managed. The nature of the information itself can change. This approach calls for a fully integrated, on-line system, involving computers and telecommunications, and networked throughout the organization. Probably the best known champion of integrated information systems in PR is Dermot McKeone of public relations consultancy Infopress (see Figure 7.6).

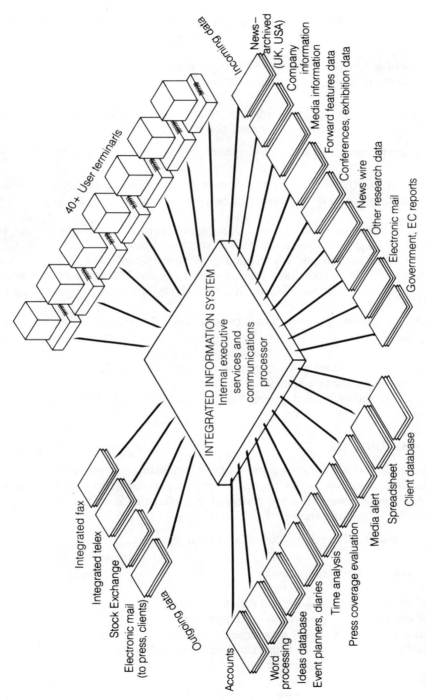

Figure 7.6 Integrated information system[15]

The chief advantages of the integrated approach to information technology are:

- Ease of access by everybody to all the on-line services.
- Combinations of and interaction between the various services.

The main disadvantage is the time you need to spend developing this integrated solution. And for small organizations, this will cost more.

Whichever approach is right for you, here are some golden guidelines.

1. Decide exactly what information inputs you need, and in exactly what form, to enable you to do a proper professional job. Make sure that is what you get.
2. Similarly, decide exactly what information outputs are required, and in exactly what form. Make sure that is what you deliver.
3. Use whatever information technology is most cost-effective in helping you attain those twin objectives, remembering that good PR has a strong strategic and planning element. Think ahead to what you will need in a few years' time.
4. At the earliest possible stage, consult and keep on consulting the three groups of people who need to be involved in information management. According to the Henley Management Centre, these are 'The senior managers concerned with the strategy of the enterprise, the IT professionals who know about the technology, and the middle- and junior-level staff who are (or may become) the major users of information systems'.[16]

Consultancies

Chapter 11 looks at the client/consultancy relationship in depth and in detail. It would be pointless to say anything here to pre-empt that. What is worth underlining is that a main function of consultancies is to act as an expert resource for and on behalf of their clients.

Here are some of the things consultancies can provide:

- Advice   —strategic
                          —tactical
- Experience   —beyond the client's own
- Expertise   —in getting things done
- Implementation   —of programmes
- Influence   —on the client's attitude to PR
                          —on the whole company culture
- Information   —fact finding
                          —baseline research
- Management   —of bought-in services

- Planning   —of specific PR programmes
- Skills   —analytical
                    —diagnostic
                    —professional
                    —specialist
- Solutions   —to problems, familiar and new
- Training/education—of client's PR and other staff

What you should not use consultants for is to manage your business. They have quite enough to do managing their own. *The Financial Times* drew attention to the danger. 'While getting closer to their clients, most consultancies . . . have avoided becoming permanent members of the corporate staff and (effectively) co-managers of their clients' businesses. Nor would most clients wish them to get that close in any case, on the grounds that a consultant is still at his most effective as an external adviser and that it is for the manager to do the actual managing.'[17]

Bear in mind that as well as providing their clients with resources, consultancies may also draw on some of their clients' own resources, for example, staff time. The traffic is by no means always one-way.

Importance versus priority

It should be clear that in any consideration of people, know-how, time, services, money, information and consultancies, the major challenge to management competence is how to ensure the best allocation of these resources. Whether you are in the PR department of a huge multinational company, or the owner-director of a tiny PR consultancy, you have only two valid reasons for committing resources—importance and urgency. It is vital to distinguish between them.

When something is both important and urgent there is not much scope for argument or even discussion about the allocation of resources. You throw in everything you need to get the job done in the required time. An obvious example is the management of PR during a crisis or a major threat to the organization—perhaps a hostile takeover bid; branded retail foods that are contaminated, accidentally or deliberately; a plane or train disaster.

In November 1989, the unfortunately named Hidden Report on the Clapham Junction rail disaster was published. It had much to say about what constitutes good and bad management. The press highlighted 'a crucial area of management responsibility' and commented that 'neither BR nor the Department of the Environment felt it appropriate to provide the necessary expertise to rank, in order of priority, special projects designed to improve safety'.[18]

Here was a case when top priority and top importance should have been one and the same thing. It is not always so. Priority is about relative urgency, ranking about relative importance. That which has top priority gets done first. That is the whole point and is what the word itself means.

Decisions about priority can be helped by the use of techniques such as critical path analysis, network analysis, timebars or linear scheduling. The aim is to highlight the latest times—deadlines—by which specific activities must be carried out. These techniques are explained in most standard management manuals.

Deadlines are about priorities rather than importance. Some urgent things may never get done because the deadline has been passed, whereas, by definition, important things should always get done, even though those with top import- ance ranking may not have top priority. The question is, how do you decide on relative importance when faced with the difficult task of allocating resources?

In Chapter 5 we looked at some techniques of decision making. One of these used the principle of comparing every option with every other option, tabulating the results to arrive at a ranking order. The same sort of approach can be used to work out a percentage basis for allocating resources. This time, let us handle the data in matrix form.

The decisional matrix

Youth training has a poor image in inner cities, especially among young people from ethnic minority backgrounds. Five specific ways of countering this poor image were identified.

A. The use of youth training development officers.
B. Contacts with community leaders.
C. Specific approaches to schools.
D. The deployment of dedicated youth employment officers.
E. Direct approaches to parents of ethnic minority youngsters.[19]

The question is—based on order of importance—what proportion of the strictly limited resources available should go to which counter-activities?

First draw a matrix listing the options, so that you can compare and assess each against all the others. Why not call it a decisional matrix (see Figure 7.7)?

For the purpose of this exercise, assume that, after a full discussion of the pros and cons, you mark A equal with B and C and E, but less important than D. Your first column would look like Figure 7.8.

Next, compare option B with all the others. Let us assume you conclude that B is less important than C or D or E. Your second column would look like Figure 7.9.

Continue in the same way until you have made a decision on each and every possible pairing (see Figure 7.10).

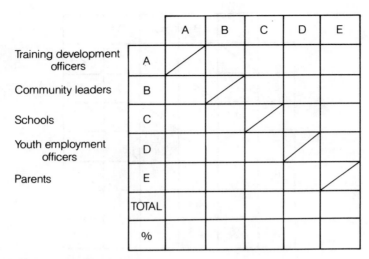

Figure 7.7 Decisional matrix—listing the options

	A	B	C	D	E
A		2	2	3	2
B	2				
C	2				
D	1				
E	2				
TOTAL	7				
%	17.5				

Figure 7.8 Decisional matrix—first column

On the basis of Figure 7.10, you might consider allocating 25 per cent of the available resources to dedicated youth employment officers and 25 per cent to approaches to parents of ethnic minority youngsters. Twenty per cent would go on tackling the schools, 17.5 per cent on youth training development officers and 12.5 per cent on contacting community leaders.

Of course, there may well be other factors to take into account, like critical mass—the level of commitment below which a particular resource could not be effective. So your percentages might not be a self-sufficient guide. But at the

	A	B	C	D	E
A		2	2	3	2
B	2		3	3	3
C	2	1			
D	1	1			
E	2	1			
TOTAL	7	5			
%	17.5	12.5			

Figure 7.9 Decisional matrix—second column

	A	B	C	D	E
A		2	2	3	2
B	2		3	3	3
C	2	1		3	2
D	1	1	1		3
E	2	1	2	1	
TOTAL	7	5	8	10	10
%	17.5	12.5	20	25	25

Figure 7.10 Decisional matrix—all columns

very least they will be a strong indication and a powerful help in coming to the right decisions on the allocation of resources.

Nevertheless, the numbers cannot make the decisions. Only you, as manager, can do that.

Sources and references

1. William F. Coventry. *Management made Simple*. W. H. Allen, London, 1975.
2. Joan Plachta. Does sweet talk pay? *Management Today*, March 1990.

3. *BIM Guide to Good Management Practice*. British Institute of Management, 1990.
4. *Professionalism in Practice*. Institute of Public Relations, London, 1990.
5. *The Survey of United Kingdom Public Relations Professionals*. Burson-Marsteller, London, 1990.
6. ibid.
7. *PRET Public Relations Education and Training Matrix*. IPR and PRCA, 1990.
8. ibid.
9. ibid.
10. ibid.
11. Sarah Barclay. The drain of overheads in industry. *The Independent*, 20 July 1988.
12. *PRET Public Relations Education and Training Matrix*. IPR and PRCA, 1990.
13. ibid.
14. John Tylee. Putting the sparkle back into Perrier. *PR Week*, February 1990.
15. Reproduced by permission of Infopress.
16. A. V. Knight and D. J. Silk. *Managing Information*. The Henley Management Series. McGraw-Hill, London, 1990.
17. Christopher Lorenz. Using consultants as managers. *The Financial Times*, 13 January 1987.
18. John Torode. Decent but dozy management team. *The Independent*, 8 November 1989.
19. Geoff Thomas. Marketing youth training to young people in inner cities. *Youth Training News*, Training Agency, February/March 1990.

CHAPTER 8

Budgeting

It's unwise to pay too much, but it's worse to pay too little. When you pay too much, you lose a little money, that is all. When you pay too little, you sometimes lose everything, because the thing you bought was incapable of doing the thing it was bought to do.

The common law of business balance prohibits paying a little and getting a lot—it can't be done. If you deal with the lowest bidder, it is well to add something for the risk you run. And if you do that, you will have enough to pay for something better.

John Ruskin

There is no doubt about the importance of sticking to your budget. Outside consultants keep contracts on the strength of it. In-house executives are dominated by it.

Not so Nicholas Dreystadt, when he was the boss of Cadillac. He is on record as saying that any fool can learn to stay within a budget, whereas he had only seen a handful of people in his lifetime who could draw up a budget worth staying within.[1] The question is how to arrive at that sort of budget for PR.

The problem may not even be admitted. Some organizations claim quite sincerely that they do no PR. They are mistaken, because they have no option. They can choose what they are going to do about PR and they can carry out those intentions more or less effectively. What they cannot choose is to have no publics and no relationship with them. If they take that line, then it can only mean that their PR is unplanned, unstructured, unbudgeted and unsuccessful: in a word, unaffordable.

Better, though not a great deal better, is the boss who says 'My secretary does the PR so it doesn't cost anything'. At least somebody is responsible and many secretaries do a surprisingly good job even though they have no training in PR and not much recognition for their efforts. Some of the lucky ones are able to turn their on-the-job training to advantage and switch to becoming PR executives and managers themselves.

Perhaps the next stage of enlightenment for businessmen is the grudging recognition that PR does cost money. Not real money, of course. Not even adequate money. To caricature them, though not by much, it is a case of 'If you really need to spend anything on PR, see what's in the petty cash'. That at least allows some expenditure and provides a heading for it in the accounts.

However, penny pinching PR only gets 'tuppeny-ha'penny' results.

What do more responsible organizations do? Major companies and government departments send out an annual written instruction to prepare and cost a PR budget. This is usually accompanied by an unwritten instruction—'don't ask how, just get on with it'. Luckily, there is no shortage of principles on which to base the budgeting process. All have their uses and there is no best way.

Budgeting is essentially a collective process. The chief value to an organization is probably in the process itself rather than any particular set of figures. Minds should focus on the arguments for and against specific objectives and strategies, and the options for achieving them.

Some approaches to budgeting are decreed or imposed from the top down. There is nothing wrong with that, as long as everybody concerned understands and agrees what is to be done and how it is to be carried out and controlled.

Other systems are generated from the bottom up. They are usually very practical, but can sometimes lose sight of the overall strategy and see only the tactical issues.

The best budgets are a mixture of top down and bottom up, with plenty of interaction and feedback among those involved, subject to the overall control of the head of public relations.

Although none of the BIM guidelines is specifically labelled 'budgeting', several of them are strongly relevant.

- Make proper use of the resources available.
- Ensure that equipment and materials are maintained and used efficiently.
- Ensure that the requirements of suppliers are properly met and that the terms of each transaction are stated clearly.
- Ensure that suppliers are informed of any action which may materially affect those terms and take all reasonable steps to minimize risk to all concerned.
- Establish and develop a continuing and satisfactory relationship with suppliers, leading to mutual confidence.
- Accept or deliver products or services within the quality, quantity, time, price and payment procedures agreed.[2]

There are not many distinctly different ways of setting out to construct a budget but all merit serious consideration. Task-based budgeting answers the question 'what will it cost to do what has to be done?' Update budgeting asks 'what shall we add to this year's budget for next year?' Percentage-based budgeting relates the PR spend to some larger figure—turnover, sales revenue, advertising, etc. Competition budgeting is shaped by the budgets of competitors. Hit-and-miss budgeting is not uncommon.

Task-based budgeting

As the name suggests, all the individual PR tasks to be carried out are identified and costed. The figures are then totalled and the sum is the budget. HM Treasury is traditionally fond of this method and it is easy to see the attractions, particularly when the budget is zero based, and not geared to what was spent in the previous year's budgets.

The most important element in a task-based budget is the time spent on the tasks, particularly thinking time. It is vital to budget for the best quality of thinking time that can be got. There are advantages and disadvantages to be weighed up when deciding on in-house time versus outside consultancy time. What is inescapable is that the amount of time budgeted for will always be underestimated.

As well as thinking time, there is operational time to be budgeted for. Bought-in time is bound to seem more expensive than the in-house variety if calculated by hourly or daily rate. But, of course, you should only pay for the outside time that is actually expended on specified tasks, whereas the in-house capability has to be funded whether it is being used fully or not. In-house time may or may not be budgeted for very precisely. Often, annual salary costs are just put in as lump sums, and for a small company this may be perfectly adequate.

Calculating true overheads on each and every occasion can be very complicated and time consuming. It is probably better to devise standard loadings and apply them consistently to costings—but see Chapter 7 for some problems associated with corporate overheads. You will want to be sure that you are not paying excessive overheads on a consultancy contract.

The next main group of tasks to be costed is to do with services and materials. Exhibitions, press conferences, booklets, videos—the variety is great and all cost money.

Is it better to go for single suppliers? That could make you a sizeable customer which ought to give you more clout on prices and priorities. There are other, less tangible, benefits to be had from the close and sustained relationship that develops between customer or client and sole provider.

On the other hand, if you keep a number of acceptable suppliers on your books, you are not dependent on any one of them, while the effect of competition should be to reduce prices and increase quality and service. What you would probably not want to be is a sole customer. That may give you a great sense of power but it is hard to justify ethically.

In spite of the pressure you may find yourself subjected to from those with a vested interest, tendering is an integral part of task-based budgeting, certainly for the major jobs. As in the architectural business, so in PR. 'There is . . . no possibility . . . that competitive tendering will be entirely superseded . . . Indeed, the persistence of competitive tendering on a substantial scale is, paradoxically, almost essential to the general acceptability of the negotiated contract procedure, because it provides a yardstick for those market factors . . . that cannot be predicted by cost analysis.'[3]

Provided every contractor is quoting from exactly the same specification, there is no reason why you should not take the lowest tender, to get the best value for money. You have to be reasonably sure that all the contractors can actually do the job properly—but that is why you chose them in the first place.

Of course, you are not bound to accept the lowest tender. Your obligation is to secure the best tender, which means 'the most reasonable price from the most suitable contractor who is likely to provide the most satisfactory results in the time available'.[4]

When time is short—it always is—telephoned quotes will do; even single tenders. If you have to do this, it is important to get confirmation on paper as soon as it is practicable.

Always earmark some of the PR budget for finding out what your relations with the public really are. Research into attitude, awareness, knowledge and behaviour can help to set a precise baseline. Evaluation studies should help to assess how successful the PR programme was. To measure is to know (see Chapter 10).

Whenever the PR budgetary system allows it, items should be charged out or recharged to some other budget, so that the cost of PR is identified with the divisions or departments on whose behalf it is done. PR consultancies adopt the same principle with their clients. The costs of implementing a programme are additional to their fees, and where other suppliers are included, the consultancy passes those costs on to the clients plus a more or less standard mark up.

One other budget item, not usually very big, could turn out to be the most significant of them all—especially if it isn't there. This is the contingency figure, to cover anything important that might emerge after the budget has been finalized and agreed. It could be an unforeseen opportunity that will never arise again. It could be a slowly developing problem that surfaces part way through the programme. Worst of all, there might be the sudden crisis everybody tries to anticipate and actually dreads.

When all these elements have been put together, costed and grossed up, there is a great feeling of confidence in the budget, even when the figures are approximate.

Table 8.1 itemizes the 1988/89 PR budget for a £25 million recruitment consultancy/employment agency with offices in several provincial cities.

Table 8.1   Budget of small in-house department

	£
1 In-house salaries	
PR Manager	18 500
PA/Secretary	5 500
2 Share of overheads	14 000
3 Outside consultancy (500 hours)	23 000
4 Bought-in services	
Press agency/monitors	10 000
Print	20 000
Exhibitions and displays	18 000
5 Client presentations	10 000
6 Special projects	27 500
7 Contingency	7 500
Total	£154 000

Case History 14
Adult training

In the early 1980s the British Government perceived the need for industry to increase the quantity and quality of adult training throughout all the sectors. Comparisons with the United States, Japan and West Germany had shown convincingly that the countries and companies which were committed to training were also those which out-performed their competitors. How could the United Kingdom do the same?

The Manpower Services Commission was made responsible for orchestrating a campaign of persuasion and cooperation intended to reshape attitudes towards training by creating awareness of the benefits to be secured. The Commission engaged Marketing Solutions as campaign consultants.

One of the key elements in a comprehensive PR package was a recommendation to stage a National Conference to focus attention on the benefits of training and to launch a programme of local activities for which others would be responsible. The Conference would also be a news event in itself, act as an accelerator to the pace of the campaign and perhaps create 'training disciples' among the decision takers in industry. The Conference budget was task based and had the potential to be self-financing (see Table 8.2).

Update budgeting

A very common method of budgeting, much used by some of the more organized organizations, relies on a well-known formula that has three great merits. It is easy to understand, operate and defend. The formula is *to arrive at next year's PR budget, add a percentage to this year's PR budget*. Between about

Table 8.2 National Training Conference budget[5]

	Approx. cost (£)
Venue—1 day	
Hall hire for 500 delegates	20 000
Exhibition hire	negotiable
Exhibition stands, etc.	3 000
Staging	
TV equipment and projection of debate and graphic logo	
Personnel	
Sound/video recording	
Vision mixers	
Screen and lighting	
Stage—2 ft raised plinth	
Lectern	
Desk for panel of six	
Steps to floor level	
Lighting	10 000–20 000
Literature	
Invitations, 50 000 light card, using ATS logo	3 000
Looseleaf insertion in magazines (25 000)	1 000
Folders, conference material	
designed and printed cover,	
word processed inside, quality paper (600)	3 500
Design (for exhibition; literature)	3 000
Expenses—1 day	
Staff (10) accommodation	2 000
Speakers (15) accommodation, meals, travel	4 500
TOTAL	50 000–60 000
Daily rate required to cover all costs	
(excluding speakers' fees, invitation, post and packing)	100–200
Potential sponsor support	
Mailing invitations—postage and packing, looseleaf insertions,	
speakers, exhibition space	

June and October every year, up and down the land, hundreds—perhaps thousands—of people are engaged in this process.

The arithmetic can be tedious. What percentage increase do you allow for inflation? Is it the same percentage for all parts of the budget, or do you accept the implications of differential inflation? Have printing costs, say, risen proportionately more than video production costs? How have the actual tasks changed? Do you go with an unchanged media mix? Are wages out of step with prices? If so, whose wages and which prices? How have commissions and fees altered?

Strange how often all these different calculations, for different organizations,

Table 8.3   Update budgeting

			This year (£)	Next year (£)
1	In-house salaries			
	PR Manager		18 500	19 000*
	PA/Secretary		5 500	6 500*
2	Share of overheads		14 000	25 000†
3	Outside consultancy (500 hours)		23 000	26 500*
4	Bought-in services			
	Press agency/monitors		10 000	12 000*
	Print		20 000	22 000*
	Exhibitions and displays		18 000	20 000*
5	Client presentations		10 000	15 000‡
6	Special projects		27 500	22 000§
7	Contingency		7 500	8 000
		TOTAL	£154 000	£176 000

* increased costs   ‡ increased activity
† new accounting system   § reduced programme

seem to come up with somewhere near the same answer, that is around 15 per cent. Table 8.3 shows how it worked out for the firm quoted in Table 8.1. The disadvantage of this approach to budgeting is that minds are directed towards the past rather than the future. But sometimes you have to do it that way.

Percentage budgeting

It is a prerequisite of the update approach that there has to be a this year's budget before any percentage can be added to make next year's.

For those who are tackling PR budgeting for the first time, and for those who are making a radical shift in direction or scale, a different approach is needed. Percentage, however, can still be the operative word.

What about costing PR budgets as a percentage of turnover? Is there a norm or mean for that, and, if so, what is it?

A survey published in May 1988 revealed what happens in practice. It was based on the responses of 600 marketing directors and managers to a detailed questionnaire. The breakdown of types of organization within this survey was as follows:

- Durables: 24 per cent
- Fast moving consumer goods (fmcg): 22 per cent
- Business-to-business: 19 per cent
- Retail/distribution: 16 per cent
- Leisure industries: 7 per cent
- Financial sector: 5 per cent
- Industrial sector: 5 per cent

Table 8.4 Industry: PR expenditure as a percentage of turnover

26% spent up to 0.1% of turnover
12% spent between 0.1% and 0.2%
 8% spent between 0.2% and 0.3%
10% spent between 0.3% and 0.5%
10% spent between 0.5% and 0.75%
 1% spent between 0.75% and 1%
 8% spent under 1% (unspecified)
 5% spent between 1% and 2%
 3% spent between 2% and 3%
 4% spent at 3% or more

Table 8.5 Industry: PR expenditure as a percentage of advertising budget

14% spent up to 2.5%
16% spent between 2.5% and 5%
 6% spent between 5% and 7.5%
14% spent between 7.5% and 10%
 6% spent between 10% and 15%
 6% spent between 15% and 20%
11% spent between 20% and 30%
 9% spent between 30% and 50%
 4% spent at 50% or more

For this mix of industries there is indeed a mean for PR expenditure as a percentage of turnover. It is 0.6 per cent. The detailed results are given in Table 8.4.[6]

Just over half of those polled used PR consultancies but 12 per cent neither used a consultancy nor had an in-house PR capability of their own. What most of them had in common was that they spent money on advertising. Table 8.5 shows their expenditure on PR as a percentage of their advertising expenditure.[7]

Other percentage approaches to budgeting include expressing PR expenditure in relation to sales revenue, or marketing costs or company profits. However, update budgeting remains the favourite.

Two other attitudes to budgeting must be considered. One is very hit-and-miss but for anyone who really knows his or her organization, whether client or consultancy, it can work well.

Comparison budgeting

But before we look at that one, there is what might be called comparison budgeting. You compare the PR needs of others with your own, and compare what they spend with what you ought to. The problem is to find out what their budgets are.

Surprisingly, doing the obvious and asking them can sometimes produce results, though you need to be careful that you are not being misled. The most likely way to get a sensible answer is to offer the same sort of information yourself. Openness can be contagious.

Failing that—or, rather, in addition to it—there is your own information intake. The press, especially the trade press like *PR Week* and *Campaign*, quite often give clues and sometimes specific figures, as in these cases.

- Dewe Rogerson's £200 000 account with Italian dairy group Parmalat represented 0.15 per cent of the £135 million of new money to be raised by a pan-European rights issue.
- When insurance brokers Willis Faber merged with Corroon and Black, the deal was worth £1000 million. Hill Murray's PR account was worth 0.1 per cent of that, at £100 000.
- The PR account won by Hill and Knowlton with steel castings giant Willian Cook worked out at 0.53 per cent of pre-tax profits of £9.5 million.[8]

The media pages of some national newspapers like *The Observer, The Independent* and *The Financial Times* can also be useful sources for these kinds of data. Less frequent, but still not negligible, are references in management magazines like *Management Today* and *The Director*. Diligent scanning of subject journals from *The Grocer* to *Accountancy Today* can be hard going, until the odd nugget is found. Then it all seems worth while, as one small company found out, based on the premise that you would not want to be spending substantially more on PR than your most successful competitors, but you dare not spend significantly less.

Case History 15
Budgeting against the competition

The sales manager of a company selling office equipment, mainly to small companies in the service sector, noticed a brief report in a trade magazine. It said that its chief competitor had engaged a public relations consultant 'to advise on their image'. A fee of £30 000 was quoted. There was no information about what further money was available for financing PR activities.

At the next directors' meeting, the company decided it would counter this PR offensive by its rivals. It was prepared to spend up to the same amount on buying advice, although it hoped it could get away with less.

Someone remembered hearing an interview on the local radio station by a consultant about business-to-business PR. The producer put the company in touch with the consultancy. Managing director met chief executive and the two businessmen got on well together.

This is the PR approach they agreed:

- Analyse the competition.
- Examine pricing policies.
- Review purchasing systems, incentives, discounts.
- Review delivery, servicing and maintenance arrangements.
- Review sales literature and trade advertising.
- Identify target audiences.
- Identify product propositions and benefits.
- Devise and cost a PR plan covering a full financial year designed to present the client in a coherent and consistent manner so as to enhance reputation and image.

The work was to be completed over a period of six months for a total fee of £20 000, including normal operating costs, up to the point of agreeing the PR programme, the costs of which would, of course, be additional to the advisory fee.

The Saki method

Finally, there is a method which is not in the least mathematical. Nor does it rely on heavy reading. It is more a matter of flair or chutzpah. However, it can be very successful and sometimes actually secures an adequate PR budget. When that happens, who is to say it is not good management practice?

The method, which owes a lot to H. H. Munro, is to *put in for the most you can possibly get away with, plus a little bit more.*

Whitehall and the stage

Government departments do not normally call their public relations officers by that name. Nor do they admit to hiring PR consultancies (see Chapter 7). Indeed, official policy forbids it though there are signs that this unnecessary self-denial may soon be over, with the Foreign & Commonwealth Office (FCO) taking the initiative. In fact, Whitehall is expert in the practice of public relations and spends large sums on it, mostly salaries and overheads but also external contracts.

Departments get their outside help from the PR capability provided via advertising agents, marketing advisers and management or communications consultants. If the FCO lead is followed, PR consultancies will gain official acknowledgement.

The public wants to know what really happens. Questions asked in Parliament

Table 8.6   Government departments: PR expenditure increases[9]

Department	PR increase (%) 1987/88–1988/89
Prime Minister's Office/Cabinet Office	53.5
Department of Employment	25.9
Department of Trade and Industry	23.4
Department of Transport	16.3
Department of Energy	12.0

Table 8.7   Government departments: PR expenditure as percentage of combined press/PR and advertising budget[10]

Department	PR (%) 1988/89
Prime Minister's Office/Cabinet Office	100
Ministry of Defence	100
Treasury	92.3
Northern Ireland	50.7
Agriculture	42.7
Lord Chancellor	36.8
Energy	11.9
Trade and Industry	11.7
Employment	7.6
Transport	7.3

about spending on press advertising and other campaigns have produced some interesting responses. There is patchiness in the data winkled out by Parliament—not all departments answered the questions fully, there was considerable variation in the criteria applied by the civil servants and in any case no comprehensive figures are kept centrally.

Nevertheless, it is clear that several departments had increased their PR budgets for 1988/89 compared with 1987/88, although the Ministry of Agriculture, Fisheries and Food had actually cut back its PR allocation by 14 per cent. Still, its total promotional spend was up by 3.7 per cent.

Of five departments quoted, the biggest increase was notched up by No. 10 Downing Street (Table 8.6).

A different approach is to compare PR spending with the total outlay on press, PR and advertising. Here again, No. 10 is at the top of the list, sharing equal billing with the Ministry of Defence, whose figures do not, of course, include recruitment advertising (Table 8.7).

Percentages are one thing, actual cash is another. At least half a dozen departments admitted earmarking sums in the region of £0.5 million to £1.5 million. The Prime Minister's Office budgeted £525 000, the Employment Department

£1.46 million. Two departments owned up to staggering expenditure. Perhaps understandably, the Ministry of Defence assigned £7.316 million, all on PR, while the Northern Ireland Office was more even-handed, at £3.713 million on PR and £3.614 million on advertising.[11]

What of the quangos? The Metrication Board's main functions were to advise, consult, coordinate and inform. The Board had no legislative powers and was not allowed to advocate going metric, only to facilitate it. Over the whole period of its life, 1969–80, more than 50 per cent of the total budget went on PR, not including the salaries and overheads of the PR Division, which probably accounted for about another 25 per cent (Figure 8.1).

As in Whitehall, so in the world of the theatre; PR has always been recognized as important. For example, the use of so-called previews to promote shows rather than criticize them is almost as old as newspapers themselves.

In Henry Irving's 20 years at the Lyceum (1879–99), total receipts came to over £1 million. Costs exceeded £880 000, and more than 11 per cent of that went into PR, including a hefty £12 000 on 'sundries', such as late night suppers where influential theatregoing opinion-formers could meet the cast.

By the 1930s, things had changed. Newton's Shilling Theatre, in Fulham, spent £30 a week on PR, and that was 12 per cent of costs. Not a lot different, per centage wise, from the Lyceum. But that same £30 a week represented only 6.25 per cent of receipts, which suggests that Mr Newton knew a thing or two about making profits in the theatre.

Only 50 years later, a typical West End musical could cost around £500 000 to set up (equivalent to ten years' box office receipts in the nineteenth century) and £50 000 a week to run. Expenditure on PR would perhaps be 13 per cent of setting up costs and 4 per cent of running costs. By contrast, a typical (non-musical) play would need maybe £95 000 to set up and £15 000 a week to run. These sums are very much smaller than for a musical: PR budgets likewise. The difference is in the ratios: 21 per cent of setting up costs and 7.5 per cent of running costs.[12]

Budget control

Every budget ought to be a target, that is the amount of money you intend to spend to achieve your objectives. That is much more positive than a budget forecast, which is the amount you expect to spend. Budget out-turn is, of course, what you actually spend. How do you control the budget so that target and out-turn are the same? Budgetary control is a continuous process. It is at its most effective when it takes place before any money is spent.

The essential point to be got across is that keeping to a budget is not an end in itself. The end is to achieve the required results from the PR programme, within the constraints that apply. The budget is one of those constraints. It is

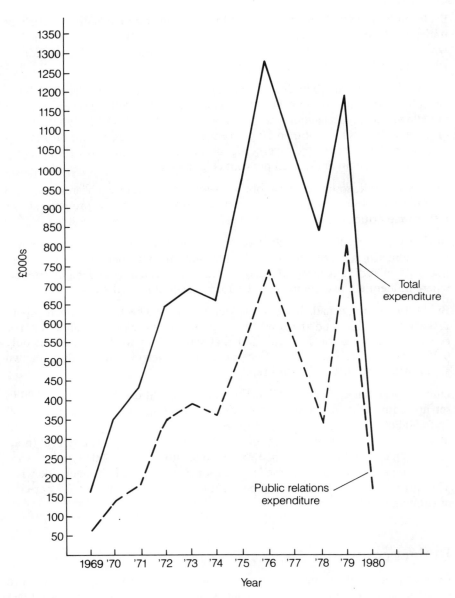

Figure 8.1 PR expenditure (excluding salaries) compared with total expenditure of Metrication Board[13]

also an aid—a tool for getting results. Expenditure has to be 'on strategy', as well as on target.

Budget tracking is something that takes place after the money has been spent. It has tactical value and is essential for accountancy purposes but it is in no real sense budget control. You cannot drive a car by following its tyre tracks.

Tracking involves comparing actual performance—budget out-turns—against intended performance—budget targets. The difference is known as 'variance' and needs to be measured more or less continuously. At certain fixed review points a 'snapshot of variance' is taken and the causes established, so that any necessary remedial action may be put in hand.

Everybody who has anything to do with budgeting knows how much time and anguish is customarily spent on making sure that expenditure does not exceed the budget. Being over budget is seen as the sin of sins, to be avoided at all costs.

But what about being under budget? That is no less significant. Under budget or over budget: both are signals. Though by no means invariably danger signals, they do call for a response. It cannot be emphasized too strongly that the response must be to do with the programme, not the budget.

Budgeting and budgetary control are not separate from the real business of PR. They are an integral part of it. Good control gives an organization better PR for its money. This is equally true of clients and of consultancies.

Budgetary control can be a spur to creative thinking. As David Wethey pointed out, 'Everyone acknowledges that a great creative idea will perform much better than an average one on the same budget . . . we have become obsessed by relative buying performance within a given range of options . . . If the discriminating shopper is totally taken up with checking out the price of apples and oranges, it is unlikely that passion fruit will find its way into the fruit bowl . . .'[14]

This book is full of examples of how budget constraints were overcome by creative thinking. But a word of warning—by all means go for passion fruit budgeting, as long as you make sure you look after the apples and oranges as well, not to mention the bread and butter.

You need to know how much time typical PR tasks actually take you and your people to plan and carry out. If you do not know, you have to find out by doing some pretty realistic measuring. It is hardly possible to give guidelines, because there are so many variables. Your typical times are specific to you alone.

Similarly, you need to be aware of what typical PR services actually cost when bought in from outside.

Sponsorship costs can range from £50 for a local activity like a Scouts' and Guides' 'At Home' to £0.25 million for a national exhibition like the Leonardo da Vinci. That is by no means the top limit.

Most sponsorships probably lie between £1000 and £2500 and there is plenty of scope at the lower end: £1000 would sponsor a Saturday morning children's creative workshop in a London fringe theatre, or a whole drama production at a provincial playhouse. At £6000–£7000 a sponsor could underwrite a major London concert.

Somewhere around that price would provide new training packs for childcare professionals.

Logica got the Photo Show for £100 000, while Barclays Bank's sponsorship of fringe dance, music and theatre companies provides £500 000 over three years.

Exhibitions At the top end—over the top, some would say—Tetrapak spent £3 million on their participation in PAKEX, the dominant exhibition about packaging. A financial exhibition during a four-day cruise on the *Canberra* cost some participants £150 000. A simple stand at a local show could cost £120 per square metre site hire.

Audio and visual Some firms pay £60 000 or more for a ten-minute promotional video, whereas you could get about the same running time for around £10 000 using a mixture of tape-slide and live action. £18 000 would buy you a three-projector audio-visual show, including hire of the equipment.

Direct mail In the educational sector, research suggests that 'if a solus mailing brings 200 purchases, a shared mailing to the same addresses would be expected to bring about 180 purchases, for about 25% of the cost . . . Medium priced items offered for sale normally gain over 2% response. Items offered free gain response rates of over 60%. School response rates are enhanced by selecting the larger schools.'[15] In other sectors the figures may be quite different. Never assume. Always check at source.

Another way of looking at costings is to know how far a certain sum would go towards paying for different types of job. In 1990, for instance, £1000 could buy any of the following:

- 20 hours of a small provincial consultancy's time
- sponsorship of a Saturday morning children's workshop at a London fringe theatre
- 10 square metres of space in a local exhibition
- 2 days' live video shooting—one location
- 1 minute of finished video production
- 3 days' still photography—indoor/outdoor
- 1½ days' studio photography in London
- 2000 good quality 8pp. one-third A4 stitched leaflets
- 1000 pictorial calendars, wire bound
- 100 hours of stretched limo hire (7 seat Merc/Jag)—mileage extra
- 3 days of 28-seater coach hire—mileage extra
- 20 000 high quality A4 letterheads
- 4545 first class stamps
- 4000 specialized direct mail addresses

- 2 places on a top London seminar
- 1 day's in-company training for five or more.

Of course, you could pay a lot more, or less, by shopping around. Making your own lists and keeping them updated will help you to control your PR budget.

Checklist

No matter what your organization's approach to budgeting may be, there are certain fundamental questions that need to be answered. They are presented here in the form of a checklist.

Is the PR budget top down or bottom up?   YES/NO

Task-based budgeting—have you allowed for the following?
In-house salaries	YES/NO
In-house overheads	YES/NO
Consultancy fees	YES/NO
Planning time	YES/NO
Implementation time	YES/NO
Programme costs	YES/NO
services (itemized)	
materials (itemized)	
Research and evaluation	YES/NO
Contingencies	YES/NO
VAT	YES/NO

Update budgeting—what percentage do you apply to each of the above? ☐

PR budget as percentage of turnover:

up to 0.2%	☐	1%–2%	☐
0.2%–0.3%	☐	2%–3%	☐
0.3%–0.5%	☐	More than 3%	☐
0.5%–0.75%	☐		
0.75%–1%	☐		

PR budget as percentage of advertising budget:

up to 5%	☐	30%–40%	☐
5%–10%	☐	40%–50%	☐
10%–15%	☐	50%–60%	☐
15%–20%	☐	60%–75%	☐
20%–30%	☐	over 75%	☐

Comparison with competitors—do you/should you spend
the same?	YES/NO
more?	YES/NO
less?	YES/NO

Budget control—do you know
    who has responsibility?   YES/NO
    who has authority?   YES/NO
    what systems are used?   YES/NO
    do *they* know?   YES/NO

Do you have a system for identifying all
    rechargeables?   YES/NO

Budget tracking—do you continuously
    check expenditure?   YES/NO
    measure variance?   YES/NO
    feed back information?   YES/NO
    apply corrections?   YES/NO

Day-to-day practice. Do you adhere to the BIM guidelines on the following?
    proper use of resources   YES/NO
    efficient use of processes and materials   YES/NO
    meeting requirements of suppliers   YES/NO
    stating clearly the terms of transactions   YES/NO
    informing suppliers of actions affecting them   YES/NO
    taking all reasonable steps to minimize risk   YES/NO
    developing continuing relationship with suppliers   YES/NO
    accepting/providing products or services to agreed   YES/NO
        standards of quality, quantity, time, price and
        payment procedures.[16]

Golden guidelines

Robert Keen, Vice-Chairman of Charles Baker Traverse-Healy, has what he describes as four commonsense rules for operating cost-control. They are simple enough and good enough to qualify as golden guidelines.

1. Always retain budget authority.
2. Recharge wherever possible.
3. Always build in a contingency reserve.
4. Argue on issue-effects, and quantify.[17]

And if, despite all your best endeavours, you find that you end up with a budget which comes to more than the total amount of money available to you, there are four more checks you can make, four more golden guidelines to follow.

First go over every programme, item by item, and cut out any fat that has been left. You cannot afford even light padding.
Next identify all the items you have no option but to keep in, for example for legal or contractual reasons.

Third protect items that give the biggest advantage to the largest number of the most important stakeholders.

Last look at what remains and agree with your management colleagues what can be abandoned or deferred.

Sources and references

1. Peter Drucker. *The Practice of Management*. Pan, London, 1968.
2. *BIM Guide to Good Management Practice*. British Institute of Management, 1990.
3. Derek Senior. *Your Architect*. Hodder & Stoughton, London, 1964.
4. Dorothy Goslett. *The Professional Practice of Design*. Batsford, London, 1980.
5. Case history authenticated by Marketing Solutions.
6. Trevor Morris and Alison Turner. Some of my best friends work in PR. *Marketing Week*, 28 May 1988.
7. ibid.
8. News items in *PR Week* during June 1990.
9. Deduced from answers to Parliamentary Questions.
10. ibid.
11. ibid.
12. Deduced from N. Marshall. *The other Theatre*, 1947. Joe Gatty. *West End Crisis*, 1982. John Pick. *West End—mismanagement and snobbery*, 1983.
13. *Final Report of the Metrication Board*, 1980.
14. David Wethey. Passion fruit marketing. *Marketing*, 16 April 1987.
15. Tony Attwood, *Hamilton House Mailings*.
16. as source 2.
17. Robert Keen. *Corporate Affairs*. Address to the London Business School, May 1989.

CHAPTER 9

Responsibility, authority and accountability

The old pyramidical or functional forms of organisation composed of groups of specialists in relatively watertight compartments are becoming more fluid models made up of accountable and multi-disciplinary teams. Operation in such environments requires enhanced teamworking skills. Rather than mechanically operating a standard management process it is increasingly recognised that different management processes may be required for different companies, sectors and projects. As a company grows and matures it is likely continually to need to refine its management processes. It may be necessary to devise a new management process, incorporating communication requirements, to apply to a particular situation or context.

Colin Coulson-Thomas[1]

To a very large extent, what a PR department does, what responsibility it bears and what authority it has, can depend on where it is, organizationally and physically.

Now, it may not matter very much into what part of an organization's structure the library fits, as long as it is physically located in a place where personal access to the material is easiest for the majority of users. The opposite is true of the computer department. Physical location may be quite irrelevant, mainly because user access is mostly through electronic means rather than in person. On the other hand, where it is positioned organizationally will determine to a great extent how it is used. It is not unusual for computer departments that come under the control of finance divisions to be dedicated largely, if not solely, to accountancy work, and this can be a severe limitation.

In much the same way, when the head of PR reports to the head of personnel as sometimes happens, the main purpose of PR may be perceived as improving staff or industrial relations—essential, but hardly the whole story.

PR managers who report to directors of advertising are in an interesting position. They are aligned with the big spenders of the communications budget and have the chance to become involved in strategy and planning. They may see rather more of top management than some of their peers, but it is likely to be in the capacity of an add-on to advertising.

In some firms PR is done by press office, as if public relations and press relations were the same thing, and PRO another name for press officer. Or there might be a press and public relations department, as if they were two quite separate, though related, activities. Either way accessibility to and by the media can be a distinct benefit, although that can lead to over-concentration on media relations.

Another common arrangement is for PR to be a subsection of marketing. The advantage of that is closeness to the customer, and also the possibility of influencing what the company actually does, rather than simply what it says. This can be very effective, as long as PR is not limited to preparing the ground for marketing and providing back-up support—two significant functions, but by no means the only ones, nor even necessarily the most important. It makes more sense to recognize that whereas PR is certainly part of the marketing mix, marketing is just as certainly part of PR. Public relations addresses a very much wider range of stakeholders than customers alone.

For an organization needing to build and maintain a relationship with central government, there are obvious advantages in being close to Whitehall and Westminster, in both senses.

As a general requirement, PR departments need to be organizationally central to the enterprise and accessible in practical ways to as many stakeholders as possible.

The ever helpful BIM guidelines are in five categories. Responsibility figures in each.

1. Self-appraisal, continuous improvement, objectivity and the pursuit of ambition are key responsibilities that managers have towards themselves, plus sensitivity and without avoidable damage to others.
2. To the organization, their responsibilities are leadership and commitment, loyalty and integrity, judgement and candour.
3. As far as colleagues and subordinates are concerned, the guidelines are consultation and communication, respect and concern for their well-being, encouragement and clear instructions.
4. Responsibility to stakeholders is particularly important in a PR manager— openness, consideration, courtesy, informativeness, confidentiality and satisfaction of needs.
5. On the environment and society, the guidelines are to do with the avoidance of harm and the conferring of benefit.[2]

Levels of responsibility

In most organizations of any size there are four levels of responsibility. These levels are not necessarily determined by formal reporting lines. They reflect the culture of the company, and how people are perceived in relation to overall business responsibilities (see Figure 9.1).

At level one are the directors and managers, who take it for granted that they

LEVEL	MANAGEMENT	SPECIALIST	TECHNICAL	OPERATIVE
Contribution	Policy	Knowledge	Know-how	Labour
People	Directors Line managers Planners	Advisers Professionals Consultants	Technologists Skilled Craftworkers	Low skilled Semi-skilled Unskilled

Figure 9.1 Perceived levels of responsibility

and only they are the policy makers, with overall responsibility for controlling how the business performs. Planners often belong in this category, if only because nobody quite knows where else to put them.

The next level is made up of specialists—the professionals, technical advisers and so on—who see their position as somewhat distant from actually making policy, but central to carrying it out, because of the knowledge that they have and which is denied to others.

Third are the craftspeople and technicians, whose skills and know-how fashion and give reality to the product or service that the business delivers. It is only in very exceptional cases that they can have any substantial effect on policy.

Underpinning all these élites are the less skilled and unskilled workers who bring varying amounts of experience to the enterprise, and do the most work, by volume and value. Policy is something that is usually done to them, occasionally for them but never by them.

Interchange between levels is not at all common. You hear of people who started at the bottom and rose to the top, but this nearly always refers to upward progress within one level or two levels only. For instance, some unskilled workers may become craftspeople or technicians. They hardly ever become professionals or technical advisers, let alone planners, managers or directors.

Most public relations people are traditionally positioned in the second and third responsibility levels. Most do not expect to move out. They should make every effort to get into the policy level of the business. They are, or ought to be, concerned with communications policy and its interaction with operational policy, and with the company culture.

Recognizing responsibility levels is one way of understanding how an organization works. Another way is to look at the chain of command. In a conventionally managed, vertical organization there is a central spine, a linear hierarchy, that represents the official way to get things done (see Figure 9.2). The chain of command runs from board of directors to unskilled operators. Off to one side

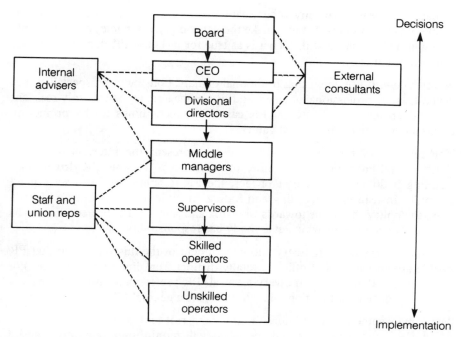

Figure 9.2 Traditional vertical organization

are the consultants, advisers and staff/union representatives who also have their own linear hierarchies, although they are not seen as being part of main line management.

Traditionally, public relations consultants input at strategic level to the client's board and chief executive, while the in-house PR department is expected to traffic in instant solutions to tactical and operational questions.

In a linear PR consultancy, assistant account executives report to account executives who report to account managers who report to account directors who report to board directors. There is the maximum possible distance between decisions, which are made on high, and their implementation by the people who will actually carry them out. The job titles may be different in-house, but the structures can be much the same, although there are signs that they are beginning to break down, to be replaced by one with far fewer links in the chain. Indeed, the whole idea of a chain, or spine, or pyramid is becoming discredited.

According to Sir Colin Marshall, 'only two levels of management are required— one level which selects long-term strategies and finds the people to effect them, and one level which deals with operational opportunities and motivates and leads the staff members who will accomplish them'.[3]

Flatness is the OK thing, and a team leader does not have to be at a higher management level than any other team member. Sir Colin Marshall again. 'While it is the systems that will make the flat company possible, it is the people who will make it successful.'[4] That is as true for in-house PR departments as it is for consultancies.

Nevertheless, it is evident that traditional demarcations between specialists and generalists, or professional advisers and line managers, are stubbornly resistant to rapid change. Good internal PR can help speed things up by promoting corporate objectives and shared values.

The real job of the PR department is to represent the interests of all the stakeholders, encouraging the entire organization to become PR driven, and enabling it do so. As a matter of fact, the PR function itself can set a good example. Instead of a 'hoarding and hiding' attitude to knowledge and know-how, the policy should be towards 'showing and sharing' PR professionalism as a common resource for which everybody has responsibility.

It is surely time to rid industry and government of the misconception that PR people are specialist staff officers, totally distinct from line managers, and not part of the real action. At the very least, all PR professionals must also have a general management function, and all managers a general PR function.

Many management experts now see this as a real and pressing need. As the *MBA Review* explains: 'Central specialists will require greater humility and a willingness to work in teams. They will need to be of a higher quality and concerned with policy, strategy and the giving of advice rather than matters of operational details. Giving absolute and off the cuff expert answers will be less important than helping colleagues to do what is best in a particular set of circumstances.'[5]

In fact, PR should have both a staff and a line function, but as is often the case in industry, the effect you have on the business is partly determined by what they call you.

The 182 respondents in Burson-Marsteller's 1989/90 survey of top companies and financial institutions showed some interesting variations. Of the people who had responsibility for PR, 30 per cent were called head of public relations and publicity or public relations manager. If you were in this category, you were more likely to employ an outside public relations agency on an ongoing basis. If you were among the 8 per cent called head of public affairs, you were more likely to be in the highest salary brackets.

Head of communications/corporate communications (7 per cent), director of corporate affairs (6 per cent), marketing director/manager (5 per cent), public relations officer (4 per cent) and press and public relations manager (3 per cent) were the other significant job titles. The biggest percentage of all (37 per cent) were described in other ways—the survey results do not say what.

A quarter of all respondents reported direct to their chairman, 22 per cent to the managing director and 19 per cent to the marketing or commercial director.

However, the survey pointed out that 'the public relations function has not normally led to the Board. Only ten respondents were Board Members—and notably none were women.'[6]

There has to come a time when directors of PR, male or female, are on the main board. It is in industry's own interests that that time should be sooner rather than later.

Exercising responsibility

A public relations manager's responsibilities are the same as any other manager's—the sum of all that he or she is required to accomplish. But by definition, managers at any level have more work to do than they can possibly accomplish themselves. It just has to be shared out with other people. There is no option. In this share out, each person's responsibilities need to be defined clearly, both as an individual who desires recognition and as a corporate stakeholder with a definite and defined value to the group.

Reporting lines ought to be short, direct and well understood by all concerned. When it comes to assigning work, it is probably more useful to think in terms of responsibility centres. Every necessary function of the PR department needs to be allocated to a specific centre. If a function is not necessary it should not be done.

That sounds obvious but may not be as easy to manage as you might think. People in PR, especially the lively self-starters, like to do what they like to do. It keeps them happy, busy, interested. The problem is how to focus all that enthusiasm and commitment on the essentials, the 25 per cent of the Stone supposition (see Chapter 2).

Responsibility is not static. The management of PR people must include the development of their ability to take more responsibility and the provision of opportunities for them to exercise it. A main aim should be to motivate them towards not only seeking but meriting greater responsibility and delivering a higher performance.

To accept responsibility willingly and discharge it effectively, people need to know just what is expected of them. What does being responsible for press notice distribution actually mean? Updating? Weeding? Selecting? Liaison with press cuttings service? Input into procedures for monitoring? What are the key results they have to deliver? Who will judge their performance? By what standards? Do they agree? Is there a built-in plan for improving the job as well as the performance?

Knowing what is wanted is all very well, but will the individual be helped or hindered by the way the organization behaves? The way that you behave? Will there be genuine opportunities, as well as problems? Are responsibilities consistent with functions and rank? You can hardly expect an assistant PR manager to deal satisfactorily, on a regular basis, with a senior account director in a consultancy or agency. Nor can you expect even the top people in a consultancy to guarantee results that are outside their own control to deliver.

People want to know how they are getting on. Consultants and in-house staff need a flow of comment and reactions in a continuous feedback that tells them when they are doing well, not just when they are doing badly. But be warned that feedback which is too late, too negative and too indirect can be dangerous.

The better their contribution, the more they should be rewarded—not necessarily in money, if only because many organizations are not geared to paying more for getting more. Appreciation—indeed approbation—can be a very effective way of helping people to meet their responsibilities and an equally effective way of rewarding them when they do.

Expectations have to be realistic. People are not likely to measure up to their responsibilities if they have too much to do—whether in terms of quantity or quality—or if too much depends on it. Nor can they do well if they are responsible for too little in the way of quantity or quality—or if too little depends on it. If it doesn't seem to matter all that much, why should they care all that much?

There is another aspect of responsibility which is to do with relationships with others at the same level as yourself. You need to be able to get information, assistance and cooperation from them, not as a favour, but as a right. These sideways responsibilities work in both directions, so that others at your level have the right to expect as much from you. Such mutual arrangements can be particularly important in the coordination of PR with other communications activities.

Authority

If responsibility is about doing things, authority is about approving things before they can be done. Whatever requires your approval to be started or stopped lies within your authority. Actions that do not require your approval are outside your authority.

True authority can come from your position or your specialism. The higher you are placed in an organization, the more authority you expect to have. The better your professional standing, the more of an authority you are. However, authority derived from what you are is not the force that it used to be, whereas authority derived from what you know and from sheer brainpower is gaining ground.

If you should happen to be a charismatic figure, your authority comes from who you are, rather than from your job title or professional qualifications. It is as if other people hand over the authority to you. But beware, they can also take it away.

The other main source of authority, and it would be foolish to deny it, is connections—who you know. That can be precarious, is often resented and rarely outlasts the tenure of the patron.

Financial authority—the amount you may sign for—is an obvious, visible indicator in that the more your signature is good for, the greater is your authority. Yet although the money expresses this, it does not necessarily confer it. Indeed, it is often the other way round, the signing level following from the responsibility level and being roughly commensurate with it.

Remember that in any client/consultancy relationship, the authority is with the client. The exception to that is when the consultancy employs sub-contractors and other outside suppliers, and therefore exercises authority over them. Although the work they do still has to be approved by the client, the consultancy carries the can for it.

Exercising authority

How an organization actually operates may not have much to do with how it is supposed to. Alongside reporting lines and formal authority, practical networks grow up which are unplanned, informal, and almost impossible to show on any organization chart, not least because they are constantly shifting.

In this shadowy environment, influential groups may be detected—social or functional or based on rank, for instance—whose common interest is self-interest.

These groups depend on the willingness of some to be told what to do and on the willingness of others to tell them. They operate through rumour, the grapevine and pillow talk, making use of personal pride, vanity and prejudice, apathy and ambition, sexual attraction, guilt—in fact, the whole range of human motivation.

It would be difficult to prove that these networks are more prevalent in the PR world than elsewhere, but they are certainly not less so. For authority to be exercised effectively in these conditions, you and your organization need to be absolutely clear about

- who has authority,
- for what,
- over whom.

And what the limits of that authority are

- downwards,
- upwards,
- sideways.

Authority should only be exercised when it is necessary and should always be at the lowest level consistent with reasonable prudence. Responsibility without authority is scapegoatism. Authority without responsibility is petty tyranny. Responsibility can and must be delegated; authority likewise.

Accountability

What cannot be delegated is accountability. The BIM guidelines are uncompromising on this—managers have to accept accountability for the actions of their subordinates as well as for their own.[7]

Ultimately, the chief executive is accountable for what is done in the name of the company. It is therefore crucially important to involve him or her in public relations. Reginald Watts notes that 'perception is no longer the most important thing, it is the only thing in the minds of most business people', and asks the question that has to be answered 'If external perception of products, of companies and their values is so important to the bottom line, why do chief executives give such a small proportion of their time to it?'[8]

The Public Relations Institute of Australia reported in the early 1980s that most chief executives of top companies spent between 10 and 50 per cent of their time on managing external affairs. Their main PR activities were meetings, seminars, speeches and media relations. Stakeholders contacted included, in descending order, clients, overseas visitors, industry and professional associations, shareholders, boards of associated companies, politicians, government administrators, consultants, the education sector, trade unions, consultative committees, statutory bodies, community groups, boards of outside companies and the mass media.[9]

In the United Kingdom, Reginald Watts highlights three acute needs for top managers:

1. To give more of their own time to communications so that these skills become as second nature as those of finance, production control and personnel.
2. To check that all current communications activity is properly managed in terms of strategic and operational control, with each constituent monitored and reviewed for effectiveness of impact.
3. To ensure that the basic principles of public relations are taught to all managers down the line. Turning a company from being product-led to marketing-driven means that everyone should understand the PR process.

Accountability requires that the top people in the company, notably the chief executive, maintain day-to-day involvement with public relations. Otherwise, they soon discover that 'strategy and operational function become divorced and one of the most complex of any management functions within the life of a company moves gently into that morass of unfulfilled hopes, conflicting orders and crossed lines that we all know so well.'[10]

I'm not too sure about that 'gently'.

Sources and references

1. Colin Coulson-Thomas. The need for PR to match management change. *Public Relations*. 40th Anniversary issue, Summer 1988.
2. *BIM Guide to Good Management Practice*. British Institute of Management, 1990.
3. Sir Colin Marshall, interviewed in *Management Today*, April 1990.
4. ibid.
5. Ray Acosta and Paul Finlay. Senior managers and their use of information technology. *MBA Review*, September 1989.
6. *The Survey of United Kingdom Public Relations Professionals*. Burson-Marsteller, London 1990.
7. as source 2.
8. Reginald Watts. Three acute needs of UK management. *Public Relations*, January 1989.
9. Discussion at the 8th National Public Relations Convention in Sydney, July 1984.
10. as source 8.

CHAPTER 10
Measuring results

While the basic philosophy and rationale behind PR is still so shrouded in confusion and ambiguity, attempts to define or measure its contribution are doomed.

Paul Winner

To measure is to know.

Lord Kelvin

Of all the facets of managing public relations, measuring results is possibly the least understood, probably the worst documented and certainly the most contentious.

In a survey of a good spread of 155 top companies, about half agreed that PR was the most cost-effective way of reaching their most important publics, like customers and consumers. Nearly two out of three thought it difficult to assess the effect of PR activities.

Measuring results may be difficult, but that is no reason for not trying. The easiest sort of assessment is subjective opinion. That is why there is a lot of it about. On the objective side, pretty well everybody tots up the press cuttings. But there is more to measuring results than gut feeling and column inches. How do you set about a more systematic approach?

The first requirement is that all concerned should be aware of the value of measurement. If you do not at least try to measure what has been achieved, how can you tell whether or not you have achieved it? How can the cost-effectiveness of a PR campaign, programme or activity be evaluated if you do not make every effort to measure the effect as well as the cost?

No matter how difficult it may be to decide what to measure and how to measure it, do not be put off. As with budgeting, so with measuring: much of the value is in making the very attempt because your mind is focused and directed back towards your objectives.

Be reassured by Judith Harper's conclusion, for the Institute of Manpower Studies, that '. . . very few of the problems normally encountered in setting up a performance measurement system are insurmountable . . .'[1]

You have, of course, already been persuaded of the importance of quantification, the process of putting numbers on those objectives. Once the value of measurement has been accepted, your next requirement is to know something about the industry, how it is made up, who does what, and what it costs. No immensely detailed knowledge is required, but PR managers should have as good a grasp of this particular industry as of, say, the printing or film-making business.

An understanding of the different types of research and techniques of measurement is very important. You do not need to be able to do it yourself, but you will want to make a definite commitment to understanding how it is done and what methods are most appropriate for any particular purpose.

Aware, knowledgeable and understanding you are now competent to advise your employers or clients on what measurements need to be done and what results may be expected. No results can be better than the raw data.

You should also be in a position to influence the selection, retrieval and analysis of the information produced from the measurements, and how it is presented.

Finally, and overridingly, there is the question of how the results will be used. It is no good thinking about that when the measurements have been made, nor even while they are being taken. The time to think about the end uses is right at the beginning, before any measurements are started or even planned. That brings you back to your objectives which should be framed in such a way that dispassionate and direct measurement of results is not only possible but unavoidable. 'Ultimately', says Michael Hingston, Chairman of Paragon, 'the key to successful evaluation is having programme objectives that can be measured'.[2]

Some options

Although in the end you may conclude that your best course is to originate the measurement you need, there are two other main options to consider first: the utilization of existing information, and syndicated research.

Existing sources can yield surprisingly satisfactory information. Studying published material is usually known as 'desk research', but that is something of a misnomer. Even in these days of computerized workstations and information technology, there is often a need to go and see something or someone for yourself. Not so much desk work as leg work, if only to the local public library or chamber of commerce.

The country is ankle-deep in research results and the level is rising. If something can be measured, it probably has been measured, and some of it is likely to be of interest to you. A proportion may actually be usable.

Here are half a dozen of the more readily accessible sources for desk research.

1. Statistical publications.
2. Trade and professional organizations.
3. Trade, technical and learned journals.
4. Directories and year books.

5. On-line data banks.

6. One-off research reports.

Press cuttings are an obvious example of published information. Analysing what the media has to say can produce hard information of practical value. A word of caution, however—do not confuse what the papers say with what their readers think. True, the more successful a newspaper or magazine is, the more likely it is that its opinions will reflect the beliefs, assumptions and attitudes of its readers. That has implications for the PR manager, who needs to know as much about readership profiles as the advertising people do. Nevertheless, interest shown by the media does not necessarily mirror interest shown by the public.

Less than a year after British Nuclear Fuels won the IPR Sword of Excellence for its open policy, a report linked the Sellafield plant with child leukaemia. BNFL, concerned that it was 'easy to jump to conclusions from . . . critical media coverage' preferred direct measurement of public opinion.[3] This was a case where desk research was not appropriate.

Even when it is appropriate one of the most important benefits of well-conducted desk research may arise not from what is in it, but what is not. The gaps can help to identify what additional measurements you may need to take, whether syndicated or originated. They may also reveal PR opportunities.

It was only when Paragon did some desk research for ICL that a significant gap was exposed. There was no single authoritative source of knowledge and advice on retail sector information technology. This led to a major strategic decision, which was to position ICL itself as the leading authority. The consequences of that decision are spelled out later in this chapter, in a case history.

Syndicated research is off-the-peg and makes use of ongoing measurements carried out for, or shared with, others. Organizations like NOP and MORI carry out more or less continuous omnibus surveys which can act as kangaroos for your own particular babies.

Some of these surveys are geared to specific activity groups, like motorists, or age groups, like pensioners. Others are more general and offer an across-the-board, large, representative sample, but not many questions. You buy in to what you want.

As well as latching on to these long-established, long-running surveys, there are other opportunities for taking advantage of syndication such as standing panels, like the National Food Survey or the Television Consumer Audit.

Originated work requires the development of a tight and specific brief leading to the deployment of techniques that are fully at your disposal and yours alone. Considerable investments of time and money can be involved, depending on how structured you want the measuring process to be.

Unstructured measurement can be relatively quick, easy and cheap. You simply measure that which happens to be both measurable and available. Results are not very reliable and they can be hard to analyse. A useful guide, they might give you some usable ideas. The risk is that a lot of the information you get could be totally irrelevant while what you really need to know gets left out.

Fully structured measurement works best for simple questions giving simple answers. Postal questionnaires and telephone surveys are normally fully structured. Results are easy to handle and analyse. Conclusions are not difficult to arrive at, as long as the questions are well designed. Fortunately, there is an immense amount of expertise and know-how to draw on when framing structured questionnaires.

Semi-structured measurement is possibly the most demanding but also the most generally useful. Incorporating some standard questions into a well-designed overall approach can mean that all the issues are covered cost-effectively. Analysis is much easier than for unstructured work and not markedly more difficult than for the fully structured.

Strategic or tactical?

Although nine out of ten in-company PR directors and managers in top firms are actively involved in media relations, and four out of five in corporate identity, employee communications, special events and/or sponsorship, only two in three are similarly involved in evaluating their campaigns.[4] That is a major weakness which ought to be corrected. They should all be involved in strategic and tactical evaluation, based on measurement.

Strategic measurement compares final achievement with original expectations. Tactical measurement compares programme results with plans and budgets.

Nationwide Anglia's Partnership strategy, was designed to change the attitude and performance of workers and management, as measured by the effect on customers.

The Puerto Rican strategy of lobbying specific US Government personnel to safeguard specific tax concessions clearly worked. They got what they wanted (see Chapter 4).

ICL electronic point of sale (EPoS) systems were in the forefront of information technology but not a lot of people knew that. As their case history shows, ICL set out to put things right, and succeeded. For them, and for Puerto Rico, the strategic results were specific.

As one element in a major PR programme to promote adult training, MSC planned to attract 500 paying delegates to a national conference. Counting the number of tickets sold would be the obvious measure of tactical success (see Chapter 8).

According to *Campaign*, 'Saatchi & Saatchi paid around £5000 for its one-week poster site on the Berlin wall . . . about 30 times the cost of a comparable UK site. The poster, booked through East German ad agency Interwerbung by Primesight International, was probably cheap at the price: it was seen by millions around the world on TV and in the press.'[5] Tactically inventive, yes, but *probably* cheap? Don't they know?

Case History 16
ICL retail unit

ICL's own independent research showed that the company was perceived by retail decision makers as No. 5 supplier of retail technology when its own marketing information showed that in reality its market share placed it as No. 2 supplier behind IBM.

Analysis

1. Paragon, PR consultants to ICL, did research among journalists, consultants and analysts which revealed lack of statistics on retail technology and the electronic point of sale (EPoS) market in particular.
2. No one EPoS supplier was regarded as an authority on the market.
3. It was Paragon's view that ICL's PR activities should concentrate on establishing ICL as the leading supplier of retail technology by positioning it as the leading authority.

Objectives

1. Establish ICL as the first choice supplier of retail systems.
2. In particular, position ICL as the leading supplier of EPoS systems.
3. Position ICL as a supplier who could satisfy all the information technology (IT) needs of retailers.

Strategy

1. Create major publicity vehicles to position ICL as the leading IT authority on retail.
2. Develop joint PR programmes with leading UK retailers to demonstrate ICL's successful track record in delivering IT solutions.
3. Underpin the above with a continuous, quality service to journalists.
4. Sustain and develop this strategic approach for a minimum of three years to effect real attitude changes.

Programme

1985

The production of *Retailing Tomorrow*, a 36-page report which looked at the future impact of technology on retailing and offered major retailers a platform to air their views on the future of retailing. The report also contained original research on the views of both shoppers and retailers on electronic funds transfer point of sale (EFTPoS), or cashless shopping as it is more commonly known.

1986

The production of a retail video to be used by ICL with customers and prospects in modular form to be relevant to individual retail sectors, for example, DIY, supermarkets.

A top level customer relations campaign with Marks & Spencer and J. Sainsbury for joint publicity on successful IT developments and milestones.

1987

The production of *Retailing Today*, a follow-up report to *Retailing Tomorrow*, which looked at the current impact of IT in retailing and detailed case histories on successful ICL installations with key retailers. Again, the report majored heavily on original research into shoppers' perceptions of the retail environment and attitudes to laser scanning, to create media interest.

1988

The development of 'Shop of the Future', a major exhibition of state-of-the-art technology to demonstrate imminent new technologies. Original research into retailers' intentions regarding IT investment was used to create briefings for all key retail trade media.

1985–88

Underpinning the major activities outlined above was a continuous national and trade media relations campaign. In addition, PR programmes were developed to support exhibition activity by ICL in retail, and a series of 'issues' luncheons was hosted by ICL to discuss topics of major interest to retailers.

Measuring results

Over a three-month period the media coverage in the press, radio and TV was analysed on a monthly basis. More than 80 million opportunities to see were produced in target business media.

ICL's own independent research shows that ICL moved from being perceived by retailers as No. 5 supplier to clear No. 1 as retail technology supplier. ICL also improved its rating versus competitors on every single factor regarded as key by customers when considering an IT supplier.

	1986 (%)	1987 (%)	1988 (%)
ICL	17	34	38
IBM	24	34	28
NCR	12	10	9

Source: Research Solutions

By 1988, journalists covering retail technology had come to view the service from ICL as better than any other supplier of IT on eight out of nine points they regard as key.

Don Jackson, principal retail consultant at ICL, said 'Paragon's campaign undoubtedly changed radically the perception of retailers towards ICL. We know that the favourable shift in attitudes was PR-led because we concentrated almost all our marketing communications budget on PR and had minimum advertising support in trade media.'

The ICL retail campaign won the IPR Sword of Excellence award for the best business-to-business PR campaign in 1986 and 1988. The campaign was voted the best overall PR campaign by the IPR in 1988.[6]

Techniques of measurement

Ideally, you want what you do to be

- *valid*, so that what is claimed to be measured is actually measured.
- *reliable*, so that what is actually measured is accurately measured.
- *consistent*, so that you get the same results no matter who does the measuring.
- *standardized*, so that the results apply to a lot of people.

In addition, you hope the work will be

- action-orientated
- anonymous
- authoritative
- cheap
- checkable
- complex
- confidential
- creative
- explanatory
- exploratory
- fast
- independent
- in-depth
- individualized
- innovative
- instant
- qualitative
- quantitative
- repeatable
- simple
- structured
- unique
- usable

Unfortunately, but obviously, no one technique can possibly do all those things. Each has its special characteristics, its own pros and cons.

The four main techniques are as follows:

* Postal questionnaires
* Telephone interviews
* One-to-one, face-to-face
* Group discussion.

Postal questionnaires can handle very large samples and cover a huge geographical area at low cost. Questions can be highly structured and are relatively easy to follow up, by a second postal questionnaire or by using one of the other techniques. Response rates tend to be low (if you can get a 10 per cent return you are doing rather well) and there is a limit to the number of questions that can be put. There is, of course, no real possibility of interaction or dialogue between you and the sample, nor do you have any idea what interaction or dialogue might be going on at the recipients' end. Postal questionnaires are hardly suitable for complex or confidential matters, but for statistical validity, authority, consistency and repeatability they are hard to beat.

Telephone surveys have many of the advantages and disadvantages of postal questionnaires, plus some of their own. They are quick to set up and operate, particularly on straightforward or routine issues, though the amount of information that can be handled in this way is rather limited. Reasonably large samples may be sounded out at reasonable cost. However, many people are resistant to unsolicited telephone interviews, which they find intrusive and irritating. The refusal rate can be high, particularly if the interviewer does not strike up a rapport very quickly. Although a telephone interview may seem more personal than a postal questionnaire, it is no more suitable for confidential matters. Nor is it easy to check the answers. Properly targeted and handled, telephone interviews are the fastest way of getting a result.

One-to-one, face-to-face interviews are very good for delving into complex matters which can be followed up then and there. They may take up a lot of time—as much as an hour or so with each person—or they may be quite brief. The larger and more expensive kind are immensely valuable for qualitative measurements. The sample, content and timing are all designed to order, and the questions can be as detailed as you like, as complex and as confidential.

Difficult concepts may be handled and ideas tested, misconceptions explored and sensitivities exposed. It is not easy to conduct these in-depth interviews but when they are successful, the potential rewards are very great.

At the other end of the scale there is the random omnibus survey. We have all been stopped in the street at some time by someone with a clipboard asking our opinion about this or that. It is sometimes possible to have additional questions slipped into surveys of this type. This can be quite cheap but the results can be non-specific and are not usually confidential. Nor do you have much control over the sample or the timing.

Group discussion is usually tailor-made and capable of yielding good qualitative information. The sample is small and individually selected. Properly managed, under the guidance of a skilled conductor, group discussions can test PR propositions for 'tone of voice'. Turns of phrase and individual words or images can be examined in unhurried depth. The results take time to interpret and they will never have the kind of statistical authenticity that a mass survey can give. Used correctly, groups can deliver the kind of value judgements that are almost impossible to arrive at in any other way.

Measuring media coverage

It is commonplace, in what might be called the press agent mode, for the effectiveness of public relations to be seen in terms of media coverage. There is much more to PR than that, but nevertheless most campaigns do include a media relations programme and this should be monitored.

The simplest and best known measure is the column inch, though increasingly these days it is the column centimetre. There are two reasons for this. Advertising space is now costed by the column centimetre so it makes sense for editorial coverage to be measured in the same units—useful to those who insist on expressing the value of editorial coverage in terms of the cost of equivalent paid-for space. You are strongly advised not to fall into that rate card trap.

As Frank Jefkins points out very firmly, programme and editorial content 'is not for sale and is priceless. The real evaluation is the effectiveness of media coverage in achieving the objectives of a PR service paid for on the basis of man hours, material and expenses.'[7]

Another reason for measuring press cuttings by the column centimetre is that there are 2.54 times as many of them as there are column inches. The figures therefore look more impressive to a client or employer—two and a half times more impressive. That may not be a serious argument for doing it, but even so it is done.

In the electronic media, the comparable units to the column centimetre are the radio minute and the TV second.

A useful way of combining all these into one unit of measurement is to focus on 'opportunities to see'—or OTS.

The origins of OTS lie in the poster business where the number of people passing a particular site—known as the traffic—was the measure of opportunities to see. Later, the idea was taken up and developed by the newspaper and television advertising people. OTS became an important part in the evaluation of campaigns and the justification for expenditure. However, there is no universally agreed and exact definition of what OTS is and how you measure it.

In the PR business, consultancies like the Quentin Bell Organisation (QBO), Paragon and Infopress use OTS or something very like it. QBO describes OTS as 'the number of chances that an average member of the target audience will have of being exposed to a media relations programme over a particular period of time'. This is in line with the way many advertising agencies calculate OTS. The Organisation also attempts to measure quality by 'relating key messages to the right audience against demographic and strategic objectives. Each cutting/transcript is scored for inclusion of key messages, multiplied by the number of items of coverage in each media sector. The actual score is then compared with the potential maximum.'[8]

Paragon's approach is in some ways closer to the traffic-based poster-site model. The key measurement factors include the total audience reach of media coverage, the quality of the audience, the impact of the coverage and delivery of the message. All these are given numerical values which form part of the final OTS calculations, as in the ICL case history, Paragon excludes incidental, irrelevant and negative coverage.[9]

Infopress, front runner in the application of information technology in the PR industry, gives a message value weighting (MVW) to the specific, pre-agreed message content of each press cutting. This qualitative information is loaded into a database along with quantitative information about the publication concerned. This is then used to 'compute visibility and message delivery statistics', and can be used to 'check the effectiveness of a given press relations strategy in delivering message A to audience B'. The system is also used to compare a client's media profile with that of competitors.[10]

Consultancies keep up with the latest readership profiles and figures. In-house PR departments need to be equally well informed. In 1990, for example, the only national dailies not to record year-on-year falls in readership were *Today*, *The Independent* and the *Daily Mirror*.[11]

In-house PR departments are also becoming more interested in the qualitative side. Several measurements of media coverage may be taken—for example, the importance or status of the place where the item appears. It is perfectly feasible to rank these in a systematic way—for one theme it would be, say, 5 for *The Financial Times* or BBC 2 *The Money Programme*; on a sliding scale down to 3 for a local radio programme and 1 for a tabloid which has a very large circulation but only a very small percentage of readers in your target group. For a message with wider relevance, the weighting might be reversed, with tabloids scoring 5 and heavies having a rating of 1 or 2. Similarly with the specialist, trade and technical media.

Here is how that might work for national daily newspapers, segmented according to the age and social class of their readers. For example, if your target audience is in the 35–44 age bracket, *The Financial Times* and the *Sun* would

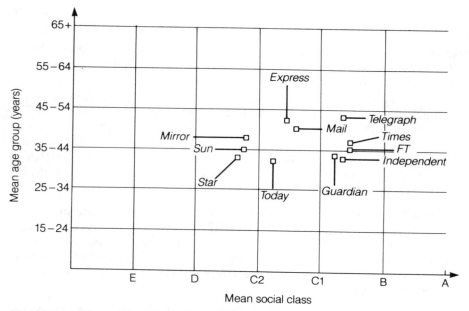

Figure 10.1 Segmentation of newspaper readership[12]

both score a maximum: weighting differentiation would be by social class. Conversely, if you need to reach the whole of the C2D social class, the *Mirror*, *Sun* and *Star* would rate maximum; differentiation could come through age. Fine distinctions can be drawn between various newspapers in the same age bracket or social class (Figure 10.1).

Distinctions can be drawn in relation to specific age brackets and specific social classes. For example, in March 1990 the *Sunday Correspondent* and *The Independent on Sunday* had a higher percentage of readers in the 15–44-year-old age bracket than any other quality Sunday, and a similar ABC1 profile to *The Sunday Times* and the (much older) *Sunday Telegraph* (Figure 10.2).

The position of the coverage can be given a numerical value—high for, say, front page or main TV news, not so high for less prominent positioning.

Wherever the message appears, it is vital that it actually is the message. Media mentions that are not on strategy are negatively weighted. Mentions that are on strategy may be positively weighted, the more important themes in the message getting the highest scores.

More subjective, and therefore harder to give a numerical value to, is assessment of the tone of the coverage—from hostile through neutral to favourable. There is a widely held belief in the PR business that the purpose of media relations is to secure favourable mention. That is understandable—who doesn't want a good image? (Did someone say 'Not Dirty Den or JR'? But the fact is that for

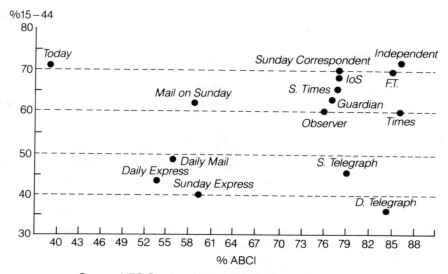

Figure 10.2 How the Age/Class Map Pans Out[13]

the professional bad guys of the soap operas, the worse their image the better—
within certain well-understood limits, that is.)

In the long run—and public relations is fundamentally a long-run business—
media relations ought to be about truth and understanding. The image cannot
convincingly be different from the reality for long. It is a matter not of securing
favourable mention but of earning it by the policies and activities of the
employer or client. As Bob Worcester, of MORI, says 'There are two types of
findings I can bring to my clients; truth and misconception'.[14]

You need to take account of everything, because the 'no' votes can tell you as
much as the 'yes' votes. Off-strategy mentions do matter, in that negative
sense.

One other measurement of media coverage deserves special mention. Known as
'share of the shout' or 'share of the voice', it involves a careful evaluation of the
total amount of media coverage of your sector or subject, estimating what share
of it you should have in the light of your standing, and comparing that with the
share you are actually getting. That provides a measure of where you are and a
target to aim for if you are falling short.

Whether in-house or bought in, these media measurement operations cost
money and need to be budgeted for.

Large companies and government departments find that the sheer volume of
material can be daunting. They subscribe to specialist bureaus for press cuttings

and broadcast monitoring. Smaller organizations find it cheaper and not too difficult to do their own.

Essentially there are three ways of tackling the job.

1. *Haphazard*, noting what happens to be seen or heard. This is the cheapest and least demanding. But it is not very useful, although it is better than nothing.
2. *Comprehensive*, taking in absolutely everything and extracting what is relevant. Can turn up the unexpected nugget but is very expensive.
3. *Planned*, aiming for coverage in specific places at specific times and checking the success or failure. The most demanding but by far the best measure.

There are occasions when the most effective score for a particular PR operation is 0. If you have a legitimate reason for keeping a story out of the media, the measure of your success is precisely nothing. If you have put a great deal of effort into listening to your customers and taking acount of their suggestions, a very good result would be very few complaints. The best result would be planned zero exposure, as long as that is what you were really aiming for.

Direct measurement

Whenever possible, measure direct. Measure what your target audience actually does, which may not be the same as what it says it does, or what you think it does.

When concern was at its height over the harmful effect on the ozone layer of the chemical CFC, used in refrigerators, air conditioners, aerosols and firefighting equipment, ICI was quick to respond. The manufacturers developed an informative and comprehensive PR programme, involving legislators, the media, the scientific community, customers, the general public and ICI's own staff. Press conferences and media briefings, videos and leaflets, facility visits, exhibitions, seminars, staff training, issues guide—it was all there. Conceding the difficulty of measuring or quantifying positive achievements in creating a balanced view, ICI believed 'we have actively moved from a poor understanding of the issue to an improved familiarity and comprehension of ICI's position in this debate'.[15] They were probably absolutely right, but it would have been better to measure that, rather than simply believe it.

What can you do in a situation like that? You can count how many people go through your exhibition turnstiles and how many copies of your stand literature they take away. Log every enquiry they make and every order you take. At Home Buyer '89, the housing and finance show in London's Barbican, 8000 potential home buyers turned up and brought £1.5 million worth of houses.

Competition entries are an obvious measure of the success of the campaigns that use them. The 'Young Ideas at Work' promotion by the non-commercial, non-profit organization Livewire, generated nearly 5000 entries.

Kwik-Fit's 'Belt Up at the Back' seatbelts campaign, by Dunseath Stephens, invited half a million children to carry out three missions designed to increase awareness among at least 10 adults. Over 2000 children completed their missions, and more than 20 000 adults got the message. The campaign developed £3 million worth of sales.[16]

Oxford Automotives was worried about its reputation for delivery of its exhaust systems and fuel tanks. The company streamlined production, transferred the responsibility for quality control to shopfloor operatives, and always kept a week's stock of finished products so that it could achieve 100 per cent delivery. That was its new measure of reputation.[17]

The measure of success of Evans Hunt Scott's direct mail campaign for Volkswagen's private contract hire-purchase plan was 50:1. 'We used the client's in-house mailing list to target likely purchasers', said Terry Hunt. 'The mail shot went to 70 000 people at a cost of £65 000 and generated £3.5 million worth of sales.'[18]

When Electricité de France was discussing its nuclear power plant programme, 1974–80, it took part in more than 2000 meetings and public debates, spent £20 million and employed scores of people, including seven or eight press attachés. Hundreds of thousands of letters were answered. By 1980 about 60 per cent of the French people were in favour of the civil nuclear programme. One particularly important direct measurement figure was three—the number of towns which refused to have a nuclear power plant. About these places EDF said 'we just gave up and left'.[19]

British Nuclear Fuels did its own direct measurements on the 300 000 visitors attracted to Sellafield. On arrival at the £3.5 million PR complex, 57 per cent said that they were already favourably inclined towards nuclear power. After the visit, the figure rose to 79 per cent. Over the same period, unfavourables dropped from 16 per cent before their visit to 9 per cent afterwards. Presumably, by inference, the 'don't knows' and 'no opinions' fell from 27 per cent to 12 per cent.[20]

Case History 17
Hampstead Health Authority

Here is the case history of a health authority making the simplest and most direct measurement of results regarding accommodation for staff.

Analysis

1. General shortage of rented accommodation in the private sector.
2. Particularly adverse effect on recruitment and retention of new entrants.

Objective

Increase the supply of suitable accommodation available to all staff.

Strategy

1. Develop links between local landlords and Hampstead Health Authority hospitals.
2. Advice and information on all aspects of housing, from council properties to mortgages.
3. Encourage initiatives to improve accommodation prospects generally.

Programme

1. One-to-one personal contact.
2. 24-hour enquiry service.
3. Posters in health centres, GP surgeries, libraries and sports centres.
4. Local press advertisements.
5. Inserts in recruitment literature.
6. Colour-coded noticeboards for easy identification of types of accommodation on offer.
7. Open days for Royal Free Hospital staff seeking local accommodation.
8. Regular visits to Friern Hospital to tell staff about local private and council accommodation for rent.
9. Liaison with Nationwide Anglia on Partnership Mortgage Scheme.
10. Information packs on housing law, housing associations and cooperatives, etc.

Resources

In-house staff—one full time
plus shared secretarial support.
Answerphone.
Budget of £14 000–£15 000.

Results

An increase of 60 per cent in amount of accommodation offered to the Authority.[21]

It is sometimes said that although you might be able to measure the effect of the total communications effort, it is almost impossible to identify the part played by PR. One way round this is to use PR in carefully selected areas only—not necessarily geographical—and compare results with those where no PR is used. At its simplest, this could involve redirecting, say, 10 per cent of the advertising budget to PR in a couple of areas and observing the effect by direct measurement.

However, there are occasions when indirect measurement at one stage removed is to be preferred. The best measure of a PR consultancy's effectiveness is not its own performance but that of its clients.

A key decision

The relationship between those making the measurements and those using them is crucial. Unless there are overwhelming reasons why not, whoever is responsible for measuring results should have no vested interest in how they turn out or how they are to be used.

You would hardly be surprised if one of the conclusions drawn from research carried out by an advertising agency is that you need to do more advertising. Nor would it be totally unheard of for a piece of research undertaken in-house to recommend that outside research contractors are not necessary.

Results may be affected not only by what is measured and by who does the measuring. A third factor is—who provides the data? It is axiomatic that anyone who aims to influence a decision has a vested interest in supplying incomplete information.

It is wise to be aware of all these possible biases and to rule them out by going to an independent operator. If this cannot be done, at least try to build in some kind of filter, to screen out the effects of self-interest, prejudice or self-deception. You could make that another golden guideline.

And if an independent research company should happen to recommend that you need to do further independent research—well, you will have to use your judgement. But this need not be unaided. The Market Research Society (MRS) and the Association of Market Survey Organisations (AMSO) are there to look after professional standards. The underlying principles are to do with cooperation between the researchers, the public and business organizations, cooperation which depends on confidence that the research is conducted honestly, objectively, without unwelcome intrusion and without harm to informants. The purpose is to collect and analyse information, not to influence opinion nor to generate sales.

The MRS and AMSO between them suggest the following checklist for anyone commissioning research. Obtaining this information will enable the potential buyer of market research to assess the general level of competence of the supplier, and will help in the decision as to whether, in principle, a particular supplier will suit requirements.

1. Evidence of the background and quality of the company's key executives from published sources and recommendations of existing clients.
2. Confirmation that key executives in the company are members of the Market Research Society and follow its Code of Conduct, and that the company conforms to the Association of Market Survey Organisation's Code of Conduct.
3. Details of any specialists—psychologists, statisticians—employed full time or on a consultancy basis.
4. Evidence of experience that may be relevant to your particular situation; work within the same market; experience of using relevant research techniques.
5. Details of the company's field operation; selection and training of interviewers; level of supervision; checks on quality and accuracy.
6. Details of editing, coding, and punching operations; quality and training of staff; supervision of these functions; checks on quality and accuracy.
7. Details of analysis and tabulation; computers and machinery used; restrictions on numbers and types of tabulations.
8. Details of normal standards of reporting; the style and content of reports.
9. Details of accounting and legal aspects and how your position will be protected; normal billing procedures.
10. Demonstration, in its statement of the research objectives and of the scope of the enquiry, that the supplier understands your problem.
11. Detailed descriptions of the research design including:
    a a statement of the scope and nature of any preliminary desk research, qualitative work or pilot studies;
    b for a quantitative study, a statement of: the data collection technique (how the information is to be obtained); the universe to be sampled (who is to be interviewed); the size of the sample (how many are to be interviewed); and the method of sample selection (how the individuals are to be chosen).
12. A statement of the cost of the project and a clear indication of the assumptions on which it is based and what is included, for example assumptions made about length of interview; assumptions made about degree of executive involvement; whether personal briefing of interviewers is included; number of copies of report envisaged; whether there will be a written interpretation of the tabulations; whether visual presentation of results is included.
13. A reasonably detailed timetable for the project and a reasonably firm reporting date.
14. A statement of the specific executive(s) responsible for the project.[22]

A summary of the AMSO Code of Standards is presented in Appendix B.

Golden guidelines

1. Be aware of the value of measurement.
2. Know about the measurement industry and understand the different techniques.

3. Advise employers/clients on the place of measurement in their thinking.
4. Put numerical values on your objectives.
5. Weigh up the pros and cons of totally independent research.
6. Influence the selection, retrieval and analysis of results.
7. Control how they are presented, so that the most significant messages are clear.
8. Measure outputs, not inputs. Use direct measurement whenever possible.
9. Count the 'no' votes as well as the 'yes' votes.
10. Never take any measurement until you know how you will use it.

The BIM guidelines for managers are disappointingly silent on the measurement of results, while the codes of IPR and PRCA understandably distance both bodies from the concept of payment by results, where the achievement of any such results is not within their members' direct control.

Judith Harper has the last word—'No measurement system will be any use . . . unless the results it produces are presented in such a way that they can be readily understood.'[23]

Sources and references

1. Judith Harper. *Measuring Business Performance*. Gower, London, 1984.
2. Michael Hingston. How we measure success. *Paraphrase*. Paragon, Spring 1988.
3. Helen Slingsby. Cancer slur blights Sellafield. *PR Week*, 22 February 1990.
4. *The Survey of United Kingdom Public Relations Professionals*. Burson-Marsteller, London, 1990.
5. *Campaign*. 6 January 1990.
6. Case history authenticated by Paragon.
7. Frank Jefkins. Theory doesn't measure up. *PR Week*, 11 June 1987.
8. PR works and that's official. *PR Solutions*. Quentin Bell Organisation, 1990.
9. Julia Thorne. *Case histories*. Presentation at Interact Seminars, 1990.
10. Dermot McKeone. How computers can help PR professionals to manage information more effectively. *International Public Relations Review*, 1989.
11. Grim news for nationals in latest figures. *Journalist's Week*, 8 June 1990.
12. Mike Gonshaw. Economics of the press. *The Economic Review*, Sept. 1989.
13. Mark Edwards. Same audience type reads Corrie and IoS. *Campaign*, 15 June 1990.
14. Robert M. Worcester. *The Image of Public Relations*. Institute of Public Relations, London, 1987.
15. Lawrie Allen. CFCs—the ICI response. *Public Relations*, February 1990.
16. The PRCA award winners. *Communicator*. Public Relations Consultants Association, Spring 1990.
17. Britain's best factories. *Management Today*, November 1989.
18. Sophie Bate. Mail Model. *Campaign*, 16 February 1990.
19. Lionel Taccoen. In France: technicians talking. *Public Relations*, February 1990.
20. Jeffrey Preece. In Britain: regaining credibility. *Public Relations*, February 1990.
21. Case history authenticated by Hampstead Health Authority.
22. Reproduced with the permission of the Market Research Society.
23. as source 1.

CHAPTER 11

The client/consultancy relationship

> Any sudden growth in a service industry is dependent on two conditions. First, there must be a need for the service. Second, there must be resources to fulfil that demand.
>
> *John Brandon*[1]

During the economic recession of the early 1980s, many companies had to rethink their business strategies. There was considerable shedding of labour. Lean payrolls became very common. Decentralization and devolution meant that operating units could no longer call so readily on central resources and corporate services. Communications policy, forward planning, long-term thinking, corporate identity—these were among the casualties of restructuring.[2]

The opportunity was there for independent consultants to identify a genuine market gap and fill it, if only they had the resources. Fortunately, at about the same time as some of the larger organizations began shedding public relations staff, a pool of experienced PR people became available on the open market. They were, of course, the same people.

Companies found that consultancies of many different sizes and specialisms were eager for their business. Not only that, the consultants often knew a good deal about the particular industrial sector. After all, in a large number of cases they had only recently left it.

However, it was not simply a matter of the mixture as before. Although the hourly or daily rates of the consultants seemed higher compared with in-house costs—indeed often substantially higher, even when all the company's overheads, etc., were taken into account—actual outlay could be less because when the consultants had finished the job for which they were hired, the company stopped paying them.

This advantage of paying only for the specific tasks or projects carried out is one of the main reasons why companies decide to employ consultancies. There are other arguments in favour of going down the consultancy road, and also some which point towards an in-house PR department. It is not a question of either/or. Some organizations rely entirely on their in-house capability, it is true. Others put all their PR in the hands of outside consultancies. Increasingly, there is a tendency to go for a blend of the two. It is not always easy to get the balance right.

Balance of PR power

In many ways, public relations consultancies bear the same relationship to their clients as any other suppliers do. They are expected to provide what the client needs, at the right time, of the required quality, for an agreed price and under mutually acceptable conditions. Those are some of the similarities.

The big difference is that as well as working *for* the client (like any other supplier) the PR consultancy also works *with* the client. That means becoming involved in business policies and objectives. It means creating and developing a partnership of shared values, common interests and joint commitment.

This can lead to serious difficulties and tensions for in-house PR departments, who tend to feel—often with some justification—that the outsiders are entrusted with strategic issues while the insiders are limited to day-to-day tactics and the run of the mill detail of relations with the media.

The problem is real. It is important enough for the leading PR magazine in the United Kingdom to express concern that 'the balance of power between in-house departments and consultancies should attain some measure of equilibrium if the industry is to develop at a more stable rate'.[3]

In a major editorial, the magazine *PR Week* went on to point out that 'in-house departments need to start becoming mini-consultancies, adopting universal standards of excellence and efficiency, attaining more power within their organisations'.[4]

Power will always be vested in those who shape strategy. In organizations that really understand PR, the in-house departments are as heavily involved in advising on policy and strategy as the outside consultancies are, although viewpoints may be different. The essential thing is to understand the respective advantages and disadvantages of in-house and of consultancy.

In-house pros and cons

The great plus of in-house PR departments lies in the general area of knowledge and experience. They should have a much firmer grasp of company policy than any outside consultancy could hope to achieve, even over a quite long period of close cooperation. In-house departments ought not to need to climb a long policy-learning curve; if they do, they are wrongly positioned within the organization.

Hand in hand with understanding policy is the understanding of how the business works. Here again, although consultancies can and do acquire a quite remarkable knowledge of what makes their clients tick, it would perhaps take an uneconomic period for them to match up to the in-house understanding of the clockwork of their own particular enterprise.

Policy grasp and business understanding presuppose a close working relationship with all strands of management and ready accessibility to the top level.

Consultancies work hard at developing this: in-house departments should already have it as a matter of course. The fact that these positions are sometimes reversed—with the consultancy on the inside track, nearer the centre than the in-house people—can be a source of tension and friction.

A source of strength for in-house PR departments is that their only corporate commitment is to their own company and its corporate objectives. Consultants have a duty of care to their clients, of course, and a professional code of practice, but that is not quite the same thing. After all, they do have corporate objectives of their own that are nothing to do with the client's.

Finally, the individuals in the in-house department have personal and career objectives which generally speaking are bound up with those of their organization, harmonizing rather than conflicting with them. The same is not necessarily true of outside consultants.

On the negative side, in-house PR departments can be too close to day-to-day problems. They can be so involved in firefighting that they cannot see what the real problems and opportunities are. They may not have the range of analytical skills needed to identify them nor the different set of skills necessary to the development of satisfactory solutions. Certainly it would be an unusual in-house capability that could provide all the skills and experience required in the implementation of PR programmes of any complexity.

And even if they know what to do and are capable of doing it, all too often in-house departments do not have the necessary clout.

Consultancy pros and cons

To a large extent, consultancy strengths are in-house weaknesses, and vice versa. Perhaps the single most important selling proposition consultancies have to offer is time. Time to look long, hard and deep at their clients, their publics and the relationships between them. Time to collect information and to probe into problem areas. Time to analyse reputations and evaluate images. Time to question, to examine, to measure. In fact, time to think.

All the best PR consultants work hard for their clients and so they should. But working hard is not at all the same thing as working long hours. Indeed, you could argue that the harder the consultancies work, the fewer hours they need to put in. That is efficient thinking.

One result of the emphasis on thinking is that consultancies can be particularly good at taking the long view, over a timespan of several years. They put considerable effort and ability into helping clients develop and sustain mutual understanding with their various publics: in short, to explain rather than explain away.

Nevertheless, clients do also have short-term problems and sudden crises. Here, the advantage of consultancies is that they can provide additional resources at short notice for the short periods necessary. Not that these resources need to be short-term only. Consultancy skills and experience, both in depth and range, are available to the client when and where needed, from analysing problems and identifying opportunities, through programme planning and creativity, to the carrying out of any and every PR programme detail.

Because consultancies normally deal with a range of client organizations, often over a range of industries or sectors, they have seen most of the game before. They can draw on parallel experience, use standard methodology, avoid obvious mistakes, and come up with tried and tested solutions in a surprisingly short space of time.

Conversely, they might be tempted to sell a client off-the-peg PR when it is really bespoke that is needed. Clients have found themselves at the receiving end of propositions so obviously word-processed that they carried no more conviction than 'personalized' mailshots for secondary double glazing that spell your name right but have not troubled to find out that only three months ago you installed factory-sealed integral double glazed windows through the entire house. Result—not only no sale now but no future business either.

One other major advantage should always be maximized when employing PR consultancies: the advantage of objectivity. Their cool, detached, impartial viewpoint cuts across inter-departmental rivalries and internal wrangles. They are well placed to steer clear of personality clashes within client organizations, although they should be aware of the more serious of these. They are able to notice what their clients may not wish to see. They can say what their clients may not wish to hear. This necessary if sometimes uncomfortable independence has two hinges—trust and information. If clients are niggardly with either, the usefulness of the consultancy is limited. But where the information is open and when trust is freely given, the objectivity of consultancies is an invaluable strength.

Some other reasons for using consultancies

There are occasions when an organization knows perfectly well what it has to do but wants to put the responsibility or blame for it on somebody else. For example, when the British arm of an American company was told by Head Office to cut its PR department staff by 30 per cent, consultants were called in to do a PR audit. This showed conclusively that the in-house department was not delivering value for money, and that a leaner, more specialized, operation was required. A detailed structure was drawn up and job specifications drafted. Within a year, by natural wastage, a ban on recruitment and the departure of some staff to new employers, the required reduction had been achieved. This helped to reduce bad feeling, and what opprobrium there was was directed at the consultants, which is what they were paid for.

Another role for consultants can be to disguise the true nature of what the client organization is up to. For instance, a foreign country wishing to secure or safeguard favourable UK legislation on trade issues affecting its interests, might conceivably commission a public relations consultancy, ostensibly because of its track record in international PR, whereas in truth it was because some MPs who specialize in trade matters happened to be on the board of the consultancy. (This is a purely hypothetical example and is not meant to imply that such a thing has ever actually happened.)

Perhaps less controversial, though no less questionable, is the cosmetic use of consultants. Hard pressed line managers might be seen to respond to adverse customer comment by calling in PR consultants—not to identify the reasons for the complaints, still less to suggest operational changes to meet consumer needs, but to show that something is being done.

That is a form of window dressing. How then does one describe the commissioning of consultants as status symbols? There is a kind of company culture—rare but not rare enough—where the presence of consultants is thought somehow to confer kudos on those to whom the consultants report. As often as not, inflated self-esteem is the only real result.

When all the arguments for and against have been worked through, a potential client will be able to answer the key question: 'Do you need a consultancy?' If yes, there are several more key questions to ask.

- What sort of consultancy?
- How can the field be narrowed?
- Who gets shortlisted?
- What kind of competitive pitching?
- Which consultancy wins?
- How much will the budget be?
- Who will do what?
- What monitoring and review procedures?

One more question will arise sooner or later:

- What do you do when it's time to part company?

What sort of consultancy?

Once a client has opted to use a consultancy, either on its own or teamed with an in-house department, the immediate decisions to be made are the following:

1. One consultancy or several?
2. What type of consultancy?
3. What level of service?

It is usually simplest, and often more effective, to have only one consultancy to do everything that is required. But it is perfectly feasible to employ more—say, one for advice and another to put the advice into effect.

Alternatively, a large client could appoint a particular consultancy to handle its international PR, another to deal with national issues and others for regional or technical PR.

Some firms might want a lobbying consultancy specifically for their relations with central or local government, and quite another for customer or consumer relations.

It is not unusual for big organizations in the private sector, or major government departments with a mixture of public responsibilities, to engage different advertising agencies for different advertising campaigns. The same is increasingly true for PR companies, though central government has never yet admitted to employing outside consultants on public relations.

The PR consultancy business is in some ways a two-tier system. Commenting on the UK top 150, *Management Today* pointed out that 'the top 15 consultancies earn more than the other 135 put together'.[5] More recent figures suggest that the top 10 earn more than the other 140 put together and the top three more than the sum of the rest of the top 50. That probably does not mean much to clients and potential clients. From their point of view there are three main types of consultancy.

At one extreme are the major firms—perhaps nine or ten altogether—who are the real heavyweights, including publicly quoted companies and multi-million pound businesses. All of these top consultancies have incomes in excess of £5 million, and some well in excess. They probably employ 100 staff on average and they offer a fully international, comprehensive PR service, in strength and in depth. Their overheads are necessarily high. So are their fees. £100 000 might buy you £25 000 of staff time. If you need this size of consultancy, whether for one special project or for a limited period of time or for sustained compaigns, there is a reasonable choice. Not all are based in London.

Next to the very top of the league, there are probably another 30 or so consultancies with operating revenues between £1 million and £5 million, and up to 100 staff (Figure 11.1). Let's call them the cruiser weights, or the 'lighter heavies'.[6]

At the opposite extreme, there is the one-man band—or very often the one-woman band. They do not have the resources to manage long-running campaigns for major clients, though their advice can be very valuable. Many of these very small consultancies, especially the very new ones, were set up by people who only a short time before were directing or managing PR divisions in very large organizations. The change of scale can be traumatic and certainly generates difficulties of adjustment. But these problems belong to the consultancies, not to the clients.

Often working from home, using their own answerphone and word processor,

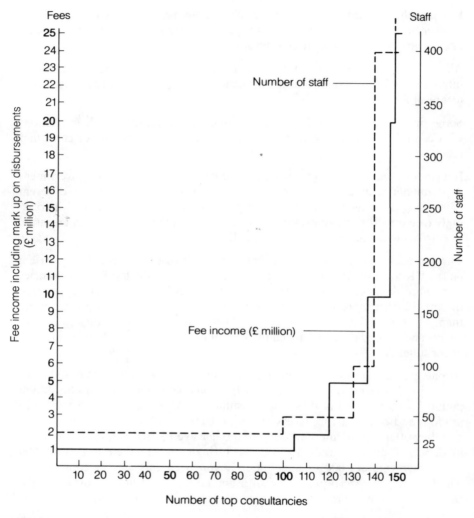

Figure 11.1 Fee income and staff numbers of top 150 PR consultancies in the United Kingdom

and perhaps sharing photocopying and facsimile machines with other local firms, they are not necessarily lightweight consultancies. The aphorism 'we didn't have any money, so we had to think' might have been coined specifically for them. They can be especially useful for one-off jobs; to relieve overloads; as trainers; for niche PR; and in a host of ways for which it would be hopelessly uneconomic to employ a large consultancy. For dedication and ingenuity they are hard to beat.

Somewhere between these two extremes sit the specialists. For example, there are PR companies specializing in

- business-to-business
- charities
- the City
- engineering
- fashion
- financial products
- food and drink
- hi-tech
- home interest

- leisure industries
- parliamentary
- pharmaceuticals
- regional
- scientific
- sponsorships
- tourism
- toy industry
- training

That list is by no means exhaustive.

Provided their specialism is exactly what you need, the specialist PR consultancies give probably the best value for money. However, if you go outside the sphere they have made their own, you tend to find that they lack both the power and the comprehensiveness of the really big consultancies. Nor do they necessarily have the agility and 100 per cent commitment of the really small ones.

Clearly, the better that clients can define their own requirements, the more likely they are to know what kind of consultancy they are looking for. When the 'possibles' have been identified, the next step is to reduce the number down to the most suitable, and put these into your 'credentials' list.

Narrowing the field: The credentials pitch

Perhaps a consultancy or two have already approached you, through a mailshot or in some other way. If the initiative was well researched and professionally carried out—in other words, if you liked what they had to say and the way that they said it—you have some obvious candidates for your 'credentials' pitches.

Either because you found out for yourself, or because you were tipped off, you may have become aware of the work of a particular consultancy. Your reaction could be favourable enough to suggest that you have got another possible contender for your business. On the other hand, the opposite may be true, in which case there would be one fewer to take into account.

Consulting the appropriate trade and professional organizations is a popular way of identifying the kind of consultancy you want on your credentials list. The Public Relations Consultants Association has a computer-based referral system now widely used by potential clients. The Institute of Public Relations is another obvious source, while the Institute of Marketing can also be useful. At least one consultancy specializes in advising on the selection of consultancies to meet specific client needs. Help in finding out about freelances and individual PR practitioners can be forthcoming from the Public Relations Division of the Institute of Journalists and from the National Union of Journalists (see Appendix D).

Publications which are good sources of information include *Hollis Press & PR Annual*, *PR Week*, *Campaign*, *Marketing* and *Marketing Week* (see Appendix A). Business directories such as *Yellow Pages* and *Directline* should not be overlooked.

For local contacts you can call on a variety of small firms advisory and information services, chambers of commerce and trade, business clubs, colleges, etc.

But probably the most common way in which a potential client makes contact with a potential consultancy is through the personal recommendation of someone whose opinion is valued, and who has direct experience of that consultancy's work.

For larger PR campaigns it would be desirable to aim for a credentials pitch by perhaps half a dozen consultancies. Four would be a good number for smaller campaigns. How do you get them?

The best thing is to ask them. A telephone call will do, explaining in very broad terms what your intentions are, and what you are looking for from a consultancy, and when, and asking on a no-commitment basis if they would be interested in being considered. You will almost certainly be asked two very important questions: What sort of budget are you talking about? Who else are you talking to? On the first of these, there is a lot of controversy, which we'll discuss later. On the second, you may reveal as much or as little as you wish. There is a lot to be said for complete openness. They'll probably find out soon enough anyway.

You will want to know who owns each consultancy and who runs it—and also if there are any connections or affiliations you might find embarrassing. How long have they been in business? What is their financial standing and their professional reputation? What jobs have they actually done? Who are their clients? What does the consultancy think it has to offer you? The manner and content of the consultancies' response can tell you a lot about them. So can the opinion of their clients.

Ask each consultancy to make a credentials pitch on its own premises. This is its opportunity to get on your short list and so be invited to make a competitive pitch. They should want to show you examples of their work and explain why and how it was successful. Make sure you give them every opportunity to do so.

Do they inspire confidence? What is their standing within their own organization? Do they seem responsive and flexible? Are they a good match for your own team? What sort of back-up do they have? Do you feel you can work with them? Do they feel they can work with you?

Always write formally to those who have been shortlisted, seeking confirmation that they wish to present competitively. When you are sure you have enough suitable contenders, close the books and write immediately to those who are not being asked to complete. These rejection letters should be friendly, leaving open the possibility of further contact. Everybody who makes it to the credentials pitch stage is potentially a future contender for a competitive pitch.

By these methods, and any others you find effective, you should end up with the two or three consultancies you are convinced can deliver what you want. Other things being equal, any one of these would be just right.

Competitive presentations

But other things hardly ever are equal and it is on the inequalities—that is the few differences, not the many similarities—that final judgement is made.

This is the time to re-define and refine your requirements. You will want to talk to each consultancy about your objectives and meet the people who would actually be working with you to attain them.

It is important they all start from exactly the same brief, with exactly the same written information and with exactly the same opportunities for further discussion and questions. If some show more initiative than others in looking into your organization and your needs, there is no need to make the results of that available to all. In fact, it would be wrong to do so. Allow the smart ones to keep whatever competitive edge they can secure for themselves by their exercise of initiative.

The brief should describe your client organization—what it is for and what it does; how it is structured; its policies and operational objectives; its key publics (customers or electorate; own staff or neighbouring community; overseas buyers or domestic investors and so on); how you want each of those publics to behave; your competitive position; indeed all the things that define your organization and its reason for being.

Following that, the next section of the brief should explain what public relations questions the consultancy should address itself to, and what the presentation is intended to achieve. Attach any relevant reports or other publications.

Finally, the brief should spell out who will be making the selection, on what basis and when.

You should not expect to get any really usable solutions out of competitive presentations. It is unreasonable to expect it and you should be very sceptical of any consultancy suggesting otherwise. The necessary investment in time and money would be unaffordable, even if practicable. After all, you would want your consultancy to be as cost-conscious as you are, wouldn't you?

Consultancies compete on a whole range of common issues, from quality of service to effectiveness of results. In addition, they compete on specialisms, from international capability to political lobbying. If they are giving their clients what they want, then within reason consultancies are not competing on *price*. But unless they are competitive on *costs*, they will find it hard to compete on anything else.

What a competitive presentation can tell you is how well the consultancies have researched you, their potential client; their grasp of your commercial/industrial/

political objectives; how they see your problems and opportunities; and what the main constraints are.

They have to demonstrate perception and understanding; intelligence and creativity; expertise and relevant experience; resources and commitment; all of which should lead to the inescapable conclusion that they are the best consultancy for your particular needs.

Some consultancies offer to produce a complete set of proposals, including strategy, plans and programmes, on the understanding that if they are not selected, the client pays a nominal fee of, say, £1000. This is a very dubious practice. Done properly, the true cost of such a set of proposals would be more than the nominal fee. Nor is it probable that the work could be done properly in the time available without affecting work for existing clients, who ought to be the prime concern of the consultancy. Better to leave all that to the consultancy which is actually appointed.

Selecting the consultancy

During the three weeks between the briefing and the competitive presentation, clients should not expect shortlisted consultancies to leave them in peace. On the contrary, there is bound to be a fair amount of interaction, with exploratory visits to be arranged, supplementary questions to be pursued, guidance to be given, misunderstandings to be cleared away and more foreplay to be indulged in. Presentations do not occur only on presentation day. They start from day one.

Equally, your evaluating faculties will not be suspended. From the moment you decide to put a consultancy on the short list you will find yourself making small judgements, often unconsciously, so that when selection day arrives, you will already have perceptions about the contenders which you almost certainly did not have when you first decided they were in the running.

It may help to clear your mind of any prejudice, one way or the other, if you write a note on your perceptions and expectations of each contender. It would certainly be of great assistance to your colleagues who will be helping you to make the selection. Be as objective as you can when comparing the consultancies' competitive pitches with each other. You will want to test their perceptions and analyses against your own. Be tough but flexible. Their vision of what is needed may be not only different from yours, but better.

Make certain that the people from the consultancy who would actually run the contract are present and take at least some part in the presentation. It does not have to be a leading part. Many consultancies field their best presenters to make the pitch and win the business. That is understandable and perfectly acceptable as long as they say so and also give you every opportunity to question and talk to the team that would be planning and doing the work after the contract has been signed. Your own knowledge of PR tactics and techniques can help you to separate the substance of a competitive pitch from its presentational aspects.

It could be helpful to insist that all the competitive pitches are made in the same format. It makes comparison so much easier and, intelligently devised, need not be an unreasonable constraint.

It is most important that your selection team should be exactly the same for all the presentations. Ideally, that team should actually make, and be fully accountable for, the final choice. That is the fairest way, and if it means that the chairman or managing director or secretary of state has to sit through three (or even more) presentations, so be it. PR is important enough to justify it.

In practice this is not always possible—that's an understatement—and the selection team could find themselves making a presentation about the presentations; and making a recommendation for somebody else to act on.

A different route for arriving at a shortlist and making your final choice is by asking an independent specialist consultant to advise you on appropriate PR consultancy resources. The practice, which is not at all uncommon in the United States, is only just beginning in the United Kingdom. PR Selection 'conduct a thorough review of a client's corporate or marketing objectives, identify communications targets, issues and priorities, and prepare the public relations brief' before suggesting a short list of consultancies.[7]

Whatever way the selecting is done, do let the contenders know when judgement day will be, so that their suspense time is limited. When you have made your choice, lose no time in telling everybody. Be courteous to the unsuccessful ones—tell them yourself, on the telephone or in person, that they haven't got the job. They are bound to ask why not. Tell them as honestly as you can. It will help them and do you no harm at all.

The brief and the budget

After the competitive pitches are over and done with, a new position arises which requires yet more work.

A certain consultancy has persuasively shown that it is the right one for your particular needs. Now comes the task of describing those needs specifically and convincingly. It is to everyone's advantage for the chosen consultancy and the client to work together on this vital stage of analysis.

Never be too proud to seek the help of the consultancy in preparing the brief. It has to satisfy both sides so it makes good sense for both sides to be involved in shaping it.

A good consultancy will always want to question many of its client's assumptions and may come up with something quite different, even surprising. Honest disagreement is but one aspect of the objectivity and independence which consultancies ought to offer and clients to demand. 'Be wary of those who agree too readily with all you have said' was the wise counsel of the Manpower Services Commission, who rarely had that problem.[8]

This kind of brief can never be too full or too detailed. Here is another approximation to a golden guideline, and it applies just as much to in-house PR divisions as to outside consultancies.

The guideline is 'Tell them all and tell them early'. It works not only at the briefing stage but at every stage. The more that PR people know, and the sooner they know it, the better job they can do—and will do. Understandably enough, one question consultants are always asking is 'what is the budget?'—at the credentials stage; before the competitive pitch; at the briefing proper. Three distinct responses are possible.

You could reply 'This is what I've got to spend on my PR consultancy contract. What can you do for the money?'. In this case, don't be surprised if you get a set of proposals that costs every penny.

Or you could say 'Here is my ballpark figure for all communications. Tell me how much of that is needed on PR, and why'. This ought to produce some interesting arguments on the pros and cons of PR as against other promotions.

The third response is to say 'When we have agreed the objectives, you tell me what it will cost to attain them. Then we'll have a dialogue about the budget.'

The matter needs to be resolved very early in the client/consultancy relationship. Whichever way you choose, you will want to make sure that the consultancy is comfortable working that way. Above all, set up a budget control system and use it. Budgeting was explored in some detail in Chapter 8. There would be little point in repeating that here.

What does bear repeating, over and over again, is that budgets are means to an end and not ends in themselves. The true aim is not keeping to budget but keeping to programme.

Some of the issues addressed by the brief could include your

- *philosophy*, for example mission in life; moral, religious or political stance; what kind of organization yours wants to be; the 'musts' and 'must nots' that really matter;
- *position*, for example market share; perceived status; relationship to competitors; what kind of business you are actually in;
- *structure*, for example how your company is put together; how it operates; what kind of outfit it really is.

The central part of the brief is about the changes that are required for the enterprise to survive, develop, shift, contract or grow; what the obstacles are; where the opportunities lie; what problems have to be solved; what results are to be obtained; what the business plan is to achieve all this. The word 'business' is here used to include the affairs of public and private sectors, non-profit-making organizations, governments, charities, etc., and not simply in the sense of buying and selling in commerce or trade.

The brief should conclude with a section on the role of the consultancy, relationships with you, the client, methods and procedures including reporting lines, responsibility, accountability and arrangements for payment. The consultancy must be absolutely clear about what is expected of it in terms of results and how they will be measured.

Typically, a consultancy in an advisory role might be briefed as follows:

- To analyse your company's strengths and weaknesses.
- To identify problems and opportunities.
- To agree objectives.
- To recommend strategy.
- To design programmes to carry out the strategy, attain the objectives, solve the problems, exploit the opportunities and so meet the needs.
- To provide information on methods and costs for implementing the programmes.
- To advise on the best ways of achieving and evaluating the above.
- To specify the timescales.

In addition, the consultancy may also be asked, in an implementation role, to put its own recommendations into effect. But this is a quite separate requirement which could perfectly well be handled by someone else and sometimes is. For example, your own in-house PR capacity may be used to carry out the programme. If this is the case, then the advisory consultancy has a clear duty to ensure that you know what in-house resources and abilities are needed to do the job successfully.

The golden guideline is that the consultancy should only do what it can do better and more cost-effectively than you can. Success is to be judged by your yardstick—that is the extent to which you are happy with the outcome. Three benefits arise from this:

1. Client satisfaction.
2. Consultancy satisfaction.
3. Improved reputation of the PR business.

The consultancy's message to the client

According to Barry Leggetter, joint Managing Director of Countrywide Communications:

> Most consultancies use a system similar to that used by legal, accountancy or management consulting firms in relation to costs. Costs consist of two elements:

A   Consultancy fees
    These are charged to cover the time input of our consultants in
    carrying out a programme for an individual client. Every agreed
    programme is accurately costed according to the executive time
    required to arrive at a total fee.

B   Operations costs
    These include all expenses incurred in carrying out the agreed
    programme, typically travel, print, postage, hire of venues or
    equipment, press release production and distribution, press cut-
    ting services and the like.

As clients, what a consultancy would ask you to remember is that the
basis of the agreement is based on the sale of time.

Consultancies commonly use a multiplier approach in costing
programmes.

Research suggests that an executive has to handle between 3.5 and 4
times his salary, to properly cover all costs and deliver an operating
profit of 20 per cent to the consultancy.

In this way the multiplier covers salary, office space, secretarial
support and so on.

Our management skill, as people running a consultancy, is therefore
to sell time in the most efficient way.

Our skill in the client/consultancy relationship is to make sure the client
has a clear understanding of what the programme fee is actually buying.

And just as important, an acknowledgement by the client that if he
asks for something to be carried out outside that programme it
represents extra work and therefore extra fee. To reprise: we are not
selling products—we are selling time.

If a client continually changes the agreed programme, it can mean that
the original programme targets are not met—because the consultancy
has been taken off the agreed course.[9]

In 1990 Countrywide Communications, the Consultancy of the Year, charged
fees that covered executive time, all overheads and 20 per cent profit. Rates
ranged from £50 per hour for an account executive to £150 for a director. *Ad
hoc* charges began at £60.

Smaller consultancies, such as Smythe Dorward Lambert, charged around £120
an hour for directors and £65 and £85 for consultants.[10]

More generally, if you assume a working day of 7 hours and a working year of
220 days, that makes the hourly salary of a £35 000 a year PR director £22.73.

Table 11.1   Effect of multipliers on salary costs

	Per year	Per day	Per hour	Per min.
	£15 000	£68.18	£9.74	16p
× 2	£30 000	£136.36	£19.48	33p
× 3	£45 000	£204.54	£29.22	49p
× 4	£60 000	£272.73	£38.96	65p
	£35 000	£159.09	£22.73	38p
× 2	£70 000	£318.18	£45.45	76p
× 3	£105 000	£477.27	£68.18	£1.14
× 4	£140 000	£636.36	£90.91	£1.51
	£50 000	£227.27	£32.47	54p
× 2	£100 000	£454.54	£64.93	£1.08
× 3	£150 000	£681.82	£97.38	£1.62
× 4	£200 000	£909.09	£129.87	£2.16

In a very small firm (overheads say 100 per cent) the salary cost becomes £45.45 an hour. In a somewhat larger concern (overheads say 200 per cent) the hourly cost rises to £68.18. A major consultancy's overheads and the need for reasonable profit push the salary cost to at least £90.91 an hour, and possibly much more.

You are likely to have a mix of people at different salary levels working on your account. Table 11.1 shows how their salary costs might work out, using multipliers of 2, 3, and 4 respectively.

Managing the contract

The same principles of management that were discussed in Chapter 1 apply here. Contracts with consultants can be managed successfully only by *consent* and by *results*.

Clients naturally want their consultancies to be effective. Ensuring that this happens is in their own hands. *Financial Times* journalist David Churchill predicts 'What will probably be the only effective means of making public relations consultancies more effective in the years ahead . . . will be the pressure that you— the client—can put on them to communicate effectively on your behalf'.[11]

Clients and consultancies should behave as partners in a highly personal, interactive and mutually beneficial relationship. Each partner has to understand fully the expectations and needs of the other, reviewing them regularly and verifying them frequently.

As far as practicable, those expectations and needs should be the same for both, so that client and consultancy are equal stakeholders. Where this cannot be so, the differences between them have to be clearly defined, precisely communicated and mutually accepted.

Rather like partners in a law firm (though without the 'all-for-one and one-for-all' legal liability) the partners in a client/consultancy relationship should consider themselves each responsible at the highest levels and to the limit of their abilities for the success of the partnership.

Adele Hargreaves, Managing Director of Attitudes PR, feels strongly that 'Senior management should not only devise an agreed strategy but be responsible for implementing it . . . There should be no reserves or substitutes; everyone should be part of the "A" team . . .' She also warns about the over-willingness of some consultancies to overload or overpromise: 'No agency can properly service its clients when executives are committed to seven, eight or even more accounts simultaneously'.[12]

Do be quite clear that while consultancies are responsible for managing their own businesses they have no responsibility whatever for managing yours unless you specifically instruct them to.

There has to be effective communication, and that means regular and frequent contact, whether in one-to-one meetings, in groups, or by telephone, letter, fax, etc. What you are after is a constant two-way flow of information, questions, ideas, problems, challenges, trial solutions and so on.

But this intellectual and creative dialogue works best within a disciplined framework, like this:

1. Specify and agree the results you need and when you need them.
2. Agree how the results will be measured.
3. Be absolutely clear about reporting lines, responsibilities, authorities and accountabilities.
4. Require contact reports after every meeting or other contact, setting out the action points, timetables, deadlines and who does what.
5. Call for regular situation reports quite independently of the contact reports, to review progress, monitor costs, and agree any necessary changes in direction, emphasis, etc.
6. Wherever possible, use numbers in the expression of what is needed to be done and in measuring what is actually done.
7. Be fully aware of the PRCA Professional Charter (see Appendix B) and ensure that your consultancy, whether a member of PRCA or not, follows the general spirit of the charter.
8. If either side is not satisfied with the way things are going, say so. Agree what corrective action is needed and allow a reasonable time for the necessary improvement to show. It is in everybody's interests to develop and sustain a lasting relationship.
9. If still not satisfied, consider dissolving the partnership, subject to any agreed period of notice.
10. Remember, clients can fire consultancies. But consultancies can also fire clients.

Checklist

1. *Pros and cons*

In-house	**Consultancy**
Advantages	*Advantages*
Policy grasp	Thinking time
Understanding the business	Long vision
Close to management	Extra resource
Corporate commitment	Range of skills
Career commitment	Broad/varied experience
Availability	Depth of support
	Objectivity
Disadvantages	*Disadvantages*
Too close to problems	Unfamiliar with policy
Narrow vision	Unfamiliar with business
Limited skills	Cost
Limited experience	Focus on inputs
Lack of clout	Window-dressing

2. *Types of consultancy*

Major	**Specialist**	**Small**
Full service	Regional knowledge	Low budget
International	Industry knowledge	Creative
Big scale	Audience knowledge	Total commitment
Wide experience	Narrow experience	Limited resources
High cost		

3. *Information sources for credentials pitch*

Approaches to consultancies

Trade and professional organizations

- PRCA; IPR; IoM; IoJ; NUJ

Publications

- *PR Week*; *Campaign*; *Marketing*
- *Marketing Week*; *UK Press Gazette*
- *Hollis Press and PR Annual*; *IPR Register*
- directories, for example *Yellow Pages* or *Directline*
- trade and business press

Local organizations

- chambers of commerce/trade; small firms advisory services
- business clubs; colleges

Personal recommendation

- satisfied clients

Exploratory visits to consultancies

- people
- premises
- resources
- atmosphere

4. *Shortlisting*
   Number required on shortlist.
   Number willing to quote.
   Consultancy owners/managers/affiliations.
   Financial standing.
   Professional reputation.
   Client list.
   Track record.
   Responsiveness.
   Acceptance and rejection letters.

5. *Competitive presentations*
   Brief
   Part 1   Client's business; organization; policies; objectives; publics; personnel; environment
   Part 2   Need for consultancy; issues to be addressed; purpose of presentations; what you will be judging on
   Part 3   Who will make the final decision? On what basis? Where? When?

6. *Selection*
   - Level of interest during three-week run-up.
   - Credentials and credibility of team.
   - Consultancy's research into client.
   - Understanding of client's business, policy, objectives.
   - Initial grasp of PR opportunities and problems.
   - Standard format for all presentations.
   - Objective comparison of consultants' performance.
   - Meet the 'A' team.
   - Tell the winners quickly—and the losers—in person.
   - Explain why the unsuccessful contenders failed.

7. *Brief and budget*
   - Budget fixed in advance?
   - Ballpark figure?
   - Task-based budget?
   - Budgetary control systems.
   - Client's philosophy; position in relation to competitors.
   - Structure and organization.
   - Specific business problems and opportunities.
   - Specific business objectives.
   - Business strategy.
   - Business plan.
   - Timescale.
   - Measurement of business results.

8. *Response to brief*
   - Analysis of client's PR needs; strengths; weaknesses.
   - Specific PR problems and opportunities.

- Specific PR strategy.
- Recommended PR programmes.
- Methods of measuring PR results.
- Client's acceptance of consultancy's proposals.
- Agreement on budget.
- Decision on who carries out the programme.

9. *Managing the contract*
- Work as a partnership.
- Specify required results, numerically where possible.
- Agree how results will be measured.
- Clarify reporting lines, responsibilities, authorities, accountabilities.
- Contact reports.
- Situation reports.
- Budget control and tracking procedures.
- Regular review procedures.
- React promptly.

10. *Termination*
- Maintain a fruitful partnership between client and consultancy for as long as practicable.
- Recognize that no relationship lasts for ever.
- Discuss any areas of dissatisfaction.
- Allow every opportunity for improvement.
- If still dissatisfied, part company.
- Do it amicably, but get it over with quickly.
- Mutual goodwill between ex-consultancies and ex-clients is a valuable asset.

11. *BIM guidelines*
At least 20 of the BIM guidelines are particularly relevant to client consultancy relationships:

- Promote effective communications; minimize misunderstandings; promote good relations; consult and communicate clearly; keep senior colleagues advised; ensure that all public communications are true and not misleading.
- Make proper use of resources; accept accountability for own and subordinates' work; direct all efforts towards success; take full account of the ideas and suggestions of others; ensure that all are aware of their duties and responsibilities.
- Ensure that consultancy's requirements are properly considered; state terms of transactions clearly; keep consultants informed of changes, development and actions affecting the contract; ensure open competition; respect confidentiality; develop continuing and satisfying relationships; refuse bribes or favours; work to agreed procedures, terms, quality, times, prices, etc.[13]

Sources and references

1. John Brandon. Where consultants fall down. *Management Today*, May 1988.
2. ibid.
3. Hanging in the balance. *PR Week*, 8 December 1988.
4. ibid.
5. Joan Plachta. Does sweet talk pay? *Management Today*, March 1990.
6. Stephen Park and Matt Fearnley. UK top 150 consultancies. *PR Week*, 24 May 1990.
7. Nicola McLaughlin. *About PR Selection*. April 1990.
8. *Choosing and Using a Training Consultant*. MSC handout, January 1986.
9. Barry Leggetter. *Choosing and using a consultancy*. Presentation at Interact seminar, January 1990.
10. *PR Week*. July 1989.
11. David Churchill (ed.). *Directors guide to choosing and using a PR consultancy*. The Director Publications Ltd., 1988.
12. Adele Hargreaves. We should all be in the A team. *PR Week*. 7 December 1989.
13. *BIM Guide to Good Management Practice*. British Institute of Management, 1990.

Further reading

These recommendations are in four categories:

1. Writers to look out for—people who usually say something useful.
2. Periodicals—a minimum list.
3. Directories and yearbooks—a representative selection.
4. Blockbusters—weighty in every sense.

1. Writers to look out for

PR, Marketing and Advertising
David Bernstein
Sam Black
Simon Broadbent
Hugh Davidson
Martyn Davis
Wayne Delozier
Jim Dunn
Norman Hart
Roger Haywood
Frank Jefkins
Philip Kotler
Stephen Morse
Reginald Watts

Management
John Adair
Igor Ansoff
Robert Appleby
Michael Armstrong
Tom Batley
Peter Drucker
Terry Farnsworth
Robert Heller
Anthony Jay
Bernard Katz
Henry Mintzberg
Michael Porter
George Steiner

2. Periodicals

W = weekly   M = monthly   Q = quarterly

Title	*Publisher*
Audio Visual (M)	EMAP MacLaren
Business (M)	Condé Nast/Financial Times
Campaign (W)	Haymarket Publications
Director (M)	The Director Publications
Economic Review (Q)	Philip Allan Publishers
Journalist's Week (W)	Maxwell Business Communications
MBA Review (Q)	Philip Allan Publishers
Management Today (M)	Haymarket Publications
Marketing (W)	Haymarket Publications
Marketing Week (W)	Centaur Communications
Media Week (W)	Maxwell Business Comunications
PR Week (W)	Haymarket Publications

Personnel Management (M)　　　Personnel Publications
Personnel Today (M)　　　　　Reed Business Publishing
Public Relations (M)　　　　　Institute of Public Relations
Sponsorship News (M)　　　　Charterhouse Business Publications
UK Press Gazette (W)　　　　Bouverie Publishing Co

3. Directories and yearbooks

Benn's Media Directory
BRAD—British Rate and Data
CEI Worldwide Conventions Yearbook
Editors Media Directories
Hollis Press & PR Annual
Institute of Sales Promotion Yearbook
Marketing and PR Guide
Marketing Director International
Marketing Executive Handbook
PIMS United Kingdom Media Director
PR Register (IPR)
Public Relations Yearbook (PRCA)

4. Blockbusters

Effective Public Relations
Cutlip, Center and Broom
Published by Prentice Hall, New York.

Management Consulting—a guide to the profession
Edited by Milan Kubr
Published by International Labour Office, Geneva.

Managers' Guidebook
Edited by Gerry Elliott
Published by Kluwer Publishing Limited, London.

Note　Other writers and titles are mentioned in Sources and References at the end of each chapter.

APPENDIX B

Professional practice

Like many others, the communications business has its various guidelines, codes of practice, professional charters, codes of standards and so on. Whatever they are called, they are not immutable. Indeed, if they are to be of real practical use, they must be able to change and adapt as circumstances change. However, all those published in this appendix were correct when the manuscript went to press.

Institute of Public Relations (IPR)
Code of Professional Conduct

By the act of accepting membership, all members of the Institute automatically subscribe to the Code. Infringements of the Code, on being brought to the attention of the Institute, are investigated. Members under investigation may be asked for explanations or to attend a meeting of the Professional Practices Committee where they can present their point of view in person. In extreme cases of abuse of the Code, members may have their membership and its privileges withdrawn. The Code itself is quite clear and specific and states:

1. Standards of Professional Conduct
A member shall have a positive duty to observe the highest standards in the practice of public relations. Furthermore a member has the personal responsibility at all times to deal fairly and honestly with his client, employer and employees, past or present, with fellow members, with the media of communication and above all else with the public.

2. Media of Communication
A member shall not engage in any practice which tends to corrupt the integrity of the media of communication.

3. Undisclosed Interests
A member shall have the duty to ensure that the actual interest of any organisation with which he may be professionally concerned is adequately declared.

4. Rewards to Holders of Public Office
A member shall not, with intent to further his interests (or those of his client or employer), offer or give any reward to a person holding public office if such action is inconsistent with the public interest.

5. Dissemination of Information
A member shall have a positive duty at all times to respect the truth and in this regard not to disseminate false or misleading information knowingly or recklessly and to use proper care to avoid doing so inadvertently.

6. Confidential Information

A member shall not disclose (except upon the order of a court of competent jurisdiction) or make use of information given or obtained in confidence from his employer, or client, past or present, for personal gain or otherwise.

7. Conflict of Interests

A member shall not represent conflicting interests but may represent competing interests with the express consent of the parties concerned.

8. Disclosure of Beneficial Financial Interests

A member with a beneficial financial interest in or from an organisation shall not recommend the use of that organisation, nor make use of its service on behalf of his client or employer, without declaring his interest.

9. Payment Contingent upon Achievements

A member shall not negotiate or agree terms with an employer or client which guarantee results beyond the member's direct control to achieve.

10. Employment of Holders of Public Office

A member who employs or is responsible for employing or recruiting a member of either House of Parliament, a member of the European Parliament or a person elected to public office, whether in a consultative or executive capacity, shall disclose this fact also the object and nature of the employment to the Executive Director of the Institute who shall enter it in a register kept for the purpose. A member of the Institute who himself falls into any of these categories shall be directly responsible for disclosing or causing to be disclosed to the Executive Director the same information as may relate to himself. (The register referred to in this clause shall be open to public inspection at the offices of the Institute during office hours.)

11. Injury to other Members

A member shall not maliciously injure the professional reputation of another member.

12. Reputation of the Profession

A member shall not conduct himself in a manner which is or is likely to be detrimental to the reputation of the Institute or the profession of public relations.

13. Upholding the Code

A member shall uphold the Code, shall co-operate with fellow members in so doing and in enforcing decisions on any matter arising from its application. If a member has reason to believe that another member has been engaged in practices which may be in breach of this Code, it shall be his duty first to inform the member concerned and then to inform the Institute if these practices do not cease. It is the duty of all members to assist the Institute to implement this Code, and the Institute will support any member so doing.

14. Other Professions

A member shall, when working in association with other professionals, respect the codes of other professions and shall not knowingly be party to any breach of such codes.

15. Professional Updating

A member shall be expected to be aware of, understand and observe this Code, any amendments to it and any other codes which shall be incorporated into this Code and to remain up-to-date with the content and recommendations of any guidance or practice papers as may be issued by the Institute and shall have a duty to take all reasonable steps to conform to good practice as expressed in such guidance or practice papers.

16. Instruction of Others

A member shall not knowingly cause or permit another person or organisation to act in a manner inconsistent with this Code or be a party to such action.

17. Interpreting the Code

In the interpretation of this Code, the Law of England shall apply.

Public Relations Consultants Association (PRCA)
PRCA Professional Charter

The Public Relations Consultancy Association Professional Charter is subscribed to by all its members (approximately 175 PR consultancies in the United Kingdom including most of the largest firms representing 85 per cent of fee income).

Potential clients should ensure, if using a consultancy that is not a member of PRCA, that the firm follows the general spirit of the PRCA Professional Charter.

A member firm shall
1. 1.1 have a positive duty to observe the highest standards in the practice of public relations. Furthermore a member has the responsibility at all times to deal fairly and honestly with clients, past and present, fellow members and professionals, the public relations profession, other professions, suppliers, intermediaries, the media of communication, employees, and above all else the public;

1.2 be expected to be aware of, understand and observe this code, any amendment to it, and any other codes which shall be incorporated into this code, and to remain up-to-date with the content and recommendations of any guidance or practice papers issued by the PRCA, and shall have a duty to conform to good practice as expressed in such guidance or practice papers.

1.3 uphold this code and co-operate with fellow members in so doing by enforcing decisions on any matter arising from its application. A member firm that knowingly causes or permits a member of its staff to act in a manner inconsistent with this code is party to such action and shall itself be deemed to be in breach of it. Any member of staff of a member firm who acts in a manner inconsistent with this code must be disciplined by the employer.

A member firm shall not:
1.4 engage in any practice nor be seen to conduct itself in any manner detrimental to the reputation of the Association or the reputation and interests of the public relations profession.

2. Conduct towards the public, the media and other professionals

A member firm shall:

2.1 conduct its professional activities with proper regard to the public interest;

2.2 have a positive duty at all times to respect the truth and shall not disseminate false or misleading information knowingly or recklessly, and to use proper care to avoid doing so inadvertently;

2.3 have a duty to ensure that the actual interest of any organisation with which it may be professionally concerned is adequately declared;

2.4 when working in association with other professionals, identify and respect the codes of these professions and shall not knowingly be party to any breach of such codes.

2.5 cause the names of all its directors, executives, and retained consultants who hold public office, are members of either House of Parliament, are members of Local Authorities or of any statutory organisation or body, to be recorded in the relevant section of the PRCA Register;

2.6 honour confidences received or given in the course of professional activity;

2.7 neither propose nor undertake any action which would constitute an improper influence on organs of government, or on legislation, or on the media of communication;

2.8 neither offer nor give, nor cause a client to offer or give, any inducement to persons holding public office or members of any statutory body or organisation who are not directors, executives or retained consultants, with intent to further the interests of the client if such action is inconsistent with the public interest.

3. Conduct towards clients

A member firm shall:

3.1 safeguard the confidence of both present and former clients and shall not disclose or use these confidences, to the disadvantage or prejudice of such clients or to the financial advantage of the member firm, unless the client has released such information for public use, or has given specific permission for its disclosure; except upon the order of a court of law;

3.2 inform a client of any shareholding or financial interest held by that firm or any member of that firm in any company, firm or person whose services it recommends;

3.3 be free to accept fees, commissions or other valuable considerations from persons other than a client, only provided such considerations are disclosed to the client;

3.4 shall list the names of its clients in the Annual Register of the Association;

3.5 be free to negotiate with a client terms that take into account factors other than hours worked and seniority of staff involved. These special factors, which are also applied by other professional advisers, shall have regard to all the circumstances of the specific situation and in particular to

a the complexity of the issue, case, problem or assignment, and the difficulties associated with its completion

b. the professional or specialised skills and the seniority levels of staff engaged, the time spent and the degree of responsibility involved

c. the amount of documentation necessary to be perused or prepared, and its importance

d. the place and circumstances where the assignment is carried out, in whole or in part

e. the scope, scale and value of the task and its importance as an issue or project to the client.

A member firm shall not:

3.6 misuse information regarding its client's business for financial or other gain.

3.7 use inside information for gain. Nor may a consultancy, its members or staff directly invest in their clients' securities without the prior written permission of the client and of the member's chief executive or chief financial officer or compliance officer.

3.8 serve a client under terms or conditions which might impair its independence, objectivity or integrity.

3.9 represent conflicting or competing interests without the express consent of clients concerned.

3.10 guarantee the achievement of results which are beyond the member's direct capacity to achieve or prevent.

3.11 invite any employee of a client advised by the member to consider alternate employment; (an advertisement in the press is not considered to be an invitation to any particular person).

4. Conduct towards colleagues

A member firm shall

4.1 adhere to the highest standards of accuracy and truth, avoiding extravagant claims or unfair comparisons and giving credit for ideas and words borrowed from others.

4.2 be free to represent its capabilities and services to any potential client, either on its own initiatives or at the behest of the client, provided in so doing it does not seek to break any existing contract or detract from the reputation or capabilities of any member consultancy already serving that client.

A member firm shall not

4.3 injure the professional reputation or practice of another member.

Association of Market Survey Organisations Summary of Code of Standards

AMSO is a voluntary association of companies of significant size engaged in market research work. Over two-thirds of all work carried out by market research practitioners in the United Kingdom is performed by AMSO members.

While the role of market research is to support and improve marketing activity it is not intended to be used for the direct creation of sales. AMSO member companies dissociate themselves from any research activity the sole or partial objective of which is to sell goods or services to informants.

A detailed Code of Standards is available on request. Its main points are given below.

The company may on occasions charge for submitting a proposal having previously informed a client. Charges will not normally be applied to responses to fixed specifications or invitations to submit cost-only information or quotations involving letters not exceeding two pages.

Proposals provided by a company remain the property of that company and their contents may not normally be revealed to third parties without the company's permission.

Unless there is an agreement to the contrary, the name of the client commissioning research and the findings of that research are confidential to the client.

The method of conducting a research project must be approved by the client in advance. Any substantial alteration to the proposed method during the course of the project, and the possible additional costs of such alteration, must also be approved by the client.

The market research techniques developed in a project are the property of the market research agency unless a specific agreement to the contrary is made.

All AMSO members work with a national field force of trained interviewers governed by an approved code of standards. Strict control is maintained over their performance by means of regional supervisors and random checks on individual interviewers.

Unless agreed to the contrary, completed questionnaires and other documents used in fieldwork, together with punched cards or any other electronic data record are the property of the research company; the company is entitled to destroy questionnaires one year, and any survey records two years, after presentation of results.

These records are kept against a client's possible future needs. He or she may obtain from the agency a duplicate set of completed questionnaires (which do not reveal the names of informants), or of punched cards or other electronic record provided the client shall bear the cost of preparing such duplicates.

The identity of informants is not normally revealed to clients or to any other third party. Where an informant is speaking not as a private individual but as the officer of an organisation, it may be desirable to list such organisations but they must not be related (even by implication) to any particular item of information. Every report issued by a member company indicates for whom and by whom the sample survey was conducted, the purpose of the survey, survey method, a definition of the population sampled, the size and nature of the sample, the number, type and geographical distribution of sampling points, the method by which the information was collected, the questions asked, the dates of the fieldwork and bases of all percentages.

Similar standards are applied to desk research based on published material.

Market survey reports are normally for use within the client's own organisation. If a wider circulation is required, the market research agency is entitled to be consulted and to approve the exact form of publication.

AMSO members are Registered Data Users as required under the Data Protection Act 1984 and operate within its relevant provisions.

Business Sponsorship Working Party
Guidelines for business sponsors of educational material

These guidelines were drawn up to assist sponsors in the production of educational material—written, visual and audio as well as learning aids such as competitions—and to tackle abuses. They were drafted by a working party, convened by the National Consumer Council, representing business, consumer interests, teachers' associations and local education authorities.

1. Sponsored material specifically for educational use should be clearly designated as such.

2. No implied or explicit sales message, exhortation to buy a product or service, merchandising slogan or other attempt to influence the purchasing decisions of children, or their families, should be included.

The name of the sponsor should be stated clearly and in a prominent place (for example, the front or back cover of publications or in the titles of videos or teaching packs). Trade names or logos should be used in these positions only to identify the sponsor with the material. Otherwise in text and illustrations, logos or trade names should be used sparingly and in a relevant context.

This does not preclude the reproduction of sales messages as examples of, for instance, advertising techniques or as part of case histories.

3. Under no circumstances should promotional material be presented as 'educational'.

Material which is promotional in content might accompany an educational pack. If so, it must be clearly identified.

4. There should be no attempt in educational material to state, imply or demonstrate that a particular product or service is superior to other similar products or services.

Where an educational purpose (oral hygiene, for example) is being promoted, it should be clearly stated that the benefits apply to the whole class of goods or services, not to an individual named product.

Illustration of the sponsor's own product or service should not be used in this context.

5. When purporting to give a balanced account of an issue, sponsors should accurately represent the broad range of informed opinion on the subject.

The presentation of an unambiguous case is preferable to spurious balance. It is, therefore, open to sponsors to put forward an argument on behalf of their industry or sector, providing it is made clear that only their own particular viewpoint is represented. The existence of contrary views should be courteously acknowledged. There is no obligation on the sponsor to argue the opposing case.

6. No unsolicited material should be distributed or direct-mailed to pupils.

7. Under no circumstances should sponsors leave samples of their product for pupils without the prior knowledge and express consent of the head teacher.

The right of head teachers and governors to control what is given to pupils must be respected.

8. In the preparation of all educational materials, sponsors should obtain advice from those actively involved in education or aware of current curricular needs. Where appropriate, sponsors should ensure that materials are tested by teachers in the classroom prior to their general release.

9. The materials should:

- carry some broad indication (for example, 'primary' or 'secondary') of the age range for which they are intended;
- be available, wherever possible, for local inspection by teachers before they are acquired by schools.

10. Material should be sensitive to the needs and expectations of all groups likely to receive it.

It is recognised that it may not always be possible to represent all minorities in each piece of resource material. Nevertheless, sponsors should at all times:

- recognise and project, through both text and illustrations, the broad range of activities and opportunities now open to both sexes and avoid sexual stereotyping;
- reflect as far as possible the races and cultures among the population of the UK and avoid racial stereotyping;
- recognise the problems and the potential of people with disabilities;
- take account of diverse family types;
- contain no express or implied prejudice in relation to politics, class or religion.

Sponsors should not only avoid prejudice but should aim positively to promote equality of opportunities. The promotion of self-esteem in each pupil should be the concern of all sponsors.

11. Educational material should carry the sponsor's name and the address and telephone number of the department responsible for receiving comments or complaints about it.

12. All material should show clearly the date of publication.

International PR groups and national associations

International groups

International Public Relations Association (IPRA)
IPRA Secretariat: 10 rue du Conseil-General 1205, Geneva, Switzerland
Letters to Case Postale 126, CH 1211, Geneva 20.
Telephone: 22910550. Telex: 428380 CRE CH. Roger Hayes FIPR, Gen. Sec.

Confédération Européenne des Relations Publiques (CERP)
General Secretary: Avenue du Rond-point 12, B1330 Rixensart, Belgium.
Telephone: (32) 02653 5239. UK: 081-674 9205.

Federation of African Public Relations Associations (FAPRA)
c/o Jesse Opembe, PO Box 30028, Nairobi, Kenya. Telephone: 29188.

Federation of Asian Public Relations Organisations (FAPRO)
c/o Samsoc Soegito, Perhumas, PO Box 2702/JKT Jakarta, Indonesia.

Inter American Federation of Public Relations Associations (FIARP)
Constitucion 2453, Pcia de Buenos Aires, Victoria 1644, Argentina.
Telephone: (54) 1-3120314

The Pacific Society of Public Relations Ltd
c/o GPO Box 2565, Hong Kong.

Pan Pacific Public Relations Federation
c/o Esko K Pajasalmi, PRESKO, GPO Box 1651, Bangkok, Thailand.

International Committee of Public Relations Consultancies Associations Ltd (ICO)
Secretary: Colin Thompson, FCA, Willow House, Willow Place, Victoria, London
SW1P 1JH. Telephone: 071-233 6026. Fax 071-828 4797

ICO represents over 400 individual member consultancies employing nearly 8000 people
in 12 member countries:

Belgium	Italy
Denmark	Netherlands
Finland	Norway
France	Sweden
Germany	Switzerland
Ireland	United Kingdom

Membership is open only to those countries where public relations consultancies are
represented by a national body, such as PRCA in the United Kingdom (see
Appendix D).

National PR associations

The following countries have their own public relations associations or institutes:*

Arab Republic of Egypt	Guyana	Norway
Argentina	Great Britain*	Panama (Republic of)
Australia	Greece*	Paraguay
Austria*	Hong Kong	Peru
Bangladesh	India	Philippines
Belgium*	Indonesia	Portugal*
Bolivia	Iran	Singapore
Brazil	Ireland*	Spain*
Canada	Israel	S. Africa (Republic of)
Chile	Italy*	Sweden*
China (People's Republic of)	Japan	Switzerland*
Columbia	Kenya	Tanzania
Costa Rica	Lebanon	Trinidad & Tobago
Cyprus*	Luxemburg*	Turkey
Denmark*	Malaysia	United States of America
Ecuador	Mexico	Uruguay
Finland*	Netherlands*	Venezuela
France*	Netherlands Antilles	Zaire
Germany (Federal Republic of)*	New Zealand	Zambia
Ghana	Nigeria	Zimbabwe

* Full member of Confédération Européenne des Relations Publiques (CERP).

Some useful addresses

Institutions and associations

Association of MBAs
15 Duncan Terrace
LONDON N1 8BZ

Association of Market Survey Organisations (AMSO)
Ince House
60 Kenilworth Road
LEAMINGTON SPA
Warwickshire CV32 6JY

British Institute of Management
Africa House
64/78 Kingsway
LONDON WC2B 6BL

Chartered Institute of Marketing
Moor Hall
COOKHAM
Berks

Institute of Journalists
Suite 2, Dock Offices
Surrey Quays
Lower Road
LONDON SE16 2XL

Institute of Public Relations
The Old Trading House
15 Northburgh Street
LONDON EC1V 0PR

Market Research Society
The Old Trading House
15 Northburgh Street
LONDON EC1V 0PR

National Union of Journalists
Acorn House
314 Gray's Inn Road
LONDON WC1X 8DP

Public Relations Consultants Association
Willow House
Willow Place
LONDON SW1P 1JH

Strategic Planning Society
17 Portland Place
LONDON W1N 3AF

Education and training

PR degree courses
College of St Mark and St John (BA)
Deriford Lane
PLYMOUTH
Devon

Dorset Institute of Higher Education (BA)
Department of Communication and Media
Wallisdown Road
POOLE
Dorset BH12 5BB

Leeds Polytechnic (BA)
Public Relations Studies
Calverley Street
LEEDS LS1 3HI

Stirling University (MSc)
STIRLING SK9 4LA

Degree courses with PR modules or elements
Cranfield School of Management (MBA)
Cranfield
BEDFORD MK43 0AL

London Business School (MBA)
Sussex Place
Regent's Park
LONDON SW1 4SA

Manchester Polytechnic (Management Diploma)
All Saints Building
MANCHESTER M15 6BH

One-year diploma in PR
Watford College
Hempstead Road
WATFORD
Herts WD1 3EZ

Non-degree education/training in PR
Ashridge Management College
BERKHAMSTEAD
Hertfordshire HP4 1NS

College of Marketing
Moor Hall
COOKHAM
Berkshire

Communications, Advertising and Marketing
(CAM) Education Foundation (Dip. Cam.)
Abford House
15 Wilton Road
LONDON SW1V 1NJ

Henley—The Management College
Greenlands
HENLEY-ON-THAMES
Oxon RG9 3AU

Institute of Public Relations
(see page 205)

Interact International
10A High Street
TUNBRIDGE WELLS
Kent TN1 1UX

Frank Jefkins School of Public Relations (Dip.Cam.)
84 Ballards Way
SOUTH CROYDON
Surrey CR2 7LA

Public Relations Consultants Association
(see page 205)

Sundridge Park Management Centre
Plaistow Lane
BROMLEY
Kent BR1 3TP

Information
Higher Education Information Services Trust
(HEIST)
Lawns Lane
Farnley
LEEDS LS12 5ET

Consultancies mentioned in this book

Attitudes PR
Asphalte House
Palace Street
LONDON SW1E 5HS

Charles Barker Traverse-Healy
30 Farringdon Street
LONDON EC4A 4EA

Quentin Bell Organisation
22 Endell Street
Covent Garden
LONDON WC2Y 9AD

Burson-Marsteller
24–28 Bloomsbury Way
LONDON W14 2PX

Countrywide Communications
Bowater House East
68 Knightsbridge
LONDON SW1X 7LH

The Dunseath Stephen Partnership
35 Alva Street
EDINBURGH EH2 4PS

Roger Haywood Associates
7 Eccleston Street
LONDON SW1W 9LX

Infopress
2/3 Salisbury Court
Fleet Street
LONDON EC4Y 8AA

Marketing Solutions
70 Salusbury Road
Queens Park
LONDON NW6 6NU

Paragon Communications
Film House
142 Wardour Street
LONDON W1V 3AU

PR Selection
40 Ravenscourt Gardens
Hammersmith
LONDON W6 0TU

The Rowland Group
67/69 Whitfield Street
LONDON W1A 4PU

Shandwick
95 Park Lane
LONDON W1Y 3TA

Sheridan Communications
15 Greenfield Crescent
BIRMINGHAM B15 3AU

Smythe Dorward Lambert
40/42 Newman Street
LONDON W1P 3PA

Valin Pollen
18 Grosvenor Gardens
LONDON SW1W 6DH

The Watts Group
52 St John Street
LONDON EC1M 4D2

Index